Defence Industrial Cooperation in the European Union

This book provides an empirical understanding of how EU-level defence industrial cooperation functions in practice.

Using the Liberal Intergovernmental theoretical model, the book argues that while national economic preferences are an essential factor of government interests they only explain part of the dynamic that leads to the development of defence industrial policy at EU level. Moving beyond a simple adumbration of economic preferences, it shows how the EU's institutional framework and corpus of law are used by governments to reaffirm their position as the ultimate arbiter and promoter of national economic preferences in the defence industrial sector. To this end, the work asks why and how EU member state governments, European defence firms, and EU institutions developed EU-level defence industrial policy between 2003 and 2009. The book also analyses significant policy developments, including the establishment of a European Defence Agency and two EU Directives on equipment transfers and defence procurement.

This book will be of much interest to students of EU policy, defence studies, security studies and International Relations in general.

Daniel Fiott is an analyst at the EU Institute for Security Studies, Brussels, Belgium, and co-editor of *The Responsibility to Protect and the Third Pillar* (2015).

Routledge Studies in European Security and Strategy
Series Editors:
Sven Biscop
Egmont Royal Institute for International Relations, Belgium
and
Richard Whitman
University of Kent, UK

The aim of this series is to bring together the key experts on European security from the academic and policy worlds, and assess the state of play of the EU as an international security actor. The series explores the EU, and its member states, security policy and practices in a changing global and regional context. While the focus is on the politico-military dimension, security is put in the context of the holistic approach advocated by the EU.

European Union Military Operations
A Collective Action Perspective
Niklas I.M. Nováky

The EU, Strategy and Security Policy
Regional and Strategic Challenges
Edited by Laura Chappell, Jocelyn Mawdsley and Petar Petrov

Europeanisation and the Transformation of EU Security Policy
Post-Cold War Developments in the Common Security and Defence Policy
Petros Violakis

EU–Japan Security Cooperation
Trends and Prospects
Edited by Emil Kirchner and Han Dorussen

European Strategy in the 21st Century
New Future for Old Power
Sven Biscop

Defence Industrial Cooperation in the European Union
The State, the Firm and Europe
Daniel Fiott

For more information about this series, please visit: www.routledge.com/Routledge-Studies-in-European-Security-and-Strategy/book-series/SESS

Defence Industrial Cooperation in the European Union

The State, the Firm and Europe

Daniel Fiott

Routledge
Taylor & Francis Group
LONDON AND NEW YORK

First published 2019
by Routledge
2 Park Square, Milton Park, Abingdon, Oxon OX14 4RN

and by Routledge
605 Third Avenue, New York, NY 10017

First issued in paperback 2020

Routledge is an imprint of the Taylor & Francis Group, an informa business

British Library Cataloguing-in-Publication Data
A catalogue record for this book is available from the British Library

Library of Congress Cataloging-in-Publication Data
Names: Fiott, Daniel, author.
Title: Defence industrial cooperation in the European Union : the state, the firm and Europe / Daniel Fiott.
Other titles: Defense industrial cooperation in the European Union
Description: Abingdon, Oxon ; New York, NY : Routledge, 2019. | Series: Routledge studies in European security and strategy | Includes bibliographical references and index.
Identifiers: LCCN 2018058883 (print) | LCCN 2019001767 (ebook) | ISBN 9780429659164 (Web PDF) | ISBN 9780429656729 (ePub) | ISBN 9780429654282 (Mobi) | ISBN 9780367109929 (hardback) | ISBN 9780429024207 (ebook)
Subjects: LCSH: Defense industries–Government policy–European Union countries. | European cooperation. | European Union countries–Military policy. | European Union countries–Economic policy.
Classification: LCC HD9743.E852 (ebook) | LCC HD9743.E852 F56 2019 (print) | DDC 338.4/73550094–dc23
LC record available at https://lccn.loc.gov/2018058883

ISBN 13: 978-0-367-73082-6 (pbk)
ISBN 13: 978-0-367-10992-9 (hbk)

Typeset in Times New Roman
by Wearset Ltd, Boldon, Tyne and Wear

Contents

Figures

Tables

Acknowledgements

No book is simply about research and writing. I would like to thank a number of people for giving up their time to help me with this book. First, those that have assisted me intellectually need thanking, first beginning with Luis Simón followed by Sven Biscop, Amelia Hadfield, Alexander Mattelaer, Sebastian Oberthür, Burkard Schmitt and Florian Trauner for giving me sustained, frank and in-depth comments and criticisms on the main argument in this book. As I was based at the Institute for European Studies, Free University of Brussels, from October 2012, I should also like to thank my former colleagues who exchanged ideas with me, criticised me for some of my approaches and celebrated my achievements.

I would also like to thank Antonio Missiroli and the entire team at the European Union Institute for Security Studies. Antonio gave me the opportunity to apply my academic skills-set in a policy setting. Having been at the Institute since September 2016, I have been able to learn more about EU policy processes with respect to defence industrial cooperation and, in some small and modest way, I hope to have influenced the policy process too. I thank my colleagues at the Institute and several other EU colleagues who have supported me in one way or another. A number of other individuals should be thanked for supporting my work by inviting me to speak at conferences, to guest lecture and write policy and/or opinion pieces on defence-related issues.

Most importantly, the bulk of my gratitude goes to my wife Juliana. I dedicate this book to her as a small token of thanks for her forbearance, especially as this book was written while having just given birth to our twin boys.

Daniel Fiott
17 September 2018
Brussels

Abbreviations

AEMGs	Military Technology and Equipment Export Authorisations
AET	Agency Establishment Team
AFET	Committee on Foreign Affairs
AIAD	Italian Aerospace, Defence and Security Industry Association
ALDE	Alliance of Liberals and Democrats for Europe
AP	Agrément Préalable
BAFA	German Federal Office for Economic Affairs and Export Control
BDSV	Federation of German Security and Defence Industries
BMF	German Federal Ministry of Finance
BMI	German Federal Ministry of the Interior
BMVg	German Federal Ministry of Defence
BMWi	German Federal Ministry for Economic Affairs and Energy
BRITE	Basic Research in Industrial Technologies for Europe
BSR	German Federal Security Council
CBRM	Chemical, Biological, Radiological and Nuclear
CDM	Capability Development Mechanism
CEO	Chief Executive Officer
CERTIDER	Register of the Certified Defence-Related Enterprises
CF	Cohesion Fund
CIEEMG	Interministerial Commission for Exports of War Material
CML	Common Military List
COMPET	Competitiveness Configuration
COREPER	Committee of Permanent Representatives
COSME	Competitiveness of Enterprises and Small and Medium-sized Enterprises
CSDP	Common Security and Defence Policy
DG	Directorate General
DGA	Direction Générale de l'Armement
DTIB	Defence Technological and Industrial Base
EBB	Electronic Bulletin Board
ECAP	European Capability Action Plan
ECJ	European Court of Justice

EDA	European Defence Agency
EDAP	European Defence Action Plan
EDC	European Defence Community
EDEM	European Defence Equipment Market
EDF	European Defence Fund
EDTIB	European Defence Technological and Industrial Base
EEA	European Economic Area
EEAS	European External Action Service
EFSI	European Fund for Strategic Investments
ENDR	European Network of Defence-Related Regions
EPP-ED	European Peoples' Party and European Democrats
ERDF	European Regional Development Fund
EDRP	European Defence Research Programme
ESDP	European Security and Defence Policy
ESF	European Social Funds
ESIF	European Structural and Investment Funds
EATF	European Air Transport Fleet
EU	European Union
EUGS	EU Global Strategy
EUISS	European Union Institute for Security Studies
EUMC	European Union Military Committee
EURAM	European Research on Advanced Materials
GDP	Gross Domestic Product
GOVSATCOM	Government Satellite Communications
HR/VP	High Representative/Vice-President
IAI	Istituto Affari Internazionali
IEPG	Independent European Programmes Group
IGCs	Intergovernmental Conferences
IMCO	Committee on Internal Market and Consumer Protection
IPRs	Intellectual Property Rights
IPSD	Implementation Plan on Security and Defence
IR	International Relations
ISAF	International Security Assistance Force
ITRE	Committee on Industry, Research and Energy
JIP	Joint Investment Programmes
KWKG	War Weapons Control Act
LI	Liberal Intergovernmentalism
LPM	Loi de programmation militaire
LoI	Letter of Intent
MEP	Member of the European Parliament
MFF	Multi-annual Financial Framework
MIC	Military-Industrial Complex
MoD	Ministry of Defence
NATO	North Atlantic Treaty Organisation
NDIAs	National Defence Industry Associations

NGO	Non-Governmental Organisation
OGTCL	Open General Trade Control Licence
OITCL	Open Individual Trade Control Licence
PASR	Preparatory Action on Security Research
PESCO	Permanent Structured Cooperation
pMS	Participating Member State
POLARM	Ad hoc Working Party on European Armaments Policy
PSC	Political and Security Committee
R&D	Research and Development
R&T	Research and Technology
SESAR	Single European Sky ATM Research
SGP	Stability and Growth Pact
SITCL	Standard Individual Trade Control Export Licence
SMEs	Small and Medium-sized Enterprises
TCE	Treaty Establishing a Constitution for Europe
TED	Tenders Electronic Daily
TFEU	Treaty on the Functioning of the EU
UK	United Kingdom
UKTI	UK Trade and Investment
US	United States
VAT	Value Added Tax
WEAG	Western European Armaments Group
WEU	Western European Union

Introduction

Given that defence industrial issues are hard-wired into traditional notions of sovereignty, it is puzzling to observe the member states of the European Union (EU)[1] cooperating on defence industrial issues. Cooperation at the EU level is founded on law and regulation, capability development programmes, financing mechanisms and policy initiatives. EU-level cooperation is designed to ensure that Europe's defence market operates efficiently; that European militaries have security of supply of defence equipment and technologies; that European-based firms can become leaders in technological innovation; and that European armed forces remain capable and ready for autonomous military action (European Defence Agency 2006a). Greater defence industrial cooperation is also seen as a way to help safeguard the more than 847,700 people directly employed in the defence sector in 2015 and the €102.3 billion generated by the European military aeronautics, land and naval sectors in the same year (ASD Europe 2016). More broadly, since the economic crisis of 2008 EU defence industrial cooperation has emerged as an important element of the EU's overall attempt to reindustrialise the European economy (European Commission 2010a). While national governments still protect their own defence technological and industrial bases (DTIBs), one observes that under certain circumstances EU member states do cooperate on defence industrial issues.

The emergence of EU defence industrial cooperation has to be seen in the broader context of the establishment of the Common Security and Defence Policy (CSDP), the 2003 European Security Strategy (ESS) and the 2016 EU Global Strategy (EUGS). Just as the first CSDP mission was being deployed to Bosnia and Herzegovina in January 2003, High Representative Javier Solana was calling for a 'more capable' Europe. As the ESS made clear, the objective for the EU in the early 2000s was to 'transform [European] militaries into more flexible, mobile forces, and to enable them to address the new threats', and to this end 'more resources for defence and more effective use of resources are necessary' (Council of the European Union 2003a: 12). In many ways, this point reinforced the long-standing assumption that on defence capability and industrial issues the '[s]ystematic use of pooled and shared assets would reduce duplications, overheads and, in the medium-term, increase capabilities' (ibid.). While some believed that the ESS was not really a strategy because it failed to bind the

EU's strategic objectives with capability development priorities (Heisbourg 2004; Toje 2005), and while the document only dealt with defence industrial issues indirectly, the ESS clearly served the purpose of trying to rationalise and bring coherence to the various initiatives being undertaken by the EU on defence (Biscop 2005; Biscop and Andersson 2008: 2).

Interestingly, the publication of the EUGS in June 2016 has seen defence industrial issues gain in importance when compared to the 2003 ESS. Not only does the EUGS call for the creation of 'a solid European defence industry' but it sees the defence sector as 'essential for Europe's strategic autonomy and for a credible CSDP' (European External Action Service 2016: 46). This logic was extended in the specific security and defence follow-up document to the EUGS in November 2016. Not only did the Implementation Plan on Security and Defence (IPSD) recognise that technologies, skills and industrial manufacturing capacities are vital for the health of the European Defence Technological and Industrial Base (EDTIB), but it called specifically for a wider 'Innovation Initiative' to keep pace with the development of new defence capabilities and disruptive technologies (Council of the European Union 2016a: 23). For the first time, therefore, the EU's overarching strategic understanding of the world comprehensively recognises the importance of the defence sector. In this way, the EUGS echoes and reinforces countless European Commission communications and documents produced by the European Defence Agency (EDA) that have all stressed the strategic importance of the defence sector. Accordingly, the idea of an EDTIB is seen to flow from, and directly support, EU efforts to develop a coherent strategic vision and defence policy through the CSDP.

The idea of the EDTIB also sits within a broader global context of shifting defence industries. In addition to the way in which defence industries can be seen as an element of a state's broader foreign policy (Neuman 2006), European defence cooperation is part of a global defence industry that is marked by interdependence and new rising centres of gravity for defence production (see, for example, Bitzinger 2017). A multitude of European countries maintain close defence industrial ties with the United States, which leads to questions about how far the EDTIB can be seen as an autonomous industrial base at all. Furthermore, many European countries are also developing defence industrial ties with non-EU countries such as Australia, India, Israel, Japan and more. While the specific focus of this book is not on the global defence industry per se, it is still important to acknowledge at this early stage that production centres and supply chains take on a global nature which may affect discussions in the EU about security of supply, export policies and technology proliferation (Bitzinger 1994; Hayward 2001; James 2002; De Vore 2015a). As Figure 1.1 below shows, defence firms can be ranked according to their global footprint.

Beyond these statements, however, how does one explain why and how European governments cooperate with one another on defence industrial issues at the EU level? Should we assume that governments still manage to protect their core interests even while cooperating through the auspices of the EU? Can member state governments use EU structures and policy frameworks to enhance national defence technological and industrial bases? If governments do manage to serve their own interests through EU cooperation, then how do they do so in a context of competing interests? Or, rather, should one point to the EU institutions as the key drivers behind defence industrial cooperation? What is the 'quality' of defence industrial cooperation in the EU? Answering such questions may raise fresh theoretical and empirical insights for European studies, defence industrial studies, strategic studies and International Relations (IR). Looking at the 2004 establishment of the EDA and the 2009 adoption of two pieces of EU legislation on defence equipment transfers and defence procurement, this book looks at the ways in which government, commercial and institutional interests intertwine to shape EU defence industrial policy.

This book argues that while national economic preferences are an essential factor of government interests they only explain part of the dynamic that leads to the development of defence industrial policy at the EU level. Moving beyond a simple adumbration of economic preferences, this book shows how the EU's institutional framework and corpus of law are used by governments to reaffirm their position as the ultimate arbiter and promoter of national economic preferences. In this sense, intergovernmental bargaining between governments at the EU level allows governments to reassert control over national DTIBs in a context where defence globalisation and broader geopolitical forces could alter the traditional links that have existed between governments and firms for decades. At face value, the adoption of defence-relevant EU legislation and the establishment of new institutions may suggest that competencies for defence market regulation are moving away from national governments and into the hands of institutions such as the European Commission. This book shows how this is not the case. Instead, the book argues that the EU's legal and institutional framework is used by governments to reassert national control over national defence markets. With a view to unpacking this broad claim, the aim of this introduction is to outline the conceptual puzzle at hand and to flesh out in more detail the main elements of the central argument of this book.

The challenge of cooperation

Even in the absence of in-depth analysis, it is not too challenging to comprehend the difficulties and sensitivities associated with EU-level defence industrial cooperation. For example, even though international armaments collaboration is relatively commonplace (De Vore 2011) it is historically not the norm for governments to cooperate with each other on defence industrial matters through institutionalised settings such as the EU; especially when such cooperation is achieved through mutually agreed law, regulations and policies (Bates 1990: 113–115; Trybus 2014). One of the major obstacles to defence industrial cooperation is the principle of *juste retour*. This is a situation where 'a national defence industry must receive work worth the full amount of its government's financial contribution to a programme' (Darnis *et al.* 2007: 25). Having to share out the proceeds of a collaborative programme among national industrial actors does not allow for proper economies of scale or cost management, which can add to the overall cost of a collaborative endeavour. This is not even to speak of the plethora of national military requirements that emerge during a joint development programme. Each military service may want a weapons system to meet specific national requirements, but this invariably adds extra costs to a programme – especially in the later stages of equipment development (see, for example, Bàngert, Davies and Watson 2017).

Given that the EU institutions are not yet able to procure weapons systems and equipment, they do not own shares in defence firms and they have no integrated military force, member state governments are still the most important actors involved in European defence industrial cooperation. In the defence sector, one would expect states to guard their sovereignty and it should not be surprising when they do so. This has led some commentators and scholars to suggest that talk about an EDTIB is misplaced given that it is largely a political vision (Briani *et al.* 2013: 17; Masson 2013: 1). It is certainly true that at present it is difficult to define the EDTIB and doing so may not actually advance our knowledge and understanding of *why* and *how* defence industrial policy is pursued at the EU level. Indeed, analysing the present-day state and form of the EDTIB with some fixed teleological point in the future, blinkers one's ability to appreciate the political constraints in which defence industrial policy is made in the EU.

Defining the EDTIB in a way that suggests some material reality does not advance our understanding of the concept much either. In a sense, one could calculate the total aggregate number of defence firms in Europe and call this the EDTIB. Such accounts of the EDTIB would start with a basic question: what is the EDTIB and what exactly is the EU seeking to safeguard? The reply: the EDTIB is the conglomeration of aerospace firms close to Toulouse in France, Linköping in Sweden, Cascina Costa in Italy; the naval shipyards on the River Clyde in the UK, the Ferrol Estuary in Spain, Karlskrona in Sweden and Sestri Levante in Italy; and the tank and infantry vehicle factories based at Kassel in Germany, Merthyr Tydfil in the UK, Hämeenlinna in Finland and Kopřivnice in the Czech Republic. Again, such an exercise would vulgarise our understanding of the political dynamics that mark European defence industrial cooperation. This exercise would assume a degree of industrial and political homogeneity in the EU that simply does not exist at present.

This book does not advance a definition of the EDTIB. Instead, it focuses on a policy framework founded on EU law and regulation, capability development programmes, financing mechanisms and policy initiatives. This policy framework is *sui generis* in nature: it helps shape the European defence sector through a range of tools and policies. By focusing on the EU's defence industrial policy framework it will be possible to go beyond the rhetoric that usually surrounds any discussion of the EDTIB. For example, the EDA's 2007 *European Defence Technological and Industrial Base Strategy* claims that the EDTIB needs to be capability-driven to improve the operational effectiveness of European armed forces; it needs to be competent to allow governments to exploit the best technologies; and it needs to be competitive inside and outside Europe (European Defence Agency 2007: 2). For its part, the European Commission has released numerous official communications that state that the EDTIB is a 'key element for Europe's capacity to ensure the security of citizens and to protect its values and interests' (European Commission 2013a: 3). Such pronouncements hide the, often contentious, nature of agreeing to EU defence industrial policy, so the focus in this book is on why and how policy is made rather than on the merit of political objectives.

Without going into too much detail here – see Chapter 1 – it is worth briefly outlining the main characteristics of the EU's defence industrial policy framework. First, it embodies elements of market liberalisation and regulation, and cooperation and information sharing. The EU has several mechanisms that can be used to simultaneously liberalise the European defence sector and move regulation from the national to the EU level. This book is explicitly interested in the interplay between national and EU levels. For example, EU primary law such as Article 346[2] of the Treaty on the Functioning of the EU (TFEU) – an article that provides the EU member states with a means of derogation from the internal market provisions of the Treaty on the grounds of national security – can be challenged by the European Commission and ruled on by the European Court of Justice (ECJ). While states may invoke Article 346 to ensure that EU law does not apply to its national defence sector, member states must prove that the invocation of Article 346 relates to their core security interests rather than the protection of national markets.

Second, it is a policy framework that is characterised by shared policy and legal competences. For example, the European Commission has exclusive competence for the EU's dual-use export policy[3] (see pages 41–42 for an elaboration on the Commission's competence for the dual-use export regime). Dual-use technologies are those that are normally used in the civilian or commercial sectors but which, with adaptation or modification, may have military application (Molas-Gallart 1997, 2002; Reppy 1999). Dual-use is one area where defence industry-relevant policy and legislation have been moved from the national to the EU level. Another example is the two specific directives on the intra-EU transfers of defence equipment (2009/43/EC)[4] and defence procurement (2009/81/EC)[5] – known collectively as the EU's 'defence package' – which were adopted in 2009 to allow for greater liberalisation and regulation of the European defence sector. We will come back to these directives in more detail later.

Third, the EU's defence industrial policy framework is also comprised of cooperative endeavours that attempt to lower the costs of defence for EU member states. In this regard, the EDA – an intergovernmental agency of the EU – is the EU's primary institution responsible for encouraging cooperation between EU member states on defence procurement and capability development programmes. The European Commission also presides over a range of financial tools such as the regional development, cohesion and research funds. These existing financial tools can support, albeit in a limited fashion, defence-relevant research and defence conversion in the EU member states (Breant and Karock 2011). In a possible evolution of these limitations, in 2016 the European Commission announced that it would launch a European Defence Fund (EDF) to invest a proportion of the EU budget into defence research[6] and defence capability development programmes.[7] The advent of the EDF represents a new method of defence industrial cooperation at the EU level because it uses financial incentives to help spur collaboration between EU member states.

The policy framework briefly outlined above raises several interesting questions. For example, if Hartley (2011) is correct to assume that EU defence industrial cooperation will inevitably result in economic winners and losers, so that the defence sector in one member state profits while others lose out, then why do EU member states persist with EU-level defence industrial cooperation at all? Surely cooperation at the EU level may mean that some governments could risk reneging on electoral pledges and/or harming job security in local and regional economies by restructuring the European defence market (Hartley 2011: 132; see also Kuechle 2006: 38; Castellacci, Fevolden and Lundmark 2014)? This is to not even consider how such cooperation could impinge upon the national security doctrines and priorities of individual European governments (Bischak 1999). To give more meaning to the notion of 'winners and losers', it is clear that while some governments and industries will stand to make economic gains through market consolidation, liberalisation and EU-level regulation, others will find it increasingly difficult to survive in the defence sector. Thus, 'winning' is about maintaining exports, increasing market share and supporting national DTIBs. 'Losing' is potentially about losing national and international market share and with it the ability to maintain some degree of national industrial and strategic autonomy.

There are many more questions. Why, when history shows that cooperation is not necessarily a panacea for overcoming issues of cost efficiency and operational autonomy (European Defence Agency 2007: 6; see also Kapstein 1991; De Vore 2011; Mawdsley 2013), do member states see the EU as a valuable venue through which to cooperate? Why, when many EU member states are also part of NATO, and given that many industrial programmes are global in nature and not necessarily delimited on a geographical basis (Bellais, Foucault and Oudot 2014: 109), does cooperation have to be just 'European' at all? Why has an EU defence industrial policy framework only emerged over the past few decades? Given the fact that many European states were facing military and economic decline in the immediate post-Second World War period, and that out of this situation their security interests were directly challenged during the Cold War, one might assume that a greater rationale for European and EU cooperation existed long before the turn of the millennium. Finally, what is the nature of EU cooperation when it does occur and does it represent a meaningful step change in EU integration on defence industrial issues? In this regard, a related question to ask is to what extent supranational institutions such as the European Commission have increased their competences in the defence sector through the EU's policy framework?

Why cooperate?

This book asks why and how EU member state governments, European defence firms and EU institutions developed EU-level defence industrial policy between 2003 and 2009. It does this by first acknowledging that the policy framework under analysis is politically contested. It is precisely because each government, defence firm and EU institution will have its own preferences to promote and protect that EU cooperation is likely to be marked by political contestation between these actors. How one disentangles government, commercial and EU institutional preferences is thus of paramount importance if one is to have a clearer understanding of how EU defence industrial cooperation has been shaped over the six-year period under examination. Such an understanding may potentially help us better comprehend the future development of EU defence cooperation. To say that governments and firms cooperate is not enough. One must show *why* and *how* they cooperate to understand how relevant EU cooperation is. Therefore, a key aim of this book is to understand how government, commercial and institutional preferences are bound up in the evolution of EU defence industrial cooperation and how these interests are specifically framed in an EU context.

A number of explanations are readily available to help one understand why and how governments, firms and institutions cooperate on defence industrial matters at an EU level. Before these explanations are addressed, however, it is important to recognise that they represent the bias of particular scholarly fields. They either opt for a predominantly *economic* (Hartley 1991, 2011; Robertson 1994), *legal* (Koutrakos 2001: 165–198; Trybus 2005; Dyson and Konstadinides 2013: 86–109), *political* (Posen 2006; Jones 2007) or *institutional* focus (Mörth and Britz 2004; Trybus 2006; Markowski and Wylie 2007; Blauberger and Weiss 2013; Strikwerda 2016; Weiss and Blauberger 2016). Notwithstanding the methodological particularities of these various explanations, this book draws on a number of them to provide a comprehensive account of why and how EU-level defence industrial cooperation occurs. An in-depth analysis of the explanations can be found in Chapter 2, but it is worth providing a brief overview here.

First, the book acknowledges structuralist explanations for EU defence industrial cooperation. More specifically, the book defines structural explanations as defence globalisation, the rising costs of defence equipment, increased international competition, decreasing defence budgets, geopolitics and the global balance of power. As far as economic factors are concerned, Hartley observes that because 'Europe's defence markets are fragmented […] there are likely to be substantial cost savings from the creation of a Single European Market for defence equipment, providing opportunities for gains from trade and economies of scale and learning' (2006: 476). Economic readings of cooperation suggest that market fragmentation and the pressures emanating from the global defence market place significant pressure on European governments to cooperate on defence industrial policy. As Guay makes clear, '[i]t seems, then, that any account of why the EU has become involved in defense industry matters must include the context-shaping role of the international economy' (1996: 412).

Taking the argument of market fragmentation further, other structuralist explanations point to the globalisation of defence markets and international competition from the United States (US) and other emerging states. When taken together with the barriers facing European firms seeking market access to these countries, structuralist explanations believe there is a strong incentive for European governments to band together (Alexander and Garden 2001; Crollen 2003; European Commission 2010b: 11; Ecorys 2010; Briani *et al.* 2013; Bellais, Foucault and Oudot 2014). There is also the argument that EU member states are cooperating because of the high and rising costs – even when adjusted for inflation – of weapons systems and R&D (Kirkpatrick and Pugh 1985; Kirkpatrick 1995, 1997, 2004; Pugh 2004, 2007; TNO 2009: 125). These scholars contend that it is the need to overcome the costs associated with the productive duplication of defence materiel across the EU that is leading to greater cooperation (Aben 1992: 136; Walker and Gummett 1993; Guay 1996; Guay and Callum 2002; Hartley 2003, 2008; Meijer 2010; Andersson 2012: 113; Balis and Heidenkamp 2014).

Another, more political, reading of structural factors posits that shifts in the global balance of power are incentivising European defence industrial cooperation. Some scholars have pointed to the post-Cold War 'peace dividend' and US unilateralism as a reason behind Europe's closer defence cooperation. The logic here is that the lower defence expenditures and shift away from focusing on hard power that have accompanied the post-Cold War period in Europe has led to a sort of de facto process of consolidation among Europe's militaries (Dyson 2010). Indeed, many of these scholars claim that greater EU cooperation is a response to the more pacific strategic landscape enjoyed by Europe since the Cold War, which has led to a depression in European defence spending, power and resources (Jones 2007; Matlary 2009; Giegerich and Nicoll 2012; McKinsey & Co. 2012: 10; Simón 2014).

Other scholars take a different approach. Looking to Washington's geopolitical shifts to the Middle East and the Asia-Pacific, post-11 September 2001, some point to a process whereby Europe is attempting to balance against US power and this is why defence industrial cooperation is being pursued in the EU (Posen 2006). The rationale is that in order to offset Europe's strategic dependence on Washington, and to cushion any blow that may come from any serious US strategic realignment away from Europe to other geopolitically relevant regions in the world, Europeans will band together on security and defence (Jones 2007). Even though Simón (2014, 2017) shows that notions of 'European balancing' often overlook the specific dynamics of the intra-European balance of power, a number of scholars insist that closer European defence cooperation can be explained by Europe's need to balance against the US (Posen 2006; Jones 2007).

Second, this book engages with the notion that EU institutions such as the Council of the EU, the European Commission, the ECJ, the EDA and the European Parliament drive forward EU defence industrial cooperation. Of the theories analysed in Chapter 2, neo-functionalism, institutionalism, Europeanisation and judicial politics are most wedded to the importance of EU institutions.

The rational choice model argues that institutions such as the Commission are vital because they can ensure the exchange of information between governments and aid in a more efficient allocation of resources (Pollack 1996, 2003). Other scholars take the importance of institutions further by showing how actors such as the European Commission can be a strategic and entrepreneurial when formulating policy (Laffan 1997; Young 1999; Zito 2001). Scholars such as Blauberger and Weiss (2013) have argued that the Commission can 'push and pull' the member states towards cooperative endeavours such as the adoption of secondary legislation. They argue that the 'Commission's role as a strategic policy entrepreneur' is crucial for closer EU defence industrial cooperation (Blauberger and Weiss 2013: 1121).

Third, ideational explanations contend that EU-level defence industrial cooperation can reflect the production of new ideas and/or a move to embed economic and political ideologies and power beyond national borders (Fairclough 2005; Glynos *et al.* 2009; Schmidt 2008, 2010). Ideational explanations are sceptical of 'rational calculations' of interests by governments, firms and institutions because it is argued that such calculations ignore the importance of language and meaning, history, culture, discourse, narratives, frames and power (Laclau and Mouffe 1985; Van Dijk 1993; Glynos *et al.* 2009). As many scholars argue, policy outcomes tend to reflect ideas or ideological preferences and the institutionalisation of these ideas and preferences can change the behaviour of states and firms over time (Skowronek 1982; Scott 1987; DiMaggio and Powell 1991; Hall and Taylor 1996; Mörth and Britz 2004).

Despite the richness of the explanations mentioned above, many of them share similar explanatory traits: first, many of them recognise that governments are still an essential actor in defence industrial policymaking; second, they allow for interaction between governments, firms and institutions; third, they can help explain the characteristics of intergovernmental cooperation in an EU setting; and finally, they can allow for structural pressures and national and European priorities to coexist as explanatory factors. These approaches may only take one so far, however, as many do not take into consideration the most recent institutional or policy developments experienced since the turn of the millennium. Furthermore, such perspectives may gloss over the significance of diverse national responses to structural factors (the major exceptions being James 2002 and Kiss 2014), they neglect EU institutions such as the European Commission and/or the EDA altogether (Bitzinger 1994, 1999; Hayward 2001; Neal and Taylor 2001), or they may give institutions too much causal relevance (Blauberger and Weiss 2013; Weiss and Blauberger 2016).

In the hope of bringing fresh insight to studies on EU defence industrial cooperation, and to make a scholarly contribution to the literature on EU integration studies, this book mainly focuses on the Liberal Intergovernmental explanation for EU defence industrial cooperation. While the word 'liberal' is not usually associated with an economic sector such as defence, Liberal Intergovernmentalism (LI) was born out of a dissatisfaction with neo-realism and the idea that cooperation must necessarily be hampered by considerations of 'national sovereignty' (Moravcsik 1990, 1991a; Cothier and Moravcsik 1991; Moravcsik 1993a). LI argues that the concept of national sovereignty is too vague because it ignores the interaction between private and public interests (Moravcsik 1993a: 157–158). While LI acknowledges that 'when domestic arms producers oppose collaboration, they are almost always successful, regardless of the interests of the military or the chief executive', this does not entirely rule out cooperation at the EU level (ibid.: 130).

At its core, LI argues that governments and firms – as rational actors that 'calculate the utility' of their actions – are central to the EU integration process rather than EU institutions (Moravcsik and Schimmelfennig 2009: 68; see also Moravcsik 1998; Schimmelfennig 2015a: 178). LI offers a 'three-step' explanation of cooperation based on several assumptions. 'Step one' argues that governments are locked in a state of economic interdependence and that governments are the arbitrators of a range of domestic economic preferences (Moravcsik 1993b, 1998: 34). 'Step two' states that governments may or may not choose to bargain on an international basis to secure their domestic preferences, especially if the prospect of cooperation results in excessive domestic costs. The results of the bargaining phase are influenced by the relative power of governments and the ability of governments to non-coercively push for a bargaining compromise. Here, compromise can be achieved based on the threat of walking away from negotiations or the threat of exclusion from policy initiatives (Moravcsik 1998: 65). 'Step three' refers to the 'outcomes' of the bargaining phase such as new or revised treaties, the establishment of new or the modification of existing institutions, codifying agreements and decision-making rules, delegating autonomous decision-making power to supranational officials and the maintenance of the status quo (Moravcsik 1993b: 508, 1999: 298; Moravcsik and Nicolaïdis 1999: 76; Guiraudon 2000; Gehring and Oberthür 2009; Moravcsik and Schimmelfennig 2009: 72).

Chapter 2 will look in more detail at the virtues and drawbacks of applying the LI model to the field of EU defence industrial policy, but it is perhaps worth tabling some initial observations here. By emphasising domestic preferences, LI affords recognition of the specificities of individual states and their political and economic systems. Understanding how these systems function and respond to structural factors and a condition of economic interdependence is something long demanded by the literature on varieties of capitalism (Crouch 2005; Bruff 2010). Focusing on domestic preference formation is a logical step if one is to understand what national defence industrial preferences are, why they have emerged considering structural pressures and how they intersect with other national preferences to produce policy outcomes. In this way, LI feeds into the broader 'agent-structure' debate that refers to the problem of sustaining state agency in the context of the structures of a world system (Wendt 1987; Wight 2004). LI also relates to two-level games that occur between domestic and international politics (Putnam 1988; Moravcsik 1993b).

Yet one must heed the criticism that LI appears to reduce national preferences to mere powerful economic interests (Forster 1998; Dover 2005; Bickerton,

Hodson and Puetter 2015a). Economic preferences are, of course, not the only preferences vying for the attention of governments. Whereas LI was originally designed to explain the EU's economic integration, one should be mindful of the fact that in the defence sector economic preferences may likely intersect with considerations of national sovereignty, military strategy and geopolitics like no other policy domain. Quite what 'domestic preferences' actually means in the context of the defence sector is a key part of the analysis in this book. The defence sector is one where governments need to balance economic considerations such as equipment costs, job protection and skills retention[8] with politico-military considerations such as equipment effectiveness, strategic autonomy and/or alliance politics. A major task ahead is therefore to analyse political preferences as well as economic ones.

Additionally, this book will contribute to refining LI's definition of relevant actors in the domestic preference phase of the model. LI's understanding has hitherto been that domestic economic actors such as firms are relatively autonomous actors pursuing their own narrow, sectional interests and that it is up to governments to arbitrate between the constellation of these domestic preferences. Yet in the defence sector one should not presume that these economic actors are as autonomous as they are in the commercial sector. Accordingly, a major question arises: does LI's assumption of the existence of a plurality of commercial interests hold in the defence sector? Given that defence firms are largely reliant on governments for demand, procurement contracts and support for exports, how does one assess 'domestic preference formation' in the defence sector? Answering this question may help to refine and expand LI by focusing on a relatively protected economic sector such as defence rather than the liberal market setting Moravcsik originally had in mind.

When viewed from a defence industrial perspective, there are also questions related to intergovernmental bargaining ('step two'). For example, how does one characterise 'bargaining power' in relation to defence industrial cooperation? What is 'relative power' when related to the defence sector? As has been previously stated, under LI power relates to the type of bargaining observed during intergovernmental negotiations with a state or group of states deciding to either: (i) walk away from the negotiations; (ii) exclude certain states by forging coalitions; or (iii) promise compromise (Moravcsik 1993b: 499). On this basis, this book will seek to understand how governments bargain when negotiating the terms of defence industrial policy. Can only certain states threaten to walk away from negotiations and would they be able to do so because they hold a competitive position in global defence markets or for other reasons?

Furthermore, LI has been criticised for its inability to explain how supranational institutions act once the member states mandate action or delegate powers (Moravcsik 1995; Wincott 1995). LI does not assume that EU integration occurs because of the actions or initiatives of EU officials (Moravcsik 1991b: 20, 1993b: 519, 1999: 268 and 298–299). However, in the field of EU defence industrial policy Blauberger and Weiss (2013) have argued that the European Commission has still been able to coerce the member states into agreeing to uphold EU law and to accept the eventual phasing out of defence offsets through the strategic use of judicial politics (see also Weiss and Blauberger 2016). In other words, the Commission aims to encourage member states to agree to EU law to provide legal certainty on defence industrial matters, but, if they decline, the Commission may threaten to leave defence industrial matters to the opinions and rulings of the ECJ. Bearing in mind this hypothesis, it is necessary to look at the role played by institutions such as the Council of the EU, the European Commission, the EDA, the European Parliament and the ECJ in shaping the EU's defence industrial policy framework. In this vein, this book seeks to understand the role of institutions in the EU defence industrial policy framework.

Another aspect of LI that needs unpacking is its focus on 'EU integration' rather than 'EU cooperation'. 'Integration' is not easy to measure and focusing exclusively on integration fails to acknowledge that EU member states are just as prone to conflict (Simón 2014: 5). Schimmelfennig and Rittberger argue that EU integration is a process of *sectoral integration* whereby policies are regulated at the EU level; of *vertical integration*, so that EU member states share competencies or delegate powers to supranational institutions; and of *horizontal integration*, when the EU expands territorially by gaining new members (2004: 74). Of course, EU defence industrial policies presume that governments are bound by mutually agreed and enforceable law; member state governments and firms engage in collaborative arms programmes and are beneficiaries of EU funds; and the European Commission and EDA guide governments through numerous policy recommendations. Yet how can one easily label this level of engagement as integration? Integration gives 'the impression of unbounded expansion of policy-making' whereas this is not always the case, especially in defence (Moravcsik 2005: 365).

Much like Jones (2007: 4) and Simón (2013: 23–26), this book draws a distinction between 'cooperation' and 'integration'. The word 'integration' is often used haphazardly in EU studies literature. It is important to keep in mind that 'cooperation' denotes a situation in which states can work together to achieve a commonly identified objective. Under 'cooperation', states are still sovereign and can choose to initiate and/or end cooperation if so required. The process of 'integration', however, implies that states incrementally pool sovereignty and a supranational authority is increasingly responsible for overall governance. In reality, the EU is marked by a combination of both cooperation and integration. In some instances, states retain a sovereign right to pursue cooperation if it is deemed beneficial to them (e.g. invoking Article 346) but in others (e.g. dual-use export policy) supranational authorities can govern policy. Understanding where the grey area between cooperation and integration sits in the defence sector is a key aspect of this book.

Conflict and cooperation in defence

Notwithstanding this list of caveats, this book contends that LI may usefully offer a more comprehensive account of EU defence industrial cooperation than has hitherto been offered by structural, institutional and/or ideational explanations. Acknowledging Rathbun's observation that liberalism expects more, rather than less, cooperation in international affairs (2010: 4), it is important to have a more nuanced point of departure that reflects the range of possible policy outcomes that may result from EU policymaking processes – that is, one must even hold out the possibility that cooperation may not be achievable at all. This book is therefore principally interested in policy outcomes and how they are achieved. When one therefore thinks about how EU-level cooperation has developed over the 2003–2009 period, one is effectively thinking about a range of negotiated outcomes that have emerged following various phases of intergovernmental bargaining (more on the specific context of such bargaining later). In this sense, the quality of EU cooperation can only be explained once a thorough study of negotiations has been conducted (Moravcsik and Schimmelfennig 2009: 69).

In this respect, great attention is paid to the bargaining process leading to policy outcomes and not just to economic interests and how governments balance them (Moravcsik 1998: 34; Moravcsik and Schimmelfennig 2009: 70; Hoeffler 2012). Indeed, intergovernmental bargaining is not only characterised by a constellation of domestic preferences but also by the relative power between the negotiating participants (Moravcsik 1991b: 25, 1993b: 499; Moravcsik and Schimmelfennig 2009: 71). Depending on the constellation of preferences and the bargaining procedures adopted, relative power may lead to non-agreement, exclusion or compromise. What is interesting, and ultimately a hallmark of LI, is that relative power is not calculated in terms of the absolute political and/or market power of individual states but rather the strongest collective preferences of a coalition of governments (Moravcsik 1993b: 499; see also Gummett and Stein 1997: 7). This definition of relative power is especially important in an EU context because a specific set of legal and decision-making processes apply that favour negotiation rather than the overt wielding of power to achieve interests.

Keeping in mind the EU's specific legal and institutional order is particularly important when analysing the three instances of EU defence industrial cooperation in this book and which span the period from 2003 to 2009. The 2003–2004 establishment of the EDA was achieved via a Council Joint Action (2004/551/CFSP) based on a unanimous decision taken by the Council of the EU on the basis of Articles 42.3 and 45 of the Treaty on European Union (TEU). Article 42.4 TEU furnishes the Council with exclusive decision-making authority for initiatives such as the creation of the EDA when they are related to the CSDP. In this regard, bargaining between member states in pursuit of a unanimous decision takes on a wholly intergovernmental form. As far as the adoption of EU secondary law is concerned, however, a different context prevails. When, for example, the 'defence package' of two directives on defence transfers (2009/43/EC) and defence procurement (2009/81/EC) were adopted over the 2007–2009 period the ordinary legislative procedure prevailed. This not only means that the European Commission was responsible for proposing both pieces of legislation, but adoption of the legislation occurred under co-decision from the Council of the EU and the European Parliament. Unlike the creation of the EDA, therefore, bargaining for the two directives took place in a hybrid context where intergovernmental and supranational actors played a prominent legislative role.

These three instances of EU defence industrial cooperation have been selected based on whether governments, firms and EU institutions were involved in the policy process. Where the 2004 establishment of the EDA is concerned (see Chapter 3), EU member state governments are important actors but firms acting through governments had an important buy-in during the establishment of the Agency too, and so did the European Commission. Studying the establishment of the EDA allows one to investigate how governments defined the purpose and scope of the Agency. In terms of the individual defence directives (see Chapters 4 and 5 respectively) governments working through the Council of the EU, defence firms, the European Commission and the European Parliament played an important role. An examination of the defence directives allows one to see how member state governments sought to put in place a legal/regulatory environment for the European defence market. They also allow for an interrogation of how the European Commission and EU governments balanced national prerogatives and market considerations.

There is a clear temporal gap between the examples proposed in this book (i.e. 2003–2004 and 2008–2009) and many of the more recent initiatives referred to in this Introduction and in the Conclusion (e.g. the EU Global Strategy, the European Defence Fund, etc.). The gap between the studies reflects the absence of major defence initiatives between 2004 and 2008. These four years were marked by the EU's adjustment to the 'big bang' enlargement of 2004, the failed EU constitution and efforts to reform the EU through the Treaty of Lisbon and the economic crisis that began in 2007. With the exception of the defence aspects of the Treaty of Lisbon – that is, in particular the crisis management structures to be established in newly created European External Action Service (EEAS) – defence was not a significant feature of EU politics during this period. The gap between 2009, when the defence directives were adopted, and present-day initiatives can be explained by an absence of major policy initiatives on defence industrial matters in the intervening years. Aside from the so-called 'Ghent Initiative'[9] in 2010, the December 2013 Council Conclusions[10] and the European Commission's 2013 'New Deal'[11] on defence, it has taken until 2016 – in the context of Russia's seizure of Crimea and the UK's decision to leave the EU – to spur further action on defence industrial policy.

Having now outlined the three focus studies in this book, it is important to recognise the limitations of the study. First, to ensure in-depth analysis of a few important instances of EU defence industrial cooperation it will not be possible to touch upon specific European capability development programmes and/or EU financial mechanisms such as the regional, structural and research funds. Of course, these specific programmes and mechanisms could be studied as part of a future research agenda. Second, it is important to note that this book cannot analyse every single defence firm based in the EU. Where required the book draws on primary sources gathered from a range of EU-based defence firms and industry associations such as Airbus Group, MBDA and the Aerospace and Defence Industries Association of Europe (ASD Europe). The companies that appear in the book reflect the fact that they are headquartered in EU member states, that they are responsible for producing finished weapons systems and that they have a vested interest in EU policies that will affect their business. To avoid bias, time has been taken to analyse defence firms that represent a range of productive activities, including: aerospace, land and naval systems, missile technology, metering and lasers for land, air defence, etc. Finally, this study does not focus on the preferences of each EU member state and it instead analyses the preferences of a range of large industrial states such as the Letter of Intent[12] countries, medium-sized countries such as Belgium, the Netherlands and Poland and smaller states such as Finland and Portugal. This is vital if one is to have a balanced picture of what preferences emerge at the EU level.

With these caveats in mind, it is also worth stating where the qualitative and quantitative sources for each of the three example studies have been attained. In terms of primary sources, national security and defence industrial policy documents and national parliamentary debates have been widely used. The book also draws on corporate documents such as annual shareholder and financial reports. Council of the EU, European Commission, EDA and European Parliament policy documents, including studies, regulations, directives, communications, working papers and guidance notes, are also analysed. Unless otherwise stated, all translations from French and Italian in this book are the author's own. For all other languages, the author has drawn on the support of native-level speakers and translation services. Several statistical compilations have been drawn on including the Stockholm International Peace Research Institute's (SIPRI) database; the International Institute for Strategic Studies (IISS); Eurostat; the EDA's defence portal; and ASD Europe's annual key defence facts and figures publication. In addition to secondary sources such as specialist journals and books, some 84 semi-structured interviews with officials from the European Commission, European Defence Agency, European Parliament, industry representatives,[13] think tank researchers and officials from eight[14] major European governments have been conducted.

Organising interviews with representatives from the defence sector was difficult, as many have a duty of confidentiality (Deschaux-Beaume 2012). Therefore, interviews in this book are cited under conditions of strict anonymity. Public and commercial representatives have been identified based on their proximity to the formation and application of the EU defence industrial policies studied in this book. Interviews were conducted with both policy officer- and director-level representatives to ensure greater representation and a spread of institutional views and nationalities. While acknowledging that deciphering responses from interviews that are conducted under conditions of confidentiality can be problematic (Leech *et al.* 2013: 222), interview responses have been compared with each other and cross-checked against primary and secondary data (Aberbach and Rockman 2002; Leech 2002; Bleich and Pekkanen 2013).

Why Europe?

One may reasonably ask why one should want to study EU defence industrial cooperation. After all, there is nothing new about European initiatives to improve defence industrial cooperation (De Vore and Eisenecker 2010; De Vore 2011; Thiem 2011). European cooperation during the 1950s – mainly between France, Germany, the Netherlands and the UK – was, under the 1954 Paris Agreements,[15] principally aimed at managing Germany's post-1945 rearmament and ensuring the market competitiveness of countries such as France and the UK in global defence markets that were, because of the Cold War, dominated by the US and the Soviet Union (Art 1991; Markusen 1992; Hacker 2005). Collaborative efforts since 1945 have demonstrated the proclivity for intergovernmentalism among European states. For example, consider the 1976 establishment of the Independent European Programme Group (IEPG),[16] the 1993 creation of the Western European Armaments Group (WEAG),[17] the 1996 formation of the Organisation for Joint Armament Cooperation (OCCAR)[18] and/or the 2000 signing of the 'Letter of Intent' between France, Germany, Italy, Spain, Sweden and the UK on the restructuring of the European defence industry. Each of these initiatives has been, or is, intergovernmental in nature and located outside of the formal structures of the EU (Mörth 2005: 123; De Vore 2011; Thiem 2011).

This book contends that, because the EU defence industrial policy framework is located inside the formal structures of the EU, defence industrial cooperation symbolises a curious political and historical development that requires further theoretical and empirical reflection. For the field of IR, steps by the EU into the defence sector not only raise questions about the interplay between economics and politics but it also potentially points to a shift in the national security preferences of particular European states. Many policy domains are marked by an interplay between economics and politics, but none impinge upon considerations of national security in the way the defence sector does. In this respect, this book feeds into the process of bridging strategic studies and international security with the theoretical approaches of the International Political Economy (IPE). As long called for by many scholars, studying the defence sector as both a strategic and economic domain is of great benefit to the field of IR (see, for example, Strange 1970; Baldwin 1985; Betts 1997: 23–24). Studying European defence industrial cooperation gives one a window into how European governments balance national security with economic interests in ways unachievable by a mere study of national defence policy and/or national security doctrines. Bringing in a discussion about the combination of economic and industrial policies gives one a much more comprehensive understanding of European states as geopolitical entities.

Analysis of European defence industrial cooperation has so far predominantly focused on how globalisation is affecting the shape of national defence industries (James 2002), or on how the interaction between firms and governments affects the shape of national defence markets (Smith 1990; Serfati 2001). However, no in-depth empirical or theoretical analysis of defence industrial cooperation has been satisfactorily conducted, and so this research promises to add to our understanding and appreciation of the defence industrial policy framework and cooperation between governments, firms and institutions at the EU level. Primarily, this book promises to make an empirical and conceptual contribution to debates surrounding defence industrial cooperation and liberal intergovernmentalism, plus a broader contribution to European and defence studies. In particular, an objective is to ground debates about the CSDP in a more empirically viable way. By focusing on industrial matters, this book hopes to move the debate about CSDP into more substantive waters. This aim is, of course, greatly aided by the fact that defence industrial matters have risen to the top of the CSDP policy agenda since the publication of the EU Global Strategy (2016) and the European Defence Action Plan (2016). If defence industrial cooperation is increasingly seen as a foundational basis of CSDP, then much greater focus on this area is required.

The originality of this book stems from its ability to draw on insights from, and make contributions to, two often separate realms of European integration: economic policy and politics. As far as the politics of European defence policy go, a focus has been placed on military operations and capability development, whereas in economic policy there has traditionally been little focus on issues related to EU defence cooperation – although Hartley (2003, 2011) has almost single-handedly tried to remedy this gap. The added value of the thoughts in this book is that in defence industrial cooperation elements of both political and economic policies come together. Defence industrial cooperation is a policy domain that demands insights from both economic policy and the politics of defence cooperation in the EU, and so this book seeks to contribute to our understanding of the interdependence that exists between both policy domains. An investigation of how economics and politics interrelate is perhaps this book's most important contribution to our understanding of European defence industrial cooperation.

Regarding this books' conceptual contribution, the research aims to build on and critique the theoretical work developed by Andrew Moravcsik. Although Moravcsik's early academic work focused on arms cooperation, it is worth considering at least three shortcomings with his belief that defence industrial cooperation in Europe was stimulated chiefly by the economic interests of firms. First, his original work only took stock of bilateral arms collaboration between select firms and governments rather than EU-level cooperation; second, it was written before some important developments in EU defence industrial policy such as the 2004 establishment of the European Defence Agency and/or the 2009 adoption of the EU's 'defence package'; and third, it did not dedicate space to understanding the role of EU institutions such as the European Commission. To build on Moravcsik's original thoughts, this book focuses on the policy outcomes on EU defence industrial policy that emerge after intergovernmental bargaining has occurred and after a time when the economic preferences of firms and the political preferences of governments have been brought together (Moravcsik 1993b: 474–479).

Furthermore, the book will ask whether EU efforts in the defence sector since 2003 represent a milestone for EU integration or whether Moravcsik and Schimmelfennig (2009) are correct to assume that only incremental and limited steps have been taken in the post-Maastricht Treaty period. As far as the first of these two objectives is concerned, Moravcsik has been clear that the existence of outcomes that result in a supranational role does not undermine his central premise that domestic preferences matter (ibid.: 507), but a clearer understanding of the unintended consequences caused by intergovernmental bargaining outcomes is still required. In terms of the second of the two observations, this book seeks to address the criticism that LI is only really suited to understanding 'grand bargains' made at the EU level, such as treaty changes. Moravcsik has himself downplayed the significance of integration in new areas of activity since Maastricht (Moravcsik 2002; Bickerton, Hodson and Puetter 2015a: 707), yet he previously stated that 'there is nothing to rule out the use of [LI] for the analysis of everyday decisions' (Moravcsik 1995: 613).

In this regard, Schimmelfennig (2015a) has recently shown how LI can help one better understand European cooperation during the recent eurozone crisis. Other studies have tested LI in other specific policy areas too: on neighbourhood policy see Gillespie 2011; on immigration see Andersson 2016; on banking regulation see Schäfer 2016. The hope here is that a similar exercise can be achieved in the field of defence industrial cooperation. Furthermore, this book may contribute to the recent debate on 'new intergovernmentalism'. New intergovernmentalism argues that EU cooperation post-Maastricht (1992) has become increasingly intergovernmental in nature even though there has been an intensification of cooperation at the EU level since this period (Bickerton, Hodson and Puetter 2015a, 2015b; Schimmelfennig 2015b). By looking at preference formation and the delegation of powers to the European Commission in the defence industrial policy realm, it may not only be possible to engage with some of the arguments forwarded under new intergovernmentalism, for example, the blurring of lines between 'high' and 'low' politics, but it may also contribute to the recent focus on 'new areas of activity' in EU policy (Bickerton, Hodson and Puetter 2015a; Schimmelfennig 2015b: 727).

Yet the objective of this book is not merely to apply the LI model to the defence sector. In critiquing and building on LI, this book seeks to add conceptual value to the debate by concentrating its analytical focus on how politics and economics interact in domestic preference formation and intergovernmental bargains. Thus far, applying LI to various areas of EU policy have failed to comprehensively engage with an important question: can economic and political preferences really be disentangled at the state level as the theory assumes? As will be shown in this book, European defence industrial cooperation is framed as a situation where governments reassert control over national DTIBs in a context where defence globalisation and broader geopolitical forces threaten to irreparably alter the traditional links that exist between governments and firms. Perhaps unlike any other application of LI, therefore, this book attempts to advance our understanding of the interplay between economic and political preferences in a policy domain that is notoriously wedded to the notion of national sovereignty.

By focusing on the policy processes involved in the development of EU defence industrial policy, this book also feeds into a broader discussion about the EU's role in the world. If, as some scholars assume (Cornish and Edwards 2001; Norheim-Martinsen 2013), the EU's legitimacy in world affairs is premised on the extent and effectiveness of its capabilities, then what might a study of the productive factors needed to generate said military capabilities imply for the EU's legitimacy? Comprehending how the EU member states cooperate on defence industrial matters may help one understand the long-term viability of the EU as an international actor and its position in the global balance of power (Taylor 1990: 59; Neuman 2006, 2009: 85–86). This takes on even more poignancy given the UK's decision to leave the EU in 2016 (Simón 2015; Biscop 2016; Heisbourg 2016; Uttley and Wilkinson 2016) and the election of an American president that has repeatedly called into question the founding principles of NATO (Allin 2016; Schake 2016). Although this book studies historical policy developments, close reading of the findings will be useful for any understanding of how EU defence industrial cooperation may evolve in the future without the UK as a member of the EU and with President Donald Trump in office in the US.

Finally, not only might this book shed light on the EU member states' stake in the European defence market, but the examples of cooperation studied in this book will also distil the major fault lines and possibilities of European defence industrial cooperation for academics, and it could also be useful for policy and commercial actors. The analysis in this book could be of use to the European Commission, which has so far largely pursued defence industrial integration without a theoretically grounded appreciation of the underlying political machinations of defence industrial politics in Europe. Likewise, the EDA stands to profit from a deeper analysis of European defence industrial cooperation. With the 2016 publication of the EU Global Strategy and its follow-on 'Implementation Plan on Security and Defence' (Council of the European Union 2016a, 2016b), and given the geopolitical changes currently being experienced in Europe, this book may usefully bridge the intellectual gap between the EU's industrial initiatives and its broader strategic aims in the field of security and defence. This book could also prove useful to actors (inside and outside the EU) involved in the defence sector – governments and firms alike – that wish to better understand defence industrial policymaking in the European Union.

Book structure

With the addition of this Introduction and a Conclusion, the book is divided into five chapters. Chapter 1 comments on the theoretical and political challenge posed by EU-level defence industrial cooperation and it maps the EU's defence industrial policy framework in more detail. Chapter 2 then outlines the conceptual aspects of the book by providing a critique of LI and by contrasting the model with competing approaches. The book then proceeds to each of the example studies. The first case study is contained in Chapter 3 and is dedicated to the establishment of the European Defence Agency (2003–2004). The second case study in Chapter 4 delineates the adoption of the EU directive on intra-community transfers of defence equipment (2008–2009). Chapter 5 develops the final case study with the example of the adoption of the EU directive for defence procurement (2008–2009). The concluding chapter compares the examples of cooperation and relates them back to the conceptual debate, while also providing some further conceptual and empirical reflections on the future development of EU defence industrial cooperation.

Notes

1 In this book, the 'European Union' refers to all EU member states except for Denmark, which has a specific opt-out on defence and defence industrial issues. EU institutions are also included in this book's definition of the EU with a specific focus on the Council of the European Union, European Commission, European Court of Justice, European Defence Agency and European Parliament.

2 Article 346 TFEU states:

> 1(a) 'no Member State shall be obliged to supply information the disclosure of which it considers contrary to the essential interests of its security'; and
>
> 1(b) 'any Member State may take such measures as it considers necessary for the protection of the essential interests of its security which are connected with the production of or trade in arms, munitions and war materiel; such measures shall not adversely affect the conditions of competition in the internal market regarding products which are not intended for specifically military purposes'.

3 The EU's dual-use export policy is presently governed by Regulation (EC) No. 428/2009 of 5 May 2009 which has set up a Community regime for the control of exports, transfer, brokering and transit of dual-use items. Following a period of public consultation, the European Commission proposed an improved and simplified system for dual-use exports on 28 September 2016 (see proposal COM (2016) 616 final).

4 Directive 2009/43/EC of the European Parliament and of the Council of 6 May 2009 simplifying terms and conditions of transfers of defence-related products within the Community.

5 Directive 2009/81/EC of the European Parliament and of the Council of 13 July 2009 on the coordination of procedures for the award of certain works contracts, supply contracts and service contracts by contracting authorities or entities in the fields of defence and security, and amending Directives 2004/17/EC and 2004/18/EC.

6 To begin its defence research investments, the European Commission launched a Preparatory Action on Defence Research (PADR) in 2017 that will see the European Commission invest €90 million on defence research between 2017 and 2019.

7 Under the proposed 2017 regulation for a European Defence Industrial Development Programme (EDIDP), the European Commission intends to invest up to 20 per cent of the total cost of capability development programmes from 2019 to 2020. The remaining 80 per cent of the programmes will be composed of member state pooled resources.

8 The issue of skills is critical but it does not just relate to the size or knowledge-base of the labour force. As one interviewee revealed, the age of the labour force is also a concern because one-third of the workforce in Europe is over 50 years of age. 'There is a need to attract young technicians into the sector but this is difficult when defence

spending is so low. Young technicians are not going to be attracted to a sector where there is inconsistent demand for orders', interview with an official, European Defence Agency, 28 March 2014.

9 The 'Ghent Initiative' emerged out of a joint German–Swedish 'Food for Thought' paper (dated November 2010) on the European imperative to intensify military cooperation. The Ghent Initiative stressed the need for a 'thorough and systematic analysis of military capabilities and support structures by all EU member states' on the basis of agreed capability development output and economic efficiency (German Government/Swedish Government 2010: 1).

10 The 19 December 2013 European Council meeting focused specifically on defence issues. This was the first such meeting and the Council meeting was consequently dubbed the 'Defence Council'. While the Council conclusions did highlight the importance of the internal–external security nexus, cyber defence, security of supply, Government Satellite Communication and RPAS technology, the main purpose of the Council meeting was to promote the member states' commitment to EU defence policy.

11 The 'New Deal' was elaborated in a Communication from the Commission on 24 July 2013 (see COM(2013) 542 final). As part of the 'New Deal' the Commission stated that it would evaluate the effectiveness of the EU 'defence package', to promote the competitiveness of SMEs, to initiate EU investment in defence research and to assist member states' armed forces to reduce their energy consumption. A follow-on Communication to evaluate the Commission's progress was published on 24 June 2014 (see COM(2014) 387 final).

12 The 'Letter of Intent Framework Agreement Treaty' on defence industrial cooperation was signed on 27 July 2000 between France, Germany, Italy, Spain, Sweden and the UK. The LoI treaty focuses on cooperation in security of supply, export procedures, security of information, research and harmonisation.

13 Representatives from firms based in the following countries were interviewed: France, Germany, Italy, Spain and the UK.

14 Finland, France, Germany, Greece, the Netherlands, Norway, Sweden and the UK.

15 The Paris Agreements were signed on 23 October 1954 and they were the result of the September 1954 London conference and the October 1954 Paris conference. The agreements resulted in full sovereignty for West Germany but they also looked at ways of integrating European armed forces.

16 With the exception of Iceland, the IEPG was established by 'NATO Europe' states to foster collaboration on armaments cooperation. On 10 December 1991 the functions of the IEPG were transferred to the structures of the Western European Union under the WEAG.

17 The WEAG was established following a meeting of WEU ministers in Rome in May 1993. The WEAG was established to harmonise defence requirements, to stimulate cross-border defence trade and to cooperate on defence R&D.

18 OCCAR (also known by its French title the *Organisation Conjointe de Coopération en matière d'armement*) was established in 1996 by the then French, German, Italian and UK defence ministers to manage European armament procurement programmes. To date, Belgium, France, Germany, Italy, Spain and the UK are OCCAR member states. Finland, Luxembourg, the Netherlands, Poland, Sweden and Turkey are participating states without being formal OCCAR members.

1 Surveying EU defence industrial policy

European defence industrial cooperation has been an important issue for many decades. In the Western European Union's 1998 *Rome Declaration* the then member states acknowledged that Europe's

> operational potential cannot be realised without an adequate purpose-adapted European defence capacity and this in turn demands harmonisation of operational requirements and rationalisation of research and technology, development and procurement as well as of the industrial base in the field of armaments.
>
> (Western European Union 1998: 3)

Even in the 1950s, Articles 107 and 109 of the failed Treaty for a European Defence Community referred to the need for European states to standardise and jointly procure defence equipment (Fursdon 1980: 163–162; Ruane 2000). In more recent times, former president of the European Council, Herman Van Rompuy, has surmised that greater cooperation is a way of strengthening Europe's broader industrial and manufacturing base because it supports scientific ingenuity and a high-skilled labour force (European Council 2013a: 6). Bodies such as the European Defence Agency support this sentiment by working to ensure that Europe produces cutting-edge defence capabilities (European Defence Agency 2006a, 2007; European Council 2013a: 6). As the Agency's 2007 *EDTIB Strategy* makes plain, if a strong European defence industrial base is to underpin the EU's CSDP then Europe 'cannot continue routinely to determine [its] equipment requirements on separate national bases, develop them through separate national R&D efforts, and realise them through separate national procurements' (European Defence Agency 2007: 1).

More recently, the EU Global Strategy makes clear that strategic autonomy is a goal for EU defence and that the industrial elements of this autonomy require sustained EU support (2016: 45). This strategy has given rise to a number of defence industrial policy initiatives. For example, the member states have agreed to a Coordinated Annual Review on Defence (CARD) which will see the EDA ensure greater synchronisation between the national defence planning processes of EU member states. The idea is for member state defence planners to share information on defence planning horizons and future technology/capability plans with the EDA in the hope that duplication can be avoided and future cooperative programmes can be defined. The hope is that CARD may lead to greater opportunities for capability development and defence research collaboration (Fiott 2017a).

Furthermore, in 2016 the European Commission established a European Defence Fund where it has committed €90 million for defence research until the end of 2019. This total is planned to rise to €500 million per year after 2020, making the European Commission the fourth largest investor in defence research in the EU when compared to the member states. Furthermore, under the fund the Commission has set aside €500 million over 2019 to 2020 to support the development of joint capability programmes in the EU, and after 2020 the Commission expects this total to rise to €1 billion per year (European Commission 2017). This initiative seeks to enhance European cooperation through the use of financial incentives. These incentives are designed to ensure that no financial support will be provided to the member states without first agreeing to standardise defence requirements at the beginning of a capability project and to develop these programmes in collaboration with two or more partner member states (De La Brosse 2017; Fiott 2017b).

One other notable initiative that emerged in December 2017 is the agreement between 25 EU member states to engage in Permanent Structured Cooperation (PESCO). As foreseen under the Lisbon Treaty, PESCO is designed as a political framework that should lead to the progressive framing of a common EU defence. PESCO is divided between two levels of cooperation. First, the participating member states – all EU states minus Denmark, Malta and the UK – agree to 20 binding commitments that are subject to a yearly review by the HR/VP (with support from the EDA and the EU Military Staff) that range from spending more on defence, enhancing European capability development to engaging with defence research endeavours. Second, the participating member states are involved in developing specific capability projects. In 2018, a first wave of 17 projects, including maritime surveillance, armoured vehicles, a medical command, etc. was agreed to with further project phases to be defined in the future. PESCO is designed to give a structured, political framework to European defence cooperation (Fiott, Missiroli and Tardy 2017; Biscop 2018).

In the face of defence market fragmentation and greater global competition, these new initiatives combine with the examples of cooperation found in this book to form the basis for the EU's defence industrial policy framework. The book opts for the notion of a 'defence industrial policy framework' (see Figure 1.1 below) instead of the often-used 'EDTIB' because the EDTIB is a contested concept.[1] Instead, this book focuses on law and regulation, capability development programmes, financing mechanisms and policy initiatives. This chapter in turn raises some of the challenges associated with national preference formation and interdependence in the European defence sector. Accordingly, this chapter takes stock of how the balancing of market openness and autarky, economic health and military strength and sovereignty and cooperation plays out in a European context. This chapter is consequently divided into four main sections that look consecutively at the constituent parts of the European defence industrial policy framework.

Law and regulation

The most developed element of the EU's defence industrial policy framework is law and regulation, or, to be more precise, EU primary and secondary law. No other defence industrial cooperative framework in Europe – not the LoI, OCCAR or NATO – embodies a legal framework such as that found at the EU level. Not only do the EU treaties frame questions about national sovereignty, defence and industry in an EU context but the European Commission plays an important role in upholding key elements of legislation that relate to the defence sector. For its part, the ECJ serves as a mediator in disputes involving the member states, firms and the Commission. The European Parliament, as a co-legislator with the Council of the EU, plays an important role in amending and agreeing to defence-relevant EU secondary law such as the 'defence package'. EU law is an important, albeit limited, mechanism through which to coerce the member states into adhering to laws that are aimed at liberalising the European defence market (Blauberger and Weiss 2013). The laws and regulations that underpin the EU's internal market are a way to break down barriers between national defence markets and to enhance cross-border trade in defence equipment, while also pushing regulation to the EU level. As Trybus remarks, '[w]hile this Internal Market or "Community" regulation and policy cannot be considered a complete success [it has] established a viable legal framework for the operation of the Internal Market' in the defence sector (2014: 222).

This is a familiar facet of European market integration. Hix and Goetz (2000) observe that the European Commission has traditionally supported a process of market liberalisation at the EU level. As they remark, 'the EU is a deregulatory project. The removal of technical, fiscal and physical barriers to the "free movement" of goods, services, capital and labour in the single market programme' has led to 'considerable deregulation and liberalisation of domestic markets' (ibid.: 4). While the drive towards more market liberalisation cannot be disputed, even in the defence sector, it is worth reflecting on the tools required to achieve greater liberalisation in Europe's defence markets. Regulation – that is, regulation at the EU rather than the national level – is a vital part of the liberalisation process (McGowan and Wallace 1996; Majone 1997; Damro 2012: 687). Thus, whereas the European Commission has pledged 'to further develop the Internal Market for defence' it can only do this via regulation that tackles persistent 'unfair and discriminatory practices and market distortions' (European Commission 2013a: 10). The European Commission favours the simultaneous liberalisation of economic activities in the internal market and greater EU-level regulation. While market liberalisation is a way to dismantle barriers to trade within the internal market, regulation at the EU level is defined as the 'promulgation of an authoritative set of rules, accompanied by some mechanism for monitoring and promoting compliance with those rules' (Levi-Faur 2008: 103).

In many ways, the liberalisation/regulation agenda is to be expected, given that 'supranational agents are characterised by a common preference for greater competences for themselves and for the European Union as a whole' (Pollack 2003: 39). Yet, the European Commission does not have a free hand in its quest for a more liberalised and regulated EU defence market. There are several factors hindering a greater regulatory role for the Commission in the European defence market. First, given the European Commission's responsibilities for a range of defence-relevant areas such as competition law, research policy, industrial policy, internal market, etc., it should not be assumed that each directorate general[2] (DG) is enthusiastic about gaining greater competences over the defence sector – especially for those DGs with an overwhelmingly civilian focus such as research policy (Mörth 2000). Second, the European Commission finds it difficult to establish links with Europe's defence firms because these firms still overwhelmingly deal with national governments – after all, governments offer procurement contracts and the Commission does not. As one official from the European Commission confirmed, 'unfortunately we still only have an indirect and partial link with the defence industry'.[3]

The European Commission's role in the formulation of defence industrial policy is therefore limited to a 'structural approach' that can be defined as the undertaking of initiatives that are designed to shape the internal market in defence via an emphasis on market regulation and competition. As the European Commission itself recognises, the best framework through which 'to implement structural change' in the European defence market is to use its regulatory, internal market-based, powers (European Commission 2013a: 8). The European Commission's policy approach to European defence industrial policy is conditioned by its own *mandate*, which emanates mainly from EU primary and

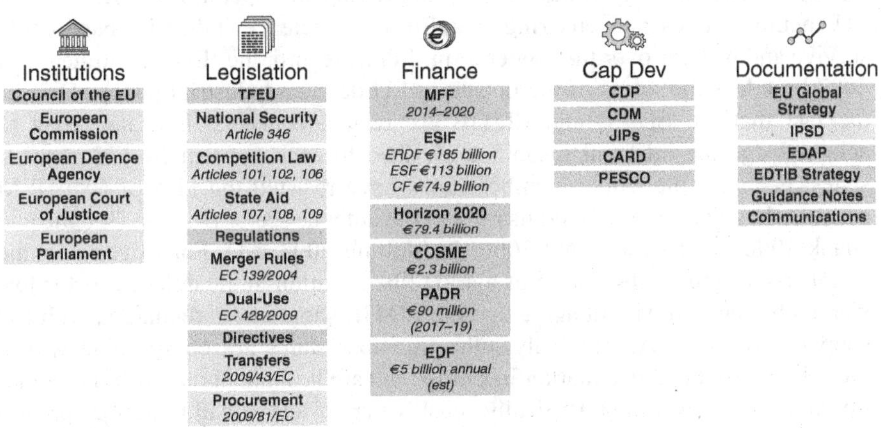

Figure 1.1 The EU Defence Industrial Policy Framework.

Source: author's own.

secondary law, and *institutional* form, because it is a supranational institution without automatic links to the defence industry or powers over national defence industrial decision-making. Confined to a specific mandate based on its position as the legal custodian of EU Treaties, the European Commission is, for now at least, largely restricted to its regulatory powers in the field of arms cooperation (Trybus 2006: 673; Britz 2010: 178; Calleja-Crespo and Delsaux 2012: 6; Hoeffler 2012).

Nevertheless, the role played by EU law and regulation in driving defence market liberalisation and enhancing EU-level regulation has long been a key element of the European Commission's strategy for the EDTIB. The Commission's own steps to create an effective European Defence Equipment Market (EDEM) reflect its desire to see an 'homogenous defence economy framework' in which the civil, internal security and military market spheres are gradually brought together to form an integrated dual-use market (Schmitt 2005a: 10–11; Aalto 2008: 39). The idea for an EDEM gained particular traction in the 1990s and the policy concept was seen as a vehicle for market liberalisation based on the principles of the EU internal market and EU law (i.e. the free movement of goods and services, open public procurement, etc.). The ethos under the EDEM was that defence market liberalisation could be achieved through market regulation; in particular, the free flow of goods and services would eventually lower the cost of defence for European states. It is important to recognise the nuanced difference in meaning between the EDEM and the EDTIB, even though the two concepts are used interchangeably in policy and academic literature.

Whereas the EDEM referred more specifically to market liberalisation and defence equipment, the EDTIB addressed more strategically salient factors such as defence research, security of supply and equipment standardisation. Whereas the EDEM was mainly focused on reducing the barriers and costs associated with intra-EU cross-border cooperation, the EDTIB concept went one step further by channelling efforts towards improving the operational autonomy of EU member states and ensuring that Europe's defence industrial base could survive and prosper over the longer term. In this regard, the 'EDTIB Strategy' of 2007 broadens the terms of the debate in EU defence industrial policy. Despite the fact that the EDEM and EDTIB are related concepts, it is important to acknowledge the different meanings ascribed to each concept by EU member states. For example, some member states have resisted the idea of an EDEM because they fear market liberalisation in the defence sector (Marks, Hooghe and Blank 1996: 342; Broomfield 2000: 2; Mölling 2008: 51). For example, some member states resist the notion of market liberalisation in the defence sector forwarded by the EDEM, but agree that the EDTIB should be safeguarded with EU support if needed. Alternatively, other member states are comfortable with a more liberalised defence market in Europe but are hesitant about pushing regulation to the EU level in strategically sensitive areas lest it lead to a more protectionist European defence market (Bitzinger 2009: 186).

Hartley (2011) has stated that any EU-level initiative designed to liberalise the defence market will potentially create 'winners' and 'losers'. As he remarks, '[c]hange is not costless [...] [i]nevitably, potential losers will oppose changes which inflict costs on the losing groups [...] [l]osers will lobby for protection; for "fair and managed" competition; and for *juste retour* in work-sharing' (Hartley 2011: 145). If one follows the respective objectives of the EDEM and EDTIB to their logical conclusions, one could have to accept the challenging side-effects of factory and shipyard closures, job losses and a range of socio-economic and strategic costs in those member states where markets are failing to create efficient defence production (Kuechle 2006: 38). The tension between greater market liberalisation and EU-level regulation in Europe's defence markets and the protection of national industries is reflected in several legal tools embedded in the EU treaties including Article 346 TFEU on national security, Articles 101, 102, 106 TFEU on competition law and Articles 107, 108 and 109 TFEU on state aid; the EU's merger regulation (EC/139/2004)[4]; the EU's 'defence package'; and the EU's dual-use export controls. Each of these tools is addressed below.

Article 346

A crucial element of EU primary law is Article 346[5] of the TFEU, as this gives EU member state governments a right of derogation from the internal market provisions of the treaties on the grounds of national security. As the TFEU states: 'any Member State may take such measures as it considers necessary for the protection of the essential interests of its security which are connected with the production of or trade in arms, munitions and war materiel' (European Union 2012: 194). Whereas some hold that the existence of Article 346 reinforces the intergovernmental nature of EU defence industrial cooperation (Edgar 2001: 130), a more nuanced state of affairs exists because Article 346 can only be justifiably invoked by member states under EU law for security rather than economic reasons (European Union 2012: 194). Thus, a government wishing to protect a niche area of production such as nuclear weapons technology from the reach of EU law may successfully invoke Article 346, but should a government invoke Article 346 for a more general move to protect jobs or to organise defence offset agreements, then this government risks infringement proceedings being brought against it by the European Commission.

In most cases brought by the European Commission before the ECJ thus far, member states have been accused of invoking Article 346 for the purposes of avoiding payments to the EU's 'own resources'. The EU's own resources are accrued to the EU Budget through customs duties on imports into the EU and/or through value added tax (VAT) levies. Some member states have used Article 346 to avoid paying these resources on imports of military equipment into the EU.[6] Two landmark judgments by the European Court of Justice – *Commission* v. *Spain* (C-414/97)[7] and *Commission* v. *Italy* (C-337/05)[8] – have enhanced the European Commission's ability to successfully challenge EU member states when invoking Article 346. As was reinforced by the ECJ in *Commission* v. *Portugal* (C-38/06):

> [a]ccording to the Court's settled case-law, although it is for Member States to take the appropriate measures to ensure their internal and external security, it does not follow that such measures are entirely outside the scope of European Union law.[9]

However, the inherent tension at the heart of Article 346 is how one defines 'essential interests'. Whereas the European Commission argues that EU law strictly prohibits an economic rationale for invoking Article 346, governments may not readily agree with a clinical division between economic and security interests (Trybus 2002, 2005: 123–125, 2009; European Commission 2006a; Randazzo 2014; Fiott 2015b: 546). The division between security and economic interests has been one of the major factors in debates about European defence industrial cooperation. On the one hand, the Commission and some member state governments and firms see the power to contest the invocation of Article 346 as a way to further liberalise the European defence market (European Council 2013b: 12). Therefore, it should not be assumed that every EU member state is hostile to the European Commission upholding EU law in the European defence market. On the other hand, certain governments are reluctant to fully adhere to the internal market provisions of the treaties so as to avoid incurring any negative impact on their national DTIBs and economies.

EU competition law

EU competition law is grounded in Articles 101, 102 and 106 of the TFEU. Article 101 specifically prohibits practices such as price fixing, resource supply restrictions and defence offsets and is therefore relevant to the defence sector (Trybus 2005: 231). Article 101(1e) refers to defence offsets when stating that it is prohibited to conclude 'contracts subject to acceptance by the other parties of supplementary obligations that, by their nature or according to commercial usage, have no connection with the subject of contracts'. Thus, Article 101 TFEU is a vital element of the EU's legal regime because it strives to ensure that the European defence market becomes more competitive. For its part, Article 102[10] specifically refers to the abuse of a dominant position within the internal market, which, given that many defence firms find themselves in a position of monopsony, is another vitally relevant part of the EU's competition law regime that affects the defence sector. As Trybus remarks, '[i]n many segments of the defence market, for example of fighter aircraft, missiles, or warships, some national producers have a dominant position even without mergers with companies from other Member States' (2005: 232–233). Finally, Article 106(3)[11] is applicable to the European defence sector because it provides the European Commission with the competence to ensure the application of the provisions of EU competition law in a sector that is traditionally dominated by governments.

In theory, therefore, once one excludes the possibility of invoking Article 346 the European Commission should be in a relatively strong position to shape the European defence market using legal tools such as Articles 101, 106 and 107

TFEU. Yet, in the context of an EU internal market where there is an increasing level of cross-border activity, firms can avoid the reach of Articles 101, 102 and 106 through various strategies. For example, defence firms can divide their economic activities into different product groups such as missiles or tanks or they may divide their business over different geographical areas in Europe (Trybus 2014: 170). In this way, they can avoid concentrating their business activities in one country/sector and they can thus avoid being accused of a dominant market position under Article 102 TFEU. Of course, this form of strategy is only successful if it has the indirect/direct backing of a government, because without government support Article 346 cannot be invoked, and neither can strategies that are designed to avoid the reach of EU law materialise (ibid.: 171). Even though the Commission and the ECJ interpret Article 346 in a far narrower way than they did during the 1990s, the ability to derogate from the provisions of the EU treaties based on 'essential security interests' is still a political device that the member states utilise (Dyson and Konstadinides 2013: 92).

State aid

The EU's state aid regime is also pertinent to European defence industrial policy because 'state aid control has a fundamental role to play in defending and strengthening the internal market, also in the defence sector' (European Commission 2013a: 6). Article 107 TFEU is clear that state aid that 'distorts or threatens to distort competition' shall be considered 'incompatible with the internal market'. There are many forms of state aid that can be considered compatible with the internal market, and as far as the defence sector is concerned Article 107(3c) allows aid if it 'does not adversely affect trading conditions to an extent contrary to the common interest'. Additionally, Article 108 TFEU confers on the European Commission the competence to 'keep under constant review all systems of aid existing' in the member states, although Article 109[12] provides the Council with the opportunity to exempt certain categories of aid from the EU's state aid regime. As the *Communication on EU State Aid Modernisation* (2012) makes clear, '[s]tronger and better targeted State aid control can encourage the design of more effective growth-enhancing policies and it can ensure that competition distortions remain limited so that the internal market remains open and contestable' (European Commission 2012a: 3). The member states 'have an obligation, under the Treaty, to notify to the Commission all state aid measures, including aid in the pure military sector' (European Commission 2013b: 6).

The EU's state aid regime can be characterised as a mixture of 'soft' and 'hard' law: 'soft' law allows for a degree of flexibility in applying EU law by relying on informal practices and discretion, whereas 'hard' law emerges in those cases 'when a touch line on member state compliance is deemed necessary' (Cini 2001: 204). Given the inherent flexibility of 'soft' law, the EU's state aid regime has been framed as a pragmatic one that has allowed for a form of 'negative integration' – one that constrains distorting behaviour without the immediate use of 'hard' law and stringent measures. While this process of 'negative integration' reflects the need to accommodate various state interests, Blauberger (2009) has interestingly observed that complex systems of 'soft' law have allowed the European Commission to not only define 'admissible state aid' but to also influence national state aid policies. Yet, because of a lack of political will or economic interest on the part of the member states, and because different ministries at the national level are responsible for state aid, influencing such policies is no easy task. Furthermore, in many cases the degree of government support afforded to firms can sometimes reflect whether the government is a shareholder of the defence firm in question or not (Trybus 2014: 38).

The EU's merger regulation

The EU's merger control regime is a further element of the legal regime applicable to the European defence market. The EU's merger regulation (EC/139/2004) (*ex* EEC/4064/89) is principally activated in those cases where a merger would result in a combined aggregate worldwide turnover of €2.5 billion, and where the combined turnover of all those entities seeking to merge represent an aggregate of €100 million in at least three member states (European Commission 2013b: 9). While it should be recalled that Recital 19[13] and Article 21 of the merger regulation grant governments a legitimate derogation from the provisions of the Regulation on the grounds of 'legitimate interests' related to public security (Trybus 2014: 237–240), the European Commission states that it 'has extensively applied the merger control rules to the defence sector' (European Commission 2013b: 6). It is mandatory for member states to notify the European Commission on mergers that have a Community dimension. The Commission can act under Article 6 of the merger regulation to ascertain whether any planned merger would be compatible with the common market, and, if it is not satisfied, it can take a final decision based on Article 8 of the Regulation to prohibit a merger altogether (ibid.: 9).

Merger control is one of the most controversial elements of the EU's corpus of competition law (McGowan and Cini 1999: 175), especially in the European defence sector, because of the variable nature of state ownership of defence industries. This is because unlike US competition laws or anti-trust policy, the primary aim of European competition policy 'is that of closer integration' (ibid.: 177). Interestingly, the European Commission's application of the merger regulation in various defence-related cases gives one an indication of precisely how EU law can affect proposed mergers. In the clear majority of merger notifications the European Commission has ruled that the proposed mergers do not adversely affect the EU single market. For example, following the invocation of Article 346 by the British and French governments in the 1990s, the European Commission did not object to the proposed merger between *British Aerospace* and *Lagardère SCA* during this period, even though the Commission studied the potential spillover effects of the merger on the dual-use market (Koutrakos 2001: 178; see also Trybus 2014: 236–237). Article 346 was yet again invoked during the 1999 proposed merger involving *Aérospatiale* and *Société Nationale*

Industrielle Aérospatiale (SNPE), but governments did so with no serious objections by the European Commission (Koutrakos 2001: 178 see also Teichler *et al.* 2010).

The EU's 'defence package'

In addition to EU primary and secondary law on competition, exist two defence-specific pieces of secondary legislation: the 'defence transfers directive' (known also as the 'ICT directive') (2009/43/EC) and the 'defence procurement directive' (2009/81/EC).[14] When taken together, these directives are referred to as the EU's 'defence package'. The two directives aim to simplify the rules and procedures, and to lower the bureaucratic costs, associated with arms transfers in the EU and with defence procurement (European Commission 1996: 6; European Commission 2003; Trybus 2014). The European Commission has an important stake in the 'defence package' because the directives represent vehicles through which national barriers to defence trade can eventually be diminished or removed altogether (European Defence Agency 2009). Taken together, the two defence directives aim to liberalise the European defence market while simultaneously improving security of supply for the member states. A more in-depth analysis of the two directives can be found in Chapters 4 and 5.

The defence transfers directive is designed to facilitate the transfer of defence-related products within the EU. Before the transposition of 2009/43/EC a multitude of national export licensing systems made the transfer of defence equipment within the EU cumbersome and costly, which added to the fragmentation of defence markets in Europe. The transfers directive has introduced a harmonised set of transfer licences for use across the EU, even though member state authorities remain solely responsible for issuing export certificates. The defence procurement directive seeks to harmonise EU rules for the procurement of arms and munitions, and related maintenance and services, within the EU. For its part, directive 2009/81/EC aims to harmonise practices when awarding defence contracts valued over €400,000 for supply and service contracts and €5 million for works contracts. The overall aim is to ensure transparency and open public tendering. Importantly, the defence procurement directive does not apply to government-to-government contracts, immovable property such as military bases, intelligence activities or where a contract would result in disclosure of sensitive security information.

Dual-use controls

In addition to the 'defence package' the European Commission also exercises regulatory responsibility over the EU's export control regime for dual-use goods and technologies. Such goods and technologies can be defined as items that are produced for civilian purposes, but which can also be utilised for military purposes. For example, telemetry systems that are used to tune motor vehicles to run at optimal performance can be adapted to fly Remotely Piloted Aircraft

Systems (RPAS). Dual-use goods and technologies represent a regulatory challenge because, given their simultaneous civilian nature, dual-use goods and technologies do not automatically fall under defence-specific EU primary and secondary law. Initially, Council Regulation 3381/94[15] (1994) and then the EU's *Code of Conduct on Arms Exports* (1998) attempted to retain the intergovernmental nature of dual-use regulation in the EU. However, following the ECJ's rulings in the *Leifer* (C-83/94)[16] and *Werner* (C-70/94)[17] cases, which stipulated that dual-use items should be considered as civilian goods, and thus treated in accordance with the EU's internal market rules, it was not possible for the member states to apply Article 346 in cases of dual-use procurement. Following the ECJ's rulings, dual-use items are considered part of the EU's Common Commercial Policy. Under Regulation 1334/2000[18] – known as the EU's dual-use regulation – and its later revision through Regulation 428/2009,[19] the Commission attained the exclusive right of initiative over dual-use transfers and it designed a harmonised licensing system based on an EU dual-use list that it manages (Schmitt 2001: 5–7).

One should not confuse the EU's dual-use control regime with conventional arms control, as conventional arms control is not included in the EU's Common Commercial Policy. The EU's Common Military List of goods is regularly updated by the member states through the Council of the EU rather than through or by the European Commission. It is the EU's Common Position (2008/944/CFSP)[20] that specifically relates to conventional arms transfers. Some see the Common Position as a basis for a harmonisation and even Europeanisation of arms controls policies across the EU, but, as Bromley and Brzoska (2008) have argued, despite some degree of agreement on the normative values espoused by the Common Position, member states still largely operate national systems (see also Hansen 2016). By agreeing to the Common Position, EU member states have pledged to exchange information on arms export licence denials and approvals as they relate to extra-EU exports and to 'controls to cover the licensing of production abroad, brokering activities, transit and transhipment, and intangible transfers of technology' (Bromley 2011: 40). In contrast to the EU's dual-use control regime 'all aspects of actual policy implementation in the field of arms exports remain firmly in the hands of member states' (ibid.: 41).

Capability development

In addition to law and regulation stand the initiatives that are designed to encourage cross-border military capability development, procurement and R&T and R&D investments. Military capability development is a crucial element of the EU's CSDP because having capabilities is a crucial way to ensure that the EU can act as both a foreign policy and defence actor in an autonomous fashion (Shepherd 2000; Britz and Eriksson 2008: 57; Duke 2017). One of the most important rationales for the CSDP is to improve the capabilities of European militaries (Shepherd 2015: 65; Duke 2017). If the EU is to live up to the promise of its own 'Petersberg Tasks' (Article 43 TEU),[21] which set out a range of military tasks such as humanitarian and rescue tasks, peacemaking and peacekeeping that the EU aspires to undertake, then this cannot be achieved if the EU member states do not have the concomitant military capabilities. Therefore, in addition to the European Capability Action Plan (ECAP),[22] the Capability Development Plan (CDP),[23] the Capability Development Mechanism (CDM)[24] and treaty innovations such as PESCO,[25] which have attempted to identify key military capability gaps and to structure/institutionalise cooperation among the EU member states, the EDTIB is a policy framework through which to stimulate European cooperation on defence capability programmes.

The EDA – as the EU's sole intergovernmental agency for defence – was established in 2004 to drive forward capability development initiatives and to encourage the pooling and sharing of military capabilities among EU member states. While the European Commission can claim to be involved in broader capability areas such as satellites (Matlary 2009: 131), it is the EDA that is mandated to focus on military capability development and to participate in defining European capabilities and armaments cooperation initiatives, identify operational requirements, evaluate the improvement of military capabilities and strengthen the EDTIB (see Council of the European Union 2011a). In contrast to the European Commission's 'structural approach' to European defence industrial cooperation, the Agency embodies a more 'ad hoc' strategy focusing on individual projects rather than on legal and regulatory instruments (Bátora 2009; Fiott 2015b). The EDA conducts its business within a specific political environment where its available financial resources are relatively low – it has an operational budget averaging €30 million per year since 2010 – and it is dependent on the member states for the initiation of capability programmes and initiatives (Fiott 2015b: 545).

The EDA has achieved limited success in stimulating cross-border capability development, although some progress has been achieved in areas such as the European Air Transport Fleet (EATF) programme, which is designed to provide common airlift services in the EU. On the one hand, the Agency has presided over projects such as air-to-air refuelling, helicopter training, maritime surveillance and satellite communications and it is currently working on helping member states develop their cyber defences, remotely piloted aircraft systems and collaborative R&D ventures. For example, in 2014 the EDA – serving as a central purchasing body – signed a contract with Saab Group to procure ammunition on behalf of the governments of the Czech Republic, Estonia, Latvia, Lithuania and Poland. On the other hand, capability development is an ongoing process fraught with numerous difficulties and 'when Member States invest in defence, they do not necessarily invest in the right capabilities, nor do they always procure capabilities in the most cost-effective manner' (Biscop and Coelmont 2013: 80). While a strong rationale for closer cooperation through the EDA should exist (Biscop 2011; Chang 2011), collaborative military capability development programmes are notoriously difficult to manage because of competing government, commercial and institutional preferences (Reynolds 2007; De Vore 2011; Fiott 2015b).

One of the chief reasons why it is difficult to develop military capabilities across member state borders is the split that loyalty European governments have towards various organisations and arrangements. Not only can several European states work through select groupings such as the LoI framework or OCCAR, but most European states can push – albeit with varying degrees of success – for capability development efforts through the EU under initiatives such as the 'Code of Conduct on Pooling and Sharing' (2012) or through NATO and the alliance's 'Smart Defence' (2012) approach. This is not even to speak of the various national capability development programmes that exist, such as the Queen Elizabeth Class aircraft carrier programme in the UK, the range of bilateral initiatives underway such as the Franco-British Lancaster House Treaties or non-EU multilateral programmes involving the United States such as the F-35 fighter programme. Indeed, 'capability development remains an almost entirely bottom-up process, nearly completely reliant on national initiative and hence protective of national industrial interests' (Biscop 2015: 37; see also Fiott 2013a). This is problematic because it is difficult to achieve a Europe-wide consensus on what capabilities are required when the member states plan on a largely national or sub-regional basis (Howorth 2014: 74; see also Yost 2000: 99–100; Zandee 2015: 106–107).

As far as the EDTIB and the CSDP are concerned the myriad of national, bilateral, EU and/or NATO capability development initiatives do not exactly lead to conditions for an EU economy of scale in the defence sector (Whitman 2004; Jones 2007: 190; Simón 2016: 148). Those who hold the view that the CSDP may eventually create enough demand to keep the European defence industry fertile should – at present at least – be disappointed.[26] Steps through the European defence industrial policy framework to liberalise and regulate the defence market will not make much sense if the CSDP is held back by no overarching commitment by the member states or industry. While the CSDP was originally established to ensure that Europeans were militarily capable of providing security, today's reality is that the CSDP is overwhelmingly geared to civilian operations that do not necessarily require military capabilities (Simón 2012; Fiott 2015a: 165). To the extent that the EU does undertake military operations it does so on a small scale and at a level that would alone fail to support the European defence market. Recognising that the CSDP is at present unable to sustain an EDTIB, this is perhaps one of the reasons why the EDTIB also relates to the defence sector more broadly so as to also serve bilateral and multilateral endeavours and NATO. As the former President of the European Council, Herman Van Rompuy, has put it, the 'main concern is not so much CSDP as such or "EU defence", but rather the state of defence in Europe' (European Council 2013a: 5).

Here, the NATO dimension should not be overlooked. Despite assurances from the NATO Secretary General that there 'is no contradiction between strong European defence and strong NATO [*sic*]', discussions about military capability development in an EU–NATO context have traditionally been challenging (Stoltenberg 2016). In theory, both organisations would benefit from more militarily capable European armed forces and the 2003 'Berlin Plus' agreement was designed to ensure a high degree of complementarity between EU and NATO assets (Cornish 2004; Whitman 2004: Rynning 2008; Hofmann 2009). A 'NATO–EU Capability Group' was established to aid this cooperation. However, despite an EU–NATO Joint Declaration in 2016 stating that the two organisations will work together on defence industrial matters, industrial and political considerations have conspired to hamper any joint EU–NATO approach to military capability development. Quite apart from the fact that a number of EU member states with relatively sizeable DTIBs (Austria, Finland and Sweden) are non-members of NATO, the overwhelming US presence within NATO is seen by many European states as a 'back door' to promote American industry. As one preparatory document for the 2013 French *Livre Blanc* made clear, it is not CSDP but NATO that favours 'American defence industries, *a fortiori* in a constrained budgetary context' (French Government 2013a: 48; see also Fiott 2013c: 24). Besides the broad appeal of the EDTIB, therefore, it has, as a concept, been closely related to EU military capability efforts rather than NATO.

Finance

Financial mechanisms are also an important feature of European defence industrial policy, and the European Commission presides over a range of funds aimed at inducing cross-border cooperation, assisting governments to specialise in niche technology areas and supporting more than 1,350 defence-relevant SMEs in the EU. The EU's Multi-annual Financial Framework (MFF) totals €960 billion in allocations over the 2014–2020 period and two components of the MFF are specifically applicable to the defence sector. The first component relates to the MFF's investments in 'Economic, Social and Territorial Cohesion'. This funding area relates to the EU's 'Structural and Investment Funds' (ESIFs), which total €454 billion over 2014–2020, and includes the European Regional Development Fund (ERDF), which represents a €185 billion share of the ESIFs over 2014–2020, the European Social Fund (ESF), with a share of €113 billion from the ESIFs, and the Cohesion Fund (CF), which amounts to €74.9 billion. The ESIFs are designed to encourage regional development and to correct economic and social imbalances between the EU member states and regions. Accordingly, the European Commission and EDA encourage SMEs to apply for funding under the ESIFs for the development of defence-relevant labour reskilling and re-training, the creation and support of regional clusters[27] of firms, research institutes and the leveraging of regional and central government financial support and investment in the defence sector.

The second component of funding relates to the MFF's investments in 'Competitiveness for Growth and Jobs'. Under this area of investment, the defence sector can draw on a range of R&D-specific funding instruments such as Horizon 2020[28] research grants worth €79.4 billion over the 2014–2020 period, and the Competitiveness of Enterprises and Small and Medium-sized Enterprises (COSME)[29] programme totalling €2.3 billion over 2014–2020. These financial mechanisms play a key role in the European Commission's ability to strategically invest in dual-use R&D programmes, the internationalisation of defence SMEs, etc. (Council of the European Union 2013; European Defence Agency 2014a). For example, several defence firms that work in the satellite and earth monitoring research sectors have benefitted from direct support under the EU's *Copernicus*,[30] with support totalling €4.3 billion over 2014–2020, and *Galileo*,[31] with support totalling €7.1 billion over 2014–2020, programmes. Yet there are important limitations on what the Commission can invest in, because investment in the production of, or trade in, weapons systems or ammunition is strictly forbidden under current EU budget rules. Despite this restriction, the European Commission, in cooperation with the EDA under the European Framework Cooperation for Security and Defence (2009),[32] is nonetheless able to indirectly invest in key technologies such as unmanned systems, satellite technologies, nanotechnologies, etc. It does this by placing emphasis on investments in dual-use R&D and technologies, which have predominantly commercial benefits rather than military payoffs (Molas-Gallart 1997, 2002; Fiott 2015b).

Defence-relevant funding at the EU level is not a new phenomenon. From the mid-1980s until the mid-1990s the EU funded two major R&D research programmes entitled Basic Research in Industrial Technologies for Europe (BRITE) and the European Research on Advanced Materials (EURAM), which each benefitted the aeronautical sector by supporting university research and collaboration with industry (Bach *et al.* 1995; Raube *et al.* 2015). Furthermore, following the Cold War and the resulting need to deal with the disarming of Europe's militaries, the EU used the structural funds to run two programmes – entitled Perifra and KONVER – on defence conversion during the 1990s in industrially declining regions (Guay 1996: 407; Hooper and Cox 1996; Markusen and Brzoska 2000). Over 2004–2006 the European Commission also launched a Preparatory Action on Security Research (PASR) that invested €65 million per annum in security-related projects. Although the PASR did invest in defence-relevant research areas such as biometrics, surveillance, critical infrastructure protection and crisis management, the PASR was predominantly geared to security and civilian research (Bigo and Jeandesboz 2008: 4; Breant and Karock 2011).

As of 2017, the European Commission is working to initiate a defence-specific PADR. The Preparatory Action was launched in 2017 and it will serve as a test-bed to prove the relevance of EU investment in defence-related research. In 2017, a total of €25 million was allocated from the EU budget towards defence research, although the plan is to allocate €90 million over a three-year period from 2017–2019 overall (EU Institute for Security Studies 2016: 26). The Preparatory Action follows on from a pilot project on CSDP research worth €1.4 million that was launched by the European Parliament to cover the 2015–2016 period. Should the Preparatory Action prove successful, the next step would be to insert a specific thematic area on defence research within the EU's next Multi-annual Financial Framework (2021–2027) worth some €3.5 billion (ibid.: 27). The idea is to refer to this thematic area as the 'European Defence Research Programme' (EDRP). While the EU's experiences with research funding have, to date, been restricted to civilian or dual-use programmes, the Preparatory Action and any future EDRP will represent a significant change in the way the EU views and invests in defence-specific R&D (Fiott and Bellais 2016).[33]

Additionally, on 30 November 2016 the European Commission published a 'European Defence Action Plan' (EDAP), which contained several new financing initiatives. While many of the initiatives contained in the EDAP will take time to materialise, the Plan contains the idea for an EDF (European Commission 2016: 5). There are two elements to the proposed Fund. First, a 'research window' that includes all the defence research-related initiatives mentioned above (i.e. the PADR and EDRP). Second, a 'capability window' that is supposed to pool national financial contributions at the EU level to invest in joint capability programmes. The Commission estimates that the 'capability window' of the EDF would be worth an average €5 billion per year, once member state contributions are added to the Commission's own commitment of €1 billion per year after 2020. As one can imagine, convincing the member states to depart with scarce public funds for the sake of EU-level capability development programmes is no easy task. To this end, the Commission aims to make participation in the EDF's 'capability window' attractive by supplementing national contributions with the EU budget and special purpose funds such as the European Fund for Strategic Investments (EFSI)[34]; exempting investments made into the 'capability window' from the Stability and Growth Pact[35] criteria; and offering the member states the Commission's own 'back office' support to manage programmes. Time will tell if the EDF proves a success.

Policy initiatives

The policy initiatives and policy publications that are intermittently developed and produced or commissioned by the European Commission and the EDA are another component of the European defence industrial policy framework (see Table 1.1 below). As far as publications go, official European Commission communications alert governments to the Commission's own thinking on defence industrial matters, and its 'non-papers' and/or 'guidance notes' on various aspects of EU defence industrial policy clarify how to apply EU legislation. For its part, the EDA has published several relevant policy communications including, most notably, an *EDTIB Strategy* (2007). The EDA has also drafted many *Codes of Conduct* to guide member states on issues related to defence procurement (2005) and the defence supply chain (2006). Annually, the EDA also publishes defence data on its participating member states including data on defence expenditure and standing forces. In addition, the European Commission, the EDA and the European Parliament have commissioned several studies that focus on various aspects of defence industrial policy (see TNO 2009; Ecorys 2010, 2012; Briani *et al.* 2013). While one can arguably contest the overall effectiveness of these publications, communication between EU institutions, governments and firms is important for the sake of common understanding about the needs of

Table 1.1 Selected list of official EU publications, 1996–2018

Document title	*Date*	*Reference*
Council Conclusions on Security and Defence in the Context of the EU Global Strategy	19.11.2018	13978/18
Regulation Establishing the European Defence Industrial Development Programme	18.7.2018	2018/1092
Council Conclusions on Security and Defence in the Context of the EU Global Strategy	25.6.2018	10246/18
Proposal for a Regulation Establishing the European Defence Fund	13.6.2018	COM(2018) 476
Council Decision Establishing Permanent Structured Cooperation and Determining the List of Participating Member States	11.12.2017	CFSP 2017/2315
Launching the European Defence Fund	7.6.2017	COM(2017) 295
European Defence Action Plan	30.11.2016	COM(2016) 950
Implementation Plan on Security and Defence	14.11.2016	14392/16
Council Conclusions on Implementing the EU Global Strategy in the Area of Security and Defence	14.11.2016	14149/16
A Global Strategy for the EU's Foreign and Security Policy	28.06.2016	–
Towards a More Competitive and Efficient Defence and Security Sector	24.07.2013	COM(2013) 542
Security Industrial Policy: Action Plan for an Innovative and Competitive Security Industry	26.07.2012	COM(2012) 417
Directive 2009/81/EC on the coordination of procedures for the award of certain works contracts, supply contracts and service contracts by contracting authorities or entities in the fields of defence and security	13.07.2009	L 216
Directive 2009/43/EC on simplifying terms and conditions of transfers of defence-related products within the Community	10.09.2009	L 146
A Strategy for a Stronger and More Competitive European Defence Industry	5.12.2007	COM(2007) 764
A Strategy for the European Defence Technological and Industrial Base	14.05.2007	–
An Initial Long-Term Vision for European Defence Capability and Capacity Needs	3.10.2006	LTV
Interpretative Communication on the Application of Article 296 of the Treaty in the Field of Defence Procurement	7.12.2006	COM(2006) 779
Results of the Consultation Launched by the Green Paper on Defence Procurement and on the Future Commission Initiatives	6.12.2005	COM(2005) 626
Green Paper on Defence Procurement	23.09.2004	COM(2004) 608
European Defence – Industrial and Market Issues: Towards an EU Defence Equipment Policy	11.03.2003	COM(2003) 113
The European Aerospace Industry Meeting the Global Challenge	24.09.1997	COM(97) 466
Implementing European Union Strategy on Defence-Related Industry	4.12.1997	COM(97) 583
The Challenges Facing the European Defence-Related Industry: A Contribution for Action at the European Level	24.01.1996	COM(96) 10

Source: author's own compilation.

the European defence market and to initiate, refine or clarify existing policies and legislation.

Yet specific policy initiatives are important too. For example, the EDA provides policy input to member states on a range of EU policies that affect the defence sector, including the European Regulation on Registration, Evaluation, Authorisation and Restriction of Chemicals (REACH)[36] and the programme for Single European Sky ATM Research (SESAR).[37] Furthermore, the EDA has developed programmes to improve the interoperability of medical equipment, expertise and training during CSDP operations, and to support the member states in their transition towards more energy efficient and sustainable armed forces. Additionally, the Agency has established Joint Investment Programmes (JIPs)[38] to strengthen the ability of European armed forces to invest in maritime systems (2009); to operate in Chemical, Biological, Radiological and Nuclear (CBRN) environments (2010); to invest in research related to RPAS (2013); and to improve the energy storage technologies of Europe's militaries (2016) (European Defence Agency 2015). These policy initiatives may have a negligible overall impact on Europe's defence markets, but it is important to remember that the EDA operates in a constrained financial environment and a political climate in which its participating member states are sometimes slow, hesitant and/or reluctant to feed more substantial policy programmes into the Agency (Bátora 2009; Bickerton, Irondelle and Menon 2011).

Beyond its legislative and regulatory duties, the European Commission is also engaged in several policy initiatives that are usually articulated through official communications. For example, in its 2013 communication on a 'New Deal' for the European defence sector, the European Commission launched a number of policy initiatives including: screening defence-relevant raw materials as part of the EU's Raw Materials Initiative; the potential use of ESIFs for defence industry restructuring; the development of a civil–military Government Satellite Communications (GOVSATCOM) system; building an EU satellite high resolution capability for the benefit of the CSDP; and supporting measures aimed at ensuring the environmental sustainability of Europe's armed forces (Fiott 2012, 2013b; European Commission 2013a). Finally, the 2016 EDAP not only reiterated the importance of the EU's 'defence package', but, as explained earlier, it articulated policy initiatives such as the EDF, which are designed to incentivise cooperation at the EU level.

Concluding observations

The aim of this chapter was to provide the reader with a more focused discussion of the European defence industrial policy. By characterising the policy framework as being comprised of four major components (law and regulation, capability development, finance and policy initiatives) the aim of this chapter has been to highlight the level of EU cooperation on defence industrial policy that already exists. This chapter has highlighted policy areas where the EU can add value to Europe's defence sector, but it has also established the limits to such policies and initiatives. When looking at each of the constituent parts of the European defence industrial policy framework, it has been possible to frame the roles of EU institutions such as the European Commission and the EDA. Interestingly, a division of labour has seemingly emerged between these two institutions and each entity has a special mandate or set of policy skills in the defence industrial policy milieu. More crucially perhaps, the inherent tensions that lie at the heart of Article 346 TFEU, export policies and EU laws on competition and defence procurement are vital to an understanding of how European defence industrial cooperation currently operates. Important elements of the defence industrial policy framework are characterised by political contestation between governments, firms and EU institutions. Understanding what role the preferences of governments, firms and institutions have played in developing European defence industrial cooperation is the specific focus of the next chapter.

Notes

1 This was revealed during a number of interviews with EU officials. One stated that the EDTIB is a convenient shorthand for all the work the EU does on defence industrial policy (interview with an official from the European Commission, 1 March 2013). Another observed that an EDTIB is difficult to define because there is no clear definition of what 'Europe' means in relation to defence industrial policy (interview with an official from the European Defence Agency, 2 October 2013). Finally, one official remarked that the EDTIB has to exist because otherwise the EU will not be able to have a credible Common Security and Defence Policy over the longer term (interview with an official from the European Commission, 4 April 2014).

2 The DGs mainly responsible for defence industrial-relevant policy at the European Commission are Budget (BUDG), Competition (COMP), Economic and Financial Affairs (ECFIN), Internal Market, Industry, Entrepreneurship and SMEs (GROW) and Research and Innovation (RTD). DG GROW is recognised as having the main responsibility for defence industrial policy within the European Commission and the DG has a dedicated 'Defence Unit' focusing on Defence, Aeronautic and Maritime Industries.

3 Interview with an official from the European Commission, 4 April 2014.

4 Council Regulation (EC) No. 139/2004 of 20 January 2004 on the control of concentrations between undertakings (the EC merger regulation).

5 Article 346 was formerly known as Article 223 under the Treaty of Rome and Article 296 under the EC Treaty.

6 See, for example, *Commission* v. *Portugal* (C-38/06), *Commission* v. *Greece* (C-409/05), *Commission* v. *Sweden* (C-294/05), *Commission* v. *Finland* (C-284/05), *Commission* v. *Germany* (C-372/05), *Commission* v. *Italy* (C-387/05).

7 Spain had unilaterally decided to exempt VAT on imports of defence equipment into Spain on the basis of the 'essential interests of their security', despite the existence of Directive 77/388/EEC. This Directive obliges member states to levy VAT on intra-Community acquisitions of goods. Spain's justification for invoking Article 346 was that the VAT levy would make the import of defence equipment more expensive and thus jeopardise the Spanish government's ability to provide for its own defence. However, as Advocate General Saggio stated in his opinion on 18 March 1999, Spain could not justifiably make this argument because the levied VAT would still make its way into the Spanish treasury's coffers (Saggio 1999: 5593).

8 Italy invoked Article 346 following its decision to award a public contract to Agusta and Agusta Bell helicopters without the prior publication of a public supply contract

notice. The European Commission argued that Italy's actions were not in line with Directive 93/36/CEE, which demanded open public tendering for civilian equipment such as helicopters. Advocate General Jan Mazak noted in his opinion dated 10 July 2007 that Italy's invocation of Article 346 on the grounds that it needed to ensure confidentiality of the contract did not warrant the disproportionate act of not having a public tender. Mr. Mazak made the point that Italy's actions were disproportionate given that the helicopters in question were procured for civil use rather than defence (Mazak 2007: 2191–2192). See also *Commission* v. *Belgium* (C-252/01).

9 Here the European Commission argued that Portugal had refused to calculate and pay to the Commission's own resources between 1998 and 2002 on imports of equipment and goods for military use. Portugal had invoked Article 346 (ex Article 296) to justify non-payment of the Commission's own resources on the grounds that imports were made costlier. The Commission rejected this claim on the basis that Portugal could not satisfactorily show that its essential security interests had been challenged. The ECJ found that Portugal could not reasonably 'plead the increase cost of military materiel' without showing how this affected its essential security interests.

10 Any abuse by one or more undertakings of a dominant position within the internal market or in a substantial part of it shall be prohibited as incompatible with the internal market in so far as it may affect trade between Member States. Such abuse may, in particular, consist in: (a) directly or indirectly imposing unfair purchase of selling prices or other unfair trading conditions; (b) limiting production, markets or technical development to the prejudice of consumers; (c) applying dissimilar conditions to equivalent transactions with other trading parties, thereby placing them at a competitive disadvantage; (d) making the conclusion of contracts subject to acceptance by the other parties of supplementary obligations which, by their nature or according to commercial usage, have no connection with the subject of such contracts.

11 'The Commission shall ensure the application of the provisions of this Article and shall, where necessary, address appropriate directives or decisions to Member States.'

12 The Council, on a proposal from the Commission and after consulting the European Parliament, may make any appropriate regulations for the application of Articles 107 and 108 and may in particular determine the conditions in which Article 108(3) shall apply and the categories of aid exempted from this procedure.

13 Furthermore, the exclusive application of this Regulation to concentrations with a Community dimension is without prejudice to Article 296 of the Treaty, and does not prevent the Member States from taking appropriate measures to protect legitimate interests other than those pursued by this Regulation, provided that such measures are compatible with the general principles and other provisions of Community law.

14 While the directives were jointly adopted in 2009, each directive was negotiated by different sets of national ministries: negotiations for the defence procurement directive were largely overseen by ministries of defence, whereas negotiations for the defence transfers directive mainly involved foreign ministries and national export authorities (interviews with officials from the European Commission on 31 May 2015 and 29 May 2016). In this regard, while the transfers directive and the procurement directive are usually bandied together, from a theoretical and empirical perspective it is sensible to study each directive.

15 Council Regulation (EC) No 3381/94 of 19 December 1994 setting up a Community regime for the control of exports of dual-use goods.

16 On 17 October 1995 criminal proceedings were brought against Peter Leifer, Reinhold Otto Krauskopf and Otto Holzer for the unlicensed exportation of dual-use goods to Iraq.

17 On 17 October 1995 the ECJ ruled against *Fritz Werner Industrie-Ausrüstungen GmbH* on the grounds that its exportation of a vacuum-induction smelting and cast oven to Libya between 1979 and 1982 was seen in breach of Germany's Law on Foreign Trade (*Aubenwirtschaftsgesetz*).

18 Council Regulation (EC) No 1334/2000 of 22 June 2000 setting up a Community regime for the control of exports of dual-use items and technology.
19 Council Regulation (EC) No 428/2009 of 5 May 2009 setting up a Community regime for the control of exports, transfer, brokering and transit of dual-use items.
20 Council Common Position 2008/944/CFSP of 8 December 2008 defining common rules governing control of exports of military technology and equipment.
21 [T]he Union may use civilian and military means, shall include joint disarmament operations, humanitarian and rescue tasks, military advice and assistance tasks, conflict prevention and peace-keeping tasks, tasks of combat forces in crisis management, including peace-making and post-conflict stabilisation.
22 The ECAP was launched in 2001 following the Laeken European Summit. The ECAP is a voluntary agreement between the member states to rationalise defence capability plans and to identify capability shortfalls based on the 1999 Helsinki European Council conclusions that specified the EU's desire to be able, by 2003, to deploy 60,000 troops within 60 days for up to a year. Since the creation of the European Defence Agency, the ECAP has been superseded by the CDM and CDP.
23 The Capability Development Plan provides the member states with an opportunity to identify future capability requirements based on an assessment of future strategic trends. The CDPs are drafted and managed by the European Defence Agency, and they are designed to help member states align national defence planning processes with future capabilities in mind. The first CDP was adopted in 2008 but it was revised in 2011. By the end of 2018, the EDA will complete its latest revision of the CDP.
24 Initially agreed at the Göteborg European Council in 2001, the CDM is designed to ensure unnecessary duplication in European capability development efforts via a system of monitoring and evaluation between the member states.
25 Article 42(6) and Protocol 10 of the Treaty on European Union allows like-minded member states to systematise defence cooperation through binding commitments on defence. PESCO is a voluntary, non-exclusionary, treaty provision that allows member states to define the concrete defence projects they want to structurally engage in. Although specific forms of structured cooperation were never adumbrated in the treaty, PESCO could be geared towards pooled financial resources, capability programmes, industrial consolidation, etc. (European Commission 2015a: 7).
26 Interviews with multiple industry representatives revealed that sections of industry do not believe that the CSDP, at least in its current form, can lead to the creation of more demand in the European defence market. On the contrary, one industrial representative stated that CSDP implies a consolidation of industry, which may not ultimately drive up demand to a level that can sustain industry (interviews with representatives from Selex ES, Avio Aero, Diehl Group and Finmeccanica during November 2014).
27 To support such efforts COSME funds have been used to establish a European Network of Defence-Related Regions (ENDR) to support SMEs and research clusters located in the EU. See: www.endr.eu.
28 'Horizon 2020' is the EU's financial instrument dedicated to research and innovation.
29 'COSME' is the EU's financial programme dedicated to making it easier for SMEs to access finance for the full life cycle of their business.
30 'Copernicus' is the European programme for earth observation and it makes use of satellites plus ground, airborne and seaborne sensors. It was previously called 'Global Monitoring for Environment and Security' (GMES).
31 'Galileo' is the European programme for global satellite navigation.
32 The Framework aims to rationalise Commission and EDA efforts in defence R&D and R&T.
33 This point was also raised during numerous exchanges with EU officials and industry representatives (interviews with officials from the European Defence Agency, 19 October 2015, the European Parliament, 7 June 2016 and European Commission, 15 June 2016).

34 The EFSI aims to leverage €315 billion worth of investment in the EU over the next three years, beginning in 2016. The EFSI should be differentiated from the EU budget as it is co-managed by the European Commission and the European Investment Bank (EIB). The EFSI is a special purpose fund designed to co-finance high-risk projects in the EU's real economy. Crucially, unlike a number of existing EU financial mechanisms, the EFSI is not solely earmarked for the commercial and/or dual-use sectors and it can technically be used to finance defence-relevant projects (Fiott and Missiroli 2016).

35 The SGP rules have long been seen in many member states as an impediment to increasing defence spending. As the argument goes, certain eurozone governments are unwilling to boost defence spending lest it lead to a deviation from a government's adjustment path target or its Medium-Term Objective (MTO) – in short, defence spending could lead to an unsustainable debt-to-GDP ratio. Nevertheless, in its regular reviews of a government's MTO, the Commission can grant a degree of flexibility should investments lead to enhanced growth. Under the EDF such flexibility is foreseen in order to encourage governments to invest in defence without the fear of running excessively high deficits (Fiott and Missiroli 2016).

36 The 'REACH Directive' (EC 1907/2006) was adopted in 2006 to regulate the production and use of chemicals.

37 The SESAR programme is a collaborative project that aims to harmonise air traffic control management in the EU.

38 JIPs denote programmes that are funded via a centrally managed budget that is funded by member states.

2 Theorising EU defence industrial cooperation

The last chapter mapped out the European defence industrial policy framework, which is comprised of law and regulation, capability development initiatives, financing mechanisms and policy initiatives. Fleshing out each of the constituent parts of the policy framework has revealed several tensions at the heart of European defence industrial cooperation. Such cooperation occurs within a political arena where debates about security of supply, market liberalisation, protectionism, national sovereignty and EU interests play out at the EU level. Yet how can one interpret how these tensions play out in a European context, and, more importantly, what gives rise to European cooperation within the context of such sensitivities? Here it is important to recall the question that drives forward this book: why and how did EU member state governments, European defence firms and EU institutions develop EU-level defence industrial policy between 2003 and 2009? To move towards an answer, this chapter will engage with various existing readings of European defence industrial cooperation. In doing so, the reader will be guided through *structuralist*, *institutional* and *ideational* understandings of defence industrial cooperation, and, finally, these approaches will be set against the arguments advanced by liberal intergovernmentalism.

Structuralist approaches

Many scholars see structural factors as the causal driver for closer European defence industrial cooperation (Aben 1992; Bitzinger 1999, 2009; Brzoska, Wilke and Wulf 1999; Guay and Callum 2002; Bellais, Foucault and Oudot, 2014). These scholars point to three main causal factors: globalisation, technological change and a changing security environment (Sandler and Hartley 1999: 119; Kiss 2014). Most, if not all, structuralist accounts begin at the end of the Cold War, which is a period that led to decreasing levels of military expenditure and defence procurement and which, in turn, led to great pressure on industry to secure contracts and profits. As several scholars show, in the absence of the Soviet threat, manufacturers of conventional arms, delivery systems and platforms had to reduce their production capacities in line with the reduction in demand. This inevitably led to job losses, factory closures, the quest for new markets, mergers and acquisitions and strategic alliances (Anthony 1998: 2;

Bischak 1999: 70; Sandler and Hartley 1999: 119). Combined with technological advances, the reduction in defence spending has meant that equipment costs have increased too, placing further strain on procurement budgets (Sandler and Hartley 1999: 119; Neuman 2006; Giegerich and Nicoll 2012).

Furthermore, structuralist approaches augur that greater market liberalisation, international competition and an international division of labour in the defence sector are factors that have also caused greater EU-level defence industrial cooperation. Beginning in the 1980s, defence firms took advantage of the liberalisation of defence markets to move capital, technology, labour and productive capacities around the world to foster a global production chain aimed at lowering costs (Hayward 2001; Neal and Taylor 2001; Kiss 2014: 14; Bellais, Foucault and Oudot 2014: 24). These same scholars claim that the globalisation of defence markets extended the competitiveness of large, relatively consolidated markets such as the US to the detriment of European firms. With increased defence orders coming from emerging economies such as the Gulf countries, India and Brazil, a fragmented market space in Europe – with its duplication, redundancies and a lack of economy of scale (Gegout 2005; Bellais and Droff 2013; Briani 2013b; Overhage 2013; Shepherd 2015) – would find it increasingly difficult to compete with the US for market share (Bellais, Foucault and Oudot 2014: 24). Thus, many see EU defence industrial policy as a way to address Europe's lack of competitiveness, ensuring a European economy of scale, offsetting a drop in domestic demand and lowering costs (Bitzinger 1999: 307, 2009: 182; Guay and Callum 2002).

The post-Cold War era has also witnessed an accelerated exploitation of technologies and industrial processes emanating from civilian markets. For some time now it has been understood that the defence market is 'even more concerned with the fast and reliable performance of electronic integrated circuits and the speedy acquisition and handling of data; developments are component-oriented, and the distinction between civil and military applications is becoming blurred' (Bates 1990: 97). Electronics and advanced technologies are therefore essential to the development and functioning of modern military capabilities (Blunden *et al.* 1989: 167; Anthony 1998: 13). This has led to an increased role for commercial actors in the defence sector. As has been observed by Gummett and Stein, 'although relatively isolated from each other in the 1950s and 1960s, technologies of civil and military origin have since gradually become more interdependent, as civil technologies have gained in strength and, in some cases, outstripped their military counterparts' (1997: 2). The existence of the EU single market, which has reduced tariff and non-tariff barriers on a range of dual-use goods and technologies, can therefore be both a potentially important tool for reducing the costs of defence and an attractive venue for defence market cooperation. Thus, the consolidation of civilian and defence markets through the EU single market is a way to drive forward EU defence industrial cooperation.

Furthermore, a number of scholars have looked at how the structure of international politics may affect European defence cooperation. For example, Jones uses a neorealist approach to argue that the post-Cold War shift from a bipolar system to US unilateralism has led Europeans to seek 'to decrease reliance on the United States' by increasing their security cooperation (2007: 222). This has become a familiar argument. As Posen (2004, 2006) has remarked, increasing defence cooperation in Europe can be explained through balance of power theory and the Europeans' deliberate steps to balance against the preponderance of US power. As structural realism foresees, '[w]hen another power increases its capacities through either internal or external efforts, others have incentives to look to their own position' (Posen 2006: 153). In contrast to these arguments, some scholars state that geopolitical shifts in US policy from Europe to the Middle East and Asia-Pacific is the main reason why the Europeans have sought closer defence cooperation (see, for example, Simón 2013: 11–12). The logic here is that as US interests are increasingly shaped by geopolitical realities such as the rise of China or the threat from terrorism, the more Europeans will have to provide for their own security. All of these international political factors are seen as a key reason why European states would enhance their cooperation on defence industrial matters.

Other realist approaches have attempted to move away from the balancing theories proposed by scholars such as Seth G. Jones and Barry Posen. For example, Tom Dyson has forwarded a neoclassical realist approach to show that material factors play an important role in driving forward EU defence cooperation (Dyson 2015; see also Hyde-Price 2007). What is more, such an account argues that instead of the EU balancing against the US, European states are more likely to be bandwagoning on US power. In the post-Cold War period, Dyson shows that the EU still relies on US power but it is filling those areas where the US might withdraw its support with its own defensive material capacities (Dyson 2015: 29–30). This has implications for any discussion about the main driving factors behind EU defence cooperation. Primarily, this theoretical proposition sees the rise of EU defence industrial cooperation as a way to hedge against any abrupt US withdrawal from European security but also to support the material capacities that EU defence needs to be able to prove the EU's seriousness in military affairs.

Despite technological and political factors, however, the bulk of structural explanations for closer European defence industrial cooperation rely on economic theory. One of the leading scholars in the field of defence economics, Keith Hartley, states that the central focus of defence economics 'is the study of scarcity and choice' (2011: 14). Under an economic approach, pressures on defence budgets are seen to push governments to seek efficiencies by either reducing or eliminating defence spending; improving value for money on procurement and the cost of the armed services; and/or, accepting that the armed services will gradually reduce operational effectiveness to save money (ibid.: 19). More specifically on the EU defence market, Hartley points out that the policy problem facing European governments is that 'there is massive duplication of defence ministries, procurement agencies, armed forces, training, infrastructure and military bases' (ibid.: 133). Per Hartley (2011), the benefits of improving efficiency in the European defence market would lead to an overall cost reduction (see also Briani 2013a). However, he acknowledges that there would be challenges too, including the need to define what the defence industry looks like, to balance liberalising and protectionist interests and to manage competition and monopolies (Hartley 2011: 148–149).

This quest for efficiency plays an important role in neo-functionalist accounts of EU defence industrial cooperation too. While neo-functionalism has been critiqued by some scholars (Hoffmann 1964, 1966; Moravcsik 1993a), at the heart of neo-functionalism is the idea that increasing levels of interdependence between EU member states will incrementally lead to a deeper level of EU integration (Niemann and Schmitter 2009). EU member states are locked into a state of interdependence because there is, as liberal theory hypothesises, 'increasing transborder flows of goods, services, factors, or pollutants' which provide incentives for cooperation between states (Moravcsik 1993a: 485; see also Haas 1970). In this regard, the EU is 'a means of co-ordinating policy to manage flows of goods, services, factors of production, and economic externalities more effectively than unilateral policies' (ibid.: 484–485). It is the necessity of solving policy problems within the framework of an interdependent economy that leads to an incremental and *sui generis* pattern of European integration (Mitrany 1965). Accordingly, neo-functionalists have argued that the EU and its institutions are a response to the purported increasing levels of interdependence between states (Haas 1970).

Neo-functionalism posits the idea of policy 'spillover', where policies that no longer function for the original purposes intended give rise to new policies, which, in turn, creates the momentum for further EU integration – this is called 'functional spillover'. What is more, neo-functionalism augurs that functional spillover needs to be managed through the empowerment of existing supranational institutions and/or the creation of new ones – this is termed 'cultivated' or 'political spillover' (Lindberg 1963: 10; Schmitter 1969; Haas 1970). In this regard, one is led to believe that economic interdependence in the single market has a growing effect on the level of interdependence among European states in the defence sector. As one scholar has observed, '[d]efence integration is at times separate and at times united or combined with economic and social integration [...] [c]onsequently, defence integration is pursued both through separate legal frameworks and combined with other aspects of integration, in particular economic integration' (Trybus 2005: 10). Accordingly, the existence of the EU's internal market plays a role in determining the policy frameworks selected by member states to engage in defence industrial policymaking.

One of the major criticisms levelled at neo-functionalism, however, is the way it posits an understanding of cooperation that demands continuous and increasing levels of EU integration. However, rather problematically, the EU has not always lived up to this neo-functionalist expectation and in the defence sector there is plenty of evidence to suggest that opportunities for EU integration have on the contrary been resisted. Indeed, '[t]o date, attempts to create a unified market and to end costly industrial duplication have foundered on concerns about national sovereignty, the security of supply, and the conflicting strategic interests of Europe's small and large countries' (Neuman 2009: 78; see also Lovering 1999). Furthermore, neo-functionalism can be critiqued for assuming that interdependence is a positive integrative variable. One should recognise that '[i]nterdependence can transmit bad influences as well as good ones' (Keohane 1984: 5) and it can result in the accrual of both 'costs and benefits' (Moravcsik 1993b: 480; see also Taylor 1980). Interdependence should certainly not give one the impression that all states are equally dependent on one another (Waltz 1979: 157). Furthermore, it should not be assumed that interdependence exists only between the states of Europe. In many respects, individual states such as the UK experience a higher level of interdependence with the US than it does with many of its European counterparts because of its extensive defence, intelligence and industrial ties to Washington (Aldrich 2004; Dumbrell 2009).

Perhaps one of the most sophisticated correctives to the neo-functionalist tradition is Terrance Guay's notion of 'reactive spillover'. This approach attempts to fuse insights from structuralism and neo-functionalism. Guay surmises that when intergovernmentalism and neo-functionalism are taken alone they omit important explanatory factors. Intergovernmental approaches are seen as being too statist and they omit the fact that EU institutions such as the European Commission can influence the defence sector (Guay 1996: 407). Why is it, Guay asks, that member states with the largest defence industries have willingly ceded influence in the armaments sector to a supranational institution such as the European Commission (ibid.: 405)? Neo-functionalism is seen as being too incomplete a theory to explain this phenomenon because, while it can 'help us to understand how the EU has become more involved in this sector', it says nothing about 'the timing or why an EU role may be preferable to state-level policies' (ibid.: 416). To answer this last point, Guay argues that one needs to factor in a structural level of analysis so that spillover into the defence sector only occurs when the costs of a national approach to factors such as the rising costs of defence equipment or international competition become too much to bear (ibid.: 412 and 414).

It is for the aforementioned reasons that structural factors are an object of study in this book. Given the importance of international economic and political stimuli, this book sees 'structural factors' as one of the approaches that should be tested against the three studies found in Chapters 3, 4 and 5. If structural pressures are indeed an essential explanation for the development of EU defence industrial policy and cooperation, then one would expect to uncover evidence of these pressures in grounded examples of cooperation.

There are, however, several problems associated with structuralist explanations. First, most structural factors rest on generalised terms. For example, to say that the globalisation of the defence industry is responsible for EU-level cooperation is to be rather imprecise about the meaning of the word 'globalisation'. As has been outlined earlier, the defence sector is so unique that the liberalisation of trade and markets, global supply chains and the emergence of a global division of labour do not easily apply as they do in other areas of economic activity. For example, while globalisation is an important part of the defence market not every element of the defence industry is affected by it in equal measure. A high degree of globalisation exists in civil avionics and electronics, but, for reasons of state secrecy and security of supply, this does not follow for, say, submarine production or the development of nuclear weapons technologies (Hayward 2001; Neuman 2009: 61–63). One therefore has to be clear about how specific structural factors affect the defence sector.

Second, most structural factors such as competition and cost have been prevalent for many years and decades, but defence markets in Europe are still overwhelmingly dominated by governments and national interests. In other words, the structural pressures for greater European defence industrial cooperation certainly exist – and they have for some time – but they have not necessarily led to closer cooperation between European governments. Structuralist accounts presume that a depression in demand and the increasing costs of defence should lead to greater European defence industrial cooperation. Yet, in many cases quite the opposite can be observed. Indeed, 'if globalization comes to mean international collaboration then the term may be contested within a European context because the level of intra-EU cooperation on defence-industrial matters is still minimal' (Neuman 2006: 430). Structural variables such as globalisation, competitiveness and the international balance of power are important elements of any explanation of European defence industrial cooperation, but in isolation they may not completely capture the reality of why and how governments, firms and institutions interact on defence industrial matters at the EU level.

Finally, the danger with taking structural causal factors alone – much like a purely economic understanding of defence industrial cooperation – is the proclivity towards 'an ahistorical and depoliticized understanding of politics' in which nation-states are the objects but not the makers of their destiny (Ashley 1984: 226; see also Morgenthau 2000: 46). Even though neorealist thinkers posit that structural factors condition the way states behave (Waltz 1979), there is a risk that focusing on those factors alone somehow loses a focus on the state itself. This is odd since structuralist approaches tend to premise their arguments on the idea that states act in their own self-interest without any overarching authority – that is, anarchy – to govern their behaviour. As Wight once remarked, in general a structuralist account 'simply does not believe its main unit of analysis [the state] exists' (2004: 270). Recognising the state as the predominant actor in international politics is still necessary, and, further still, so is an understanding of the differences between states in terms of interests, economic systems and policy processes (Crouch 2005).

Without considering the specific material and historical specificities of individual states, it is difficult to account for the national policies that help states respond to structural pressures. It is therefore worth asking how national responses to structural factors emerge over time (Bischak 1999: 70). National interests and national idiosyncrasies – and the choices governments make – tend to be absent from structuralist accounts, even though government policy and resource allocation may afford a state the means to tame and influence structural factors such as globalisation and international competitiveness. As Kiss argues, the 'decisions of national governments are still the basis for an arms industry firm's existence and are of primary importance' to any understanding of defence markets despite globalisation and the post-Cold War security environment (2014: 26). This is not to claim that one should discriminate between national responses or structural factors. As has been made clear in the 'agent-structure' literature (Wendt 1987; Bieler and Morton 2001), there are explanatory limits to treating agents and structures as individual, unconnected, units of analysis. It is, instead, far more profitable to study the ways in which agents and structures interact (Putnam 1988; Moravcsik 1993c: 7; Fearon 1998). These preliminary observations about structural and economic approaches must be born in mind during the examples studied in later chapters.

Institutionalist approaches

Institutionalist theories are also applicable to debates about European defence industrial cooperation. Such theories afford institutional bodies the agency to devise policy and to influence the domestic preferences of states. There are, however, many institutionalist schools of thought. First is the historical institutionalist approach, which studies patterns of behaviour and stresses the importance of rules and processes over time (Krasner 1989; Thelen and Steinmo 1992; Levi 1997; Pierson 2000: 253; Gorges 2001: 138). As Hay and Wincott argue, historical institutionalism is concerned 'with contingency and the unintended consequences of strategic action', plus 'a focus on the path dependency of institutional change' (1998: 952). In this regard, it might be argued that future initiatives to stimulate defence cooperation in Europe may take on the experiences and path dependencies of past decisions and processes. Accordingly, it is important to understand the historical context in which institutions are established because this is an effective way to analyse how an institution and/or policy functions in the present time. More specifically on the EU's defence industrial policy framework, the existence of institutions such as the European Commission raises questions about how the processes that led to that institution's creation (and the existing treaty-based parameters in which it operates) feed into present-day policy initiatives (i.e. how practices from other policy domains bleed into the defence sector).

The rational choice model, however, posits that institutions are important because they are designed to overcome market failures and the problems associated with collective action by providing rules, procedures and enforcement mechanisms (Pollack 1996). For adherents of the rational choice approach, ideas and shared norms cannot entirely explain why certain institutions become important actors in the policy process and neither can they explain why institutions change over time (Garrett and Weingast 1993; Pollack 1996). The rational choice approach argues that institutional change occurs because of changes in the policy environment and in the relative power of actors, and an improvement in the quality of information guiding the policy process (Pollack 1996: 438–439; see also Searing 1991). Accordingly, the rational choice model borrows from the field of economic theory and the quest to ensure that resource allocation is organised for optimum benefit – known also as Pareto optimality. The rational choice approach assumes that the rising costs and duplication of defence equipment and R&D in Europe serve as a strong rationale for closer collaboration between European states. However, it also posits that if this collaboration is to achieve optimal benefits for all participants, collaboration should be institutionalised to enhance information sharing and learning processes (Hartley 2011: 143).

Another, more recent, legalistic-institutionalist approach that has done much to enhance scholarly debates about European defence industrial cooperation is Blauberger and Weiss's notion of 'judicial politics' (2013; Weiss and Blauberger 2016). Under their approach it is argued that the reason why member states eventually moved highly sensitive issues such as defence procurement to the EU level can be explained through 'the combination of the Court's jurisprudence and the Commission's consecutive strategies of judicial politics' (Weiss and Blauberger 2016: 447). Far from norm diffusion or Pareto optimality, this type of legalistic-institutionalist approach shows how the European Commission could cajole member states into accepting defence-relevant EU law through a dual process of 'judicialised law-making' and 'opportunistic enforcement' (ibid.: 448–449). In other words, the European Commission threatens the EU member states with ECJ-driven integration in the defence sector 'under the influence of actual or potential ECJ case law', but it simultaneously offers EU member states legal certainty and political control over EU defence market legislation so as 'to anticipate and avoid further strategic litigation' (ibid.: 448–449; see also Strikwerda 2016). Under Weiss and Blauberger's theoretical approach, the European Commission serves as a driver for EU integration in the defence sector.

These approaches to EU defence industrial cooperation make a strong case for the importance of EU institutions as the main drivers of cooperation. Accordingly, this book looks at the role of EU institutions during the three studies that follow later. Based on the tenets of various institutionalist approaches, one would expect EU institutions such as the European Commission, EDA and/or the European Parliament to drive forward EU defence industrial cooperation.

It is worth recognising here the limits to the explanatory power of such institutionalist approaches. While it is true that such approaches are alive to the importance of states, firms and institutions, they treat institutions as the main variable behind defence industrial cooperation, and they also assume the 'continuation of institutions' without acknowledging that institutions can also succumb to 'decadence or decay' (Gorges 2001: 140–141; see also Immergut 1998; Peters and Pierre 1998). Historical institutionalist approaches stress the importance of ideas, yet these explanations do not say much about why these ideas emerge in the first place, how successfully they can be diffused and adopted and why a select institution is chosen as a venue for policymaking (Gorges 2001: 141–142). Thus, while the European Commission may be an advocate for market liberalisation, there is little in these institutionalist approaches to tell one why this is so. Moreover, these approaches do not say much about why the European Commission – rather than, say, the EDA – should become a venue for policymaking. As is the case with the rational choice approach, while it is correct to assume that institutions can play a key role in achieving Pareto optimality, this approach does not say why, when efficiency can be achieved at the EU level, governments are still reluctant to collaborate at this level.

Ideational approaches

Instead of a rational calculation of interests on the part of policymakers, adherents to a more interpretative, discourse-based or constructivist policy analysis argue that what is important is the production of and contestation over the justification for a policy (Glynos *et al.* 2009). As Schmidt argues through her work on 'discursive institutionalism', rationalist accounts of policy formation and institutional agency fail to 'explain the origins of or shifts in interest-based preferences, historical paths, or cultural frames' (2010: 2, 2008). In this sense, Schmidt argues that it is more profitable to understand how certain ideas emerge and are sustained through discourse, frames, narratives, myths, collective memories, stories and scripts (2010: 3; see also Fairclough 2005: 77–78). More specifically, sociological approaches contend that '[s]ingle-factor theories are usually not rich enough to capture the dynamics of complex processes' (Kitschelt 1986: 65–66). Instead, the sociological institutional approach studies how institutions mimic and/or produce new norms, ideas and practices, which, in turn, can alter the behaviour of actors such as states (Skowronek 1982; Scott 1987; DiMaggio and Powell 1991; Hall and Taylor 1996). As Mörth and Britz claim, institutions have facilitated 'the spread of ideas' about the European defence market at the national and European levels, which has subsequently informed regulatory efforts and led to 'the development of European institutional structures' (2004: 968).

Other forms of interpretative or discourse-based approaches also stress the importance of how certain ideologies and meanings can become embedded in power relations between political elites, institutions and groups (Van Dijk 1993: 250). Far from the positive ontology promoted by positivists and rationalists, critical approaches argue that society and meaning are in a constant state of flux and so language, symbols and signs are part of a broader societal struggle over power, ethics and norms (Laclau and Mouffe 1985; Glynos *et al.* 2009: 13). As Van Dijk remarks, 'critical discourse analysts want to know what structures, strategies or other properties of text, talk, verbal interaction or communicative events play a role in' power relations between actors (1993: 250). In particular, Norman Fairclough explains that social actions and meanings 'tend very much to cluster in terms of institutions' such as families, schools, workplaces, courts, government and/or other institutions (2013: 39).

It is worth considering the merits of these approaches for one can observe specific ideas and concepts embedded in the EU defence industrial policy framework. Expressions such as 'market liberalisation' or 'strategic autonomy' are politically loaded terms that warrant critical examination because they relate to dominant economic and political discourses. Not every member state would subscribe to the need to liberalise the European defence market, whereas others would certainly hold to the notion of strategic autonomy. The idea of market liberalisation also raises the possibility of a critical examination of power relations between governments, industry and international institutions. As Britz (2010) shows, the type of marketisation being promoted at the EU level through ideas such as 'liberalisation' and 'competitiveness' played a key role in reforming Sweden's defence sector (see also Barrinha 2010; Castellacci, Fevolden and Lundmark 2014: 1222). Likewise, in the case of France's decision to procure the A400M aircraft, Joana and Smith show how a more privatised and commercial cognitive, normative and symbolic framework guided relations between French industrialists and the government (2006: 82–83). There are advantages to uncovering embedded power relations and critiquing often taken-for-granted ideas and speech acts. Furthermore, it is important to keep in mind that individual speech acts such as 'liberalisation' can in themselves play a constructive role within the broader processes of European integration (Diez 1999, 2001).

Yet, even if they are currently in vogue, discourse-based approaches can only take one so far. Ideas, norms and language clearly matter but there are limits to their explanatory power. First, interpretative approaches may very well 'explain existing conventions as the outcome of power relations and power struggle', but is this enough and/or a problem-free assertion (Fairclough 1989: 2; see also Hammersley 1997; Breeze 2011: 498)? What is supposed to be 'critical' in interpretative approaches tends to mean a critique of a specific ideology, policy and/or social practice from another, not necessarily disinterested, stand-point based on heterogeneous intellectual and political biases (Breeze 2011: 498–499; see also Gallie 1956 and Gray 1977). Thus, one can make the case for understanding EU defence industrial policy as driven by neo-liberal ideological preferences such as competitiveness and liberalisation. However, how far does this take one in understanding why these preferences exist in the first place and how they play out in a context where multiple preferences – be they from government, industry or institutions – meet? Indeed, ideologies and/or dominant discourses are not necessarily negative if enough members of a given social group agree to them (Geuss 1981: 12 and 22). Notwithstanding the existence of various and diverse schools of discourse analysis, such an approach is useful as a method of analysis but not as a device that explains why social phenomena occur.

This is a problem that also afflicts Europeanisation studies. This approach posits that two distinct political processes explain greater European integration. First, 'national adaptation': a 'top-down' or vertical policy process through which EU norms, policies and practices are 'downloaded' by governments from the EU level to reorient national policies and practices (Ladrech 1994: 69; see also Olsen 2002; Quaglia *et al.* 2007: 406). Second, 'national projection': a 'bottom-up' process where national policies and preferences are 'uploaded' to the EU level and adopted by several other member states (Radaelli 2003: 27, 2006: 62). While the Europeanisation approach can simultaneously accommodate the role of states, institutions and firms (Coen and Dannreuther 2003: 258; Vink and Graziano 2008), it embodies many shortcomings. Predominantly, Europeanisation relates to processes of change rather than the causes of change (Bulmer 2008; see also Exadaktylos and Radaelli 2009: 521–526). Even though Europeanisation has done much to stimulate inter-disciplinary debate between comparative politics and European studies, the approach is blighted by problems of definition and application (Mair 2004). Europeanisation approaches tend to stress the importance of the European level of policymaking when this 'only explains one part of the story' because 'going European does not imply decreasing national interests in armament matters' (Hoeffler 2012: 437).

In this regard, perhaps the most insightful approach that emerges from the Europeanisation tradition is Hoeffler's (2012) elaboration of the idea of 'economic patriotism'. Hoeffler's basic question is whether European market-oriented rules and organisations are 'curtailing governments' capacity to pursue national industrial policy strategies in the defence sector' (ibid.: 436). Hoeffler answers in the negative. By looking at European defence industrial cooperation as a form of national interest projection, Hoeffler argues that 'arms producing countries have promoted market-oriented procurement and liberalization at the European level as industrial strategies intended to support national and European firms' (2012: 436). Accordingly, Hoeffler does not believe that national defence industrial strategies have been subsumed under a supranational space. Rather, the uploading of defence industrial policy to the EU level is not 'functional and automatic' but rather politically problematic because member states contest issues such as market liberalisation, regional integration and/or protectionism (ibid.: 438). The strength of Hoeffler's approach is that national preferences are key to explaining the nature and extent of EU defence industrial policy. However, the two major shortcomings associated with the approach are, first, that preferences are defined in broad terms as either protectionism or liberalisation and, second, that it does not explain what preferences emerge at any given point in time or how and why these preferences emerge in the first place.

Liberal intergovernmentalism

To innovate in the field of defence industry studies, this book will also apply a hitherto untested model to EU defence industrial cooperation: liberal intergovernmentalism (LI). At its heart, LI posits that the EU is 'a successful intergovernmental regime designed to manage economic interdependence through negotiated policy co-ordination' (Moravcsik 1993b: 474). As Figure 2.1 shows, the model forwards three broad theoretical claims. First, a critical driver of EU cooperation is domestic preferences, which are rationally negotiated at a national level between government and numerous economic actors. Second, governments will bargain with one another on an intergovernmental basis in the hope of resolving 'distributional conflicts' between various competing domestic preferences. Third, the outcomes of intergovernmental bargaining should be optimal to manage various preferences and to ensure compliance with bargaining outcomes

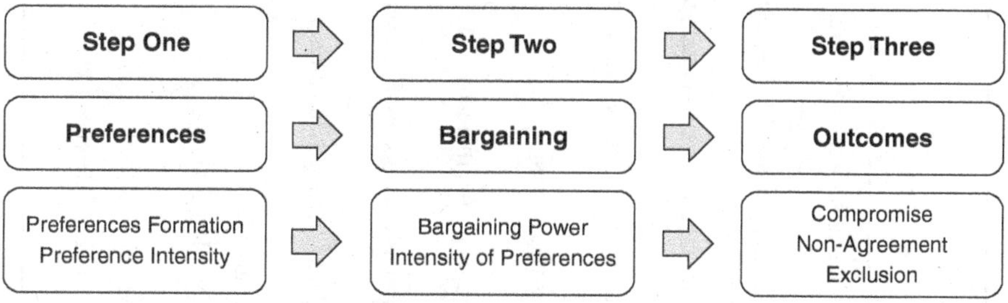

Figure 2.1 The liberal intergovernmental model.
Source: author's adaptation of Moravcsik (1993b: 482).

(ibid.: 480; Moravcsik 1998: 18 and 23). What follows from these theoretical assumptions is that: (1) economic interests play a central role in determining government policy; (2) governments are ultimately the most important actors steering the direction of EU integration; (3) EU institutions play a minimal role in 'causing' EU cooperation; and (4) relative power between governments is a major factor in determining the possibility for, and potential shape of, EU cooperation.

With a view to ascertaining the explanatory power of LI during the three examples that follow, and comparing it to competing explanatory approaches, it is important here to have a better understanding of the inherent strengths and weaknesses of LI. As stated earlier, LI is a multi-causal 'grand theory' which brings together and synthesises several theories into a single, supposedly parsimonious, model (Moravcsik 1998; Moravcsik and Schimmelfennig 2009: 68; Schimmelfennig 2015a: 178). Whereas Moravcsik was initially interested in studying the Treaties of Rome, the Single European Act and the Maastricht Treaty rather than the negotiation of specific EU directives or regulations (Moravcsik 1993b: 517, 1998, 1999: 268), this book contends that LI could be a suitable explanatory model for more 'day-to-day' EU policy processes such as defence industrial policymaking. After all, liberal intergovernmentalism is about understanding and explaining EU cooperation and it does so through three distinct, yet interrelated, explanatory steps.

'Step one' – domestic preference formation

Taking its cue from the Foreign Policy Analysis tradition (Moravcsik 1997; Hudson 2014), 'step one' of the LI model positions the domestic preferences of states as the key driver behind European cooperation. As Table 2.1 shows, LI posits that 'groups of private individuals and voluntary associations with autonomous interests, interacting in civil society' help form national preferences (Moravcsik 1993b: 484). LI assumes that governments play the role of arbiter between a range of economic, social and political preferences, which they

Table 2.1 Theoretical approaches to EU defence industrial cooperation

Theory/approach	*Independent variable/s*	*Principal agent/s*			*Process*
		States	*Firms*	*Institutions*	
Structural/economic	Globalisation/costs/ security environment				Structural pressures give rise to market liberalisation, cooperation and market consolidation
Neo-functionalism	Economic interdependence	x	x	x	Search for functionality and efficiency leads to deeper EU integration
Reactive spillover	Rising defence costs/ timing	x		x	European cooperation occurs when structural costs are too much to bear for governments
Historical institutionalism	Practices/rules/processes			x	Institutions embed patterns of behaviour, rules and processes over time
Sociological institutionalism	Norms/ideas/practices			x	Institutions mimic or produce new ideas and norms
Rational choice institutionalism	Rules/procedures/ enforcement			x	Improves policy information, resource allocation efficiency and Pareto optimality
Judicial politics	Judicialised law-making Opportunistic enforcement			x	ECJ-driven integration and legal certainty is provided by European Commission
Discursive institutionalism	Ideas/frames/narratives	x		x	Policy change results from interest shifts and changes to cultural frames
Interpretative	Ideas/symbols/norms	x	x	x	Policy change results from shifting narrative frames
Europeanisation	Ideas/interests	x	x	x	Policy formulation at EU level guided by 'downloading' and 'uploading' of norms and ideas
Economic patriotism	Interests	x	X	x	National interests 'uploaded' to EU level by powerful states
Liberal	Interests	x	X		Commercial interests favour resisting closer EU defence industrial cooperation

Source: author's own.

eventually represent based on the urgency of the preferences and how concentrated they become in a domestic setting (Moravcsik 1998: 34; Moravcsik and Schimmelfennig 2009: 70). Accordingly, the 'liberal' element of LI alludes to the fact that '[g]roups articulate preferences; governments aggregate them' (Moravcsik 1993b: 484, 1998: 35). Moravcsik forwarded this more fluid notion of preferences because of his dissatisfaction with the fixed interests of wealth, power and security that are normally associated with states under the neo-realist paradigm. Moravcsik has argued that neo-realism's contention that state interests are fixed over time and are uniform across all states is too simplistic and static (Moravcsik 1993b: 480, 1998: 26; Moravcsik and Schimmelfennig 2009: 68). What is more, LI is built on the assumption that states behave rationally, or, that they work purposively towards an ordered goal or objective (Moravcsik 1993b: 480–481).

Yet several scholars have questioned whether LI provides a more comprehensive account of domestic preferences. For example, Forster has critiqued LI because he feels that it does not adequately 'disaggregate the concept of the state' (1998: 364–365). Furthermore, in Dover's (2005) study of the LI model in relation to UK defence policy towards Europe he argues that UK policy was not defined by interest groups, but, rather, by the Prime Minister directly. More recently, in their ongoing research on 'new intergovernmentalism' Bickerton, Hodson and Puetter argue that preference formation under the liberal intergovernmental model is 'unnecessarily reductive' because beyond economic actors exist other interest groups such as the media and mass political movements (2015a: 714). One of their key objections to preference formation under liberal intergovernmentalism is that preferences are largely seen as economic interests, which, they argue, omits the 'problems of legitimacy and authority' often bound up in preference formation (ibid.: 707). Research on 'new intergovernmentalism' has also questioned LI's parsimonious divide between domestic preference formation and intergovernmental bargaining. Bickerton, Hodson and Puetter hasten to point out that EU policymaking today is marked by a 'dynamic and unstable set of relationships' between actors that increasingly blurs the line between the domestic and the international levels (2015a: 707).

In any national defence market a range of actors seeks to influence government policy (see Figure 2.2 below). National parliaments can help shape defence industrial policy; NGOs can pressure governments over a specific procurement dossier and/or over arms exports; and unions have a vested interest in new contracts and where defence industrial production centres are geographically located in any given country (Ball 1986; Markusen 1986; Paukert and Richards 1991). The 'new intergovernmentalism' literature argues that such actors should play an equally prominent role in determining national policy, although in the defence sector – which is still marked by a relatively high degree of monopsony – one should immediately question the degree to which NGOs and unions influence government policy when compared to industry, the military or central government. Given that the defence sector is 'the most nationalistic of all economic activities' the preferences of government and defence firms should play the most

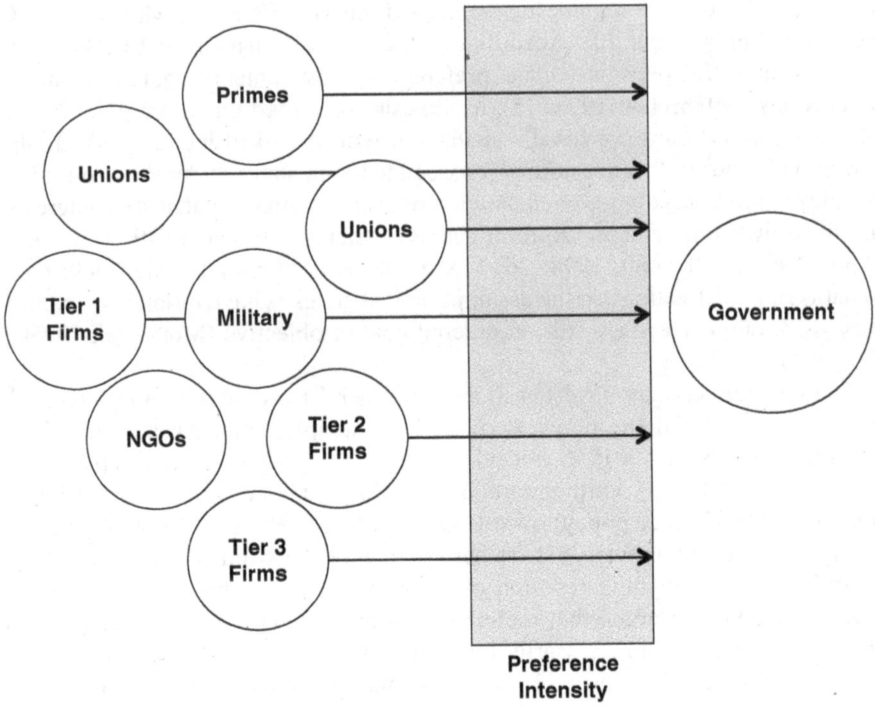

Figure 2.2 'Step one' – domestic preference formation.
Source: author's own.

prominent role in formulating defence industrial policy (Walker and Gummet 1989: 419). Part of the rationale behind the testing of the liberal intergovernmental model in this book is to observe what combination of preferences comes to the fore during EU defence industrial cooperation.

Similarly to economic patriotism, therefore, LI argues that one of the most important drivers behind EU cooperation on defence industrial matters is national economic preferences. Indeed, according to LI one would expect to see intense national preferences reflect the economic interests of defence firms rather than the political, industrial and strategic considerations of governments and armed forces.

LI is undoubtedly interest-centric because it argues that the pursuit 'of international objectives depends meaningfully on domestic politics and economics' (Mastanduno, Lake and Ikenberry 1989: 458). However, it is worth considering what Moravcsik actually wrote about domestic preference formation. For example, he has conceded the fact that there is nothing to prevent other, non-economic, preferences from feeding into government policy. Moravcsik understands that security preferences may equally vie for the attention of government, and he acknowledges that 'economic interests do not tell the whole story'

(Moravcsik and Schimmelfennig 2009: 70). Moravcsik has also acknowledged that there might even be occasions when security considerations trump even rationally determined economic preferences (1998: 34). Therefore, when examining the LI model later in this book it will be important to recognise that national preferences are 'not limited to commercial and economic policy integration' because in the defence industrial domain politico-strategic considerations can sit alongside, and/or compete with, economic considerations (Moravcsik 1998: 47; Schimmelfennig 2015b: 5).

Following on from this point, during the examples of EU cooperation studied below it will also be worth considering the extent to which other, non-economic, preferences manage to influence government policy. If government, armed services and industry are important actors in forging domestic preferences in the defence sector, it will be instructive to observe the ways in which they balance economic and security considerations. The three example studies will highlight the most intense preferences that emerged during the establishment of the EDA and the adoption of the EU's 'defence package'. Testing the liberal intergovernmental model in this way will allow one to understand how economic and non-economic preferences were calibrated during the intergovernmental bargaining phase. Finally, the three studies will also allow the reader to see how the domestic and international levels interacted with each other during the preference formation phase. In directly responding to the healthy criticism provided by 'new intergovernmentalism', it will be instructive to observe to what extent the domestic and EU levels bleed into one another during EU defence industrial policymaking.

One of the benefits of this first step in the LI model when compared to other theories and approaches is its more sophisticated treatment of domestic preferences and government positions. Step one of the model forces one to be rather more precise about the type of preferences that governments try to secure and what policies and/or structures they subsequently agree to. Again, LI does not undermine the importance of the state in policymaking and it is fully conscious of structural factors that may stimulate certain preferences at the domestic level. The LI model is thus appreciative of the importance of 'two-level games' and the interrelationship between agency and structure. Domestic actors respond to international stimuli but governments decide on the preferences they will bargain for at the international level. Crucially, unlike approaches such as reactive spillover, judicial politics, neo-functionalism and institutionalism, the liberal intergovernmentalist model begins its level of analysis with the state rather than institutions. This explanatory basis is certainly in keeping with the broader literature on defence industrial politics and the overwhelming importance it affords to the state over other actors (Lovering 1999; Sandler and Hartley 1999; Heidenkamp, Louth and Taylor 2013). Furthermore, unlike the Europeanisation approach or even neo-realism the LI model does not take preferences or interests as pre-defined factors. Rather, domestic preferences need to be rationalised and the process of preference formation needs to be explained.

'Step two' – intergovernmental bargaining

The next step after domestic preference formation is for governments to engage, if required, in intergovernmental bargaining (see Figure 2.3 below). The LI model holds that intergovernmental 'negotiations can be viewed as a co-operative game in which the level of co-operation reflects the patterns in the preferences of national governments' (Moravcsik 1993b: 499). Note the importance of potential cooperation under the liberal intergovernmental model: '[n]ational governments have an incentive to co-operate where policy co-ordination increases their control over domestic policy outcomes, permitting them to achieve goals that would not otherwise be possible' (ibid.: 485). The need for cooperation occurs where there are two or more conflictual sets of domestic preferences, so, for example, when the preferences of country A impose negative costs on country B. Policy cooperation or policy harmonisation may result in a more efficient management of the distribution of domestic preferences in the EU. However, the LI model does not view cooperation as an automatic policy avenue because should policy

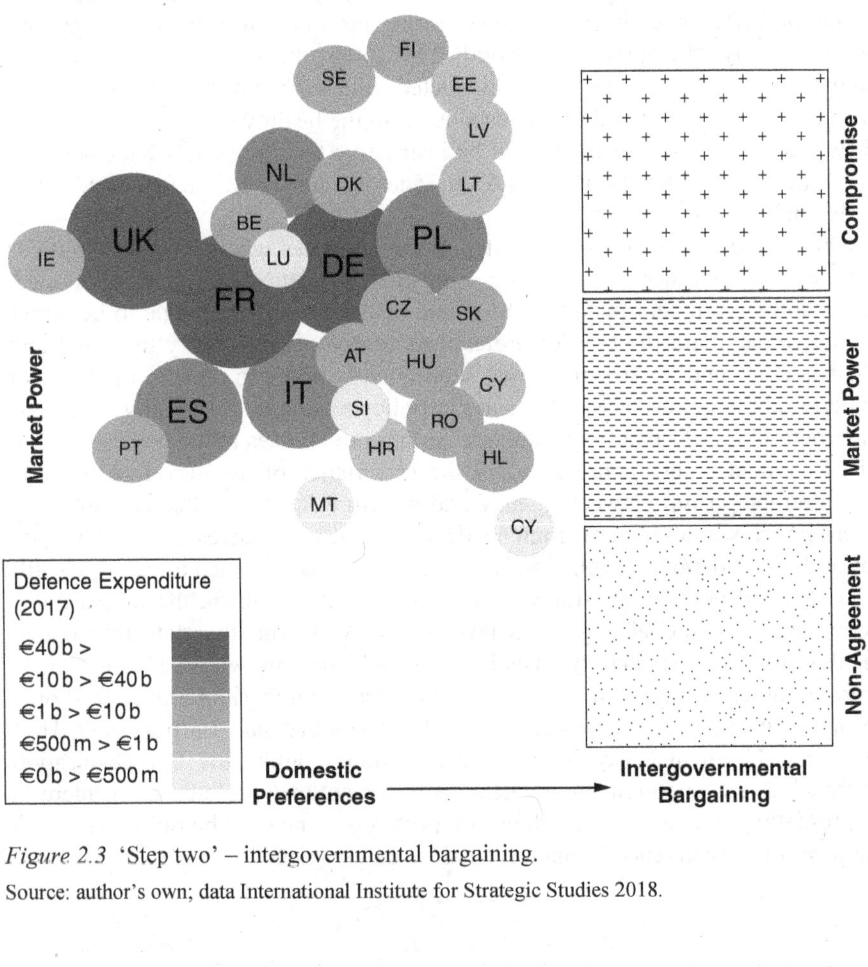

Figure 2.3 'Step two' – intergovernmental bargaining.

Source: author's own; data International Institute for Strategic Studies 2018.

cooperation impose too high a cost on a government then intergovernmental bargaining may be completely forgone in favour of a national response to a policy dilemma. Governments – presumed to be behaving and acting rationally – will assess whether a national or international response is worth pursuing based on the perceived costs that would result from intergovernmental bargaining.

It is important to understand why and how governments decide to engage in intergovernmental bargaining. In this sense, a key element of step two of the LI model is the relative power of governments (Moravcsik 1993b: 499). The term 'power' should be used with caution here, as one is not talking about military power or coercion. Instead, governments voluntarily engage in intergovernmental bargaining under the LI model (ibid.: 498). Accordingly, the risks involved in misinterpreting opposing domestic preferences are decreased because EU member states operate in an 'information-rich' environment where they possess knowledge of other state preferences (ibid.). 'Bargaining power' under the liberal intergovernmental model relates to the intensity of domestic preferences and the desire to conclude an efficient round of intergovernmental bargaining. 'Market power' plays a role during negotiations. For example, France and the UK may hold more intense preferences than Hungary and Slovenia because their respective defence markets are larger. Market size is not the only determinant of relative power, however. This may seem counter-intuitive given that 80 per cent of defence production in the EU is bound up in France, Germany, Italy, Spain, Sweden and the UK (Briani *et al.* 2013: 9). However, the unique legal and procedural structures and methods of the EU mean that governments cannot overtly wield market power. The need for consensus at the EU level ensures that national market power is usually constrained.

A government can achieve its goals by threatening non-agreement, threatening exclusion and finding a compromise (Moravcsik 1993b: 499). These various strategies are crucial when one considers that several existing EU defence industrial initiatives have been agreed to in the Council of the EU either unanimously or with QMV. For example, if country A can unilaterally find a solution to satisfy its domestic preferences then it can threaten to walk away from negotiations. However, despite this possibility it may still be in the interests of country A to negotiate to extract concessions from country B and country C, especially if these two countries stand to lose more from non-agreement. Country A may also threaten exclusion by looking for alternative policy venues for cooperation that exclude certain countries. Again, such a strategy would only be pursued if it did not imply negative costs for country A, but the threat of exclusion may yet again lead to increased leverage and further concessions. As Moravcsik states, 'the threat of exclusion from a coalition is a more powerful incentive to co-operation than a single state's threat of non-agreement' (1993b: 503). Finally, compromise may be found during intergovernmental bargaining if the agreed policy outcomes do not overly jeopardise the domestic preferences of EU member states.

Furthermore, another potentially important element during the bargaining phase relates to 'issue linkage'. Moravcsik explains that where governments share almost identical preferences there is little need for issue linkage, but where preferences are highly asymmetrical then issue linkage can lead to, and help seal, compromise between governments (Moravcsik 1998: 65). Liberal intergovernmentalism expects that issue linkage will become a possible bargaining strategy only if the domestic costs of agreeing to link issues are not too high. In respect of intergovernmental bargains at the EU level, liberal intergovernmentalism expects issue linkage to take 'the form of financial side-payments or symbolic concessions on the design of institutions' (ibid.: 65). Importantly, the LI model does not predict that issue linkage will play a prominent role during intergovernmental bargains. To the extent that issue linkage does play a role then it is normally minimal, issue-specific and used to equalise the gains among participating governments rather than to 'balance gains and losses' (ibid.: 67). Accordingly, issue linkage is a useful tool to move towards compromise so long as it does not impose domestic costs on any of the relevant parties.

In pointing to the importance of relative bargaining power, the liberal intergovernmental model reveals another important factor that may help explain why and how EU defence industrial cooperation has developed over time: namely, relative bargaining power. Indeed, if LI is right then one would expect relative bargaining power – or the ability to force either exclusion, compromise or to abandon negotiations altogether – to condition whether EU defence industrial cooperation is possible.

Before moving on to the final step in the LI model, it is worth considering some of the purported weaknesses with the concept of relative bargaining power. For example, in his study of Intergovernmental Conferences (IGCs) Slapin contests the hypothesis that member states with the largest volume of economic resources shape the direction and extent of EU cooperation (2008: 132; see also Tallberg 2008). Drawing on institutional theories, Slapin instead argues that smaller and medium-sized states can affect the pace and direction of EU cooperation because '[v]eto rights are a much more important source of power than resources' (2008: 133; see also Bailer 2010). This is an interesting and important point to take on board for the example studies that follow later, especially because member states in the Council of the EU do effectively wield a veto over EU defence industrial policy when unanimity or QMV in the Council of the EU are used. Thus, while the concentration of defence industrial production in the EU is in the hands of a minority of states, it will be important to understand the motivations and preferences of some of the EU's smaller and medium-sized defence industrial actors during the case studies.

'Step three' – outcomes

The final stage of the liberal intergovernmental model focuses on the 'outcomes' that emerge after intergovernmental bargaining. Recall that the study of policy outcomes is the main focus of the analysis in this book. LI claims that it is only through bargaining outcomes that governments can continue to secure their domestic preferences (Moravcsik 1995: 621, 1999: 298; Moravcsik and Schimmelfennig 2009: 72; Schimmelfennig 2015a: 178). Depending on the outcome, the LI model states that the results of intergovernmental bargaining may require institutional arrangements to ensure compliance with what is agreed upon between member states. The most obvious set of outcomes from intergovernmental bargaining are new or revised treaties, new regulations and/or directives, the establishment of new institutions or the selection of pre-existing institutions to undertake new mandates. Yet LI challenges the assumption that supranational institutions such as the European Commission are – once brought into the bargaining process by governments – fully autonomous actors that can work for objectives other than those set down by governments. LI argues that EU cooperation is not advanced because of 'an elite alliance between EC officials and pan-European business interest groups', but rather because of domestic preferences and bargaining power (Moravcsik 1991b: 20, 1993b: 519, 1999: 268).

LI assumes that supranational institutions are not as important as national preferences and relative power is perhaps the model's most salient and contentious feature. Even though some scholars have claimed that the LI model is practically indistinguishable from neo-functionalism (Haas 2001: 30; Rosamond 2005: 243), LI differs from neo-functionalism in that it places much more emphasis on 'traditional conceptions of national interests and power' rather than with neo-functionalism's focus on supranational institutions (Moravcsik 1991b: 21, 1993b: 473–474). When designing LI, Moravcsik sought to differentiate the model from neo-functionalism by contesting the notion that there was some 'preordained movement toward federal union', and he instead argued that 'a series of pragmatic bargains among national governments based on concrete national interests, relative power, and carefully calculated transfers of sovereignty' steered EU cooperation (Moravcsik 1998: 142). All of this presumes a minimal role for institutions such as the Commission, and LI stands in contrast to those theories that argue that such institutions are 'entrepreneurs' or 'managers' of policy (Guay 1996; Laffan 1997; Blauberger and Weiss 2013).

Yet all of this is not to say that institutions do not matter. As Moravcsik argues,

> [s]trong supranational institutions are often seen as the antithesis of intergovernmentalism. Wrongly so [...] [i]n the intergovernmentalist view, the unique institutional structure of the [EU] is acceptable to national governments only insofar as it strengthens, rather than weakens, their control over domestic affairs, permitting them to attain goals otherwise unachievable.
>
> (Moravcsik 1993b: 507 and 514; see also Moravcsik 1998: 9 and 73; Moravcsik and Nicolaïdis 1999; Moravcsik and Schimmelfennig 2009: 72)

Supranational institutions such as the European Commission are a key feature of the LI model because they may strengthen the power of governments by increasing the efficiency of intergovernmental bargaining and by ensuring that governments do not deviate from agreed policy outcomes (Moravcsik 1993b: 507). In this regard, it is claimed that EU institutions are 'deliberately designed to assist national governments' achieve their national preferences (ibid.: 515). Therefore, in contrast to scholars who believe that the role of EU institutions such as the European Commission is to somehow single-handedly drive forward the defence industrial cooperation process (Guay 1996; Blauberger and Weiss 2013), LI assumes that institutions are put in place to 'credibly lock in compliance against defection by future unsatisfied governments' (Moravcsik and Schimmelfennig 2009: 75).

One major criticism of this perspective is that LI presents a rather linear view of EU cooperation, whereby closer cooperation occurs through a rational process of managing domestic preferences and bargaining. For some, the three-step model presented by LI may appear to be far too parsimonious, when, arguably, policy processes tend to be marked by instability and variation. Socio-economic factors and actors that are initially located outside of the policy process can punctuate the process and alter its characteristics (Baumgartner and Jones 2009; Bertelli and John 2013). In this sense, the LI model can be contested for not being open to sporadic change. As Kingdon (1984) states, policy processes tend to be 'messy' with policy ideas only taking hold through luck and 'windows of opportunity'. Pierson (1996) takes up this point by inferring that LI does not adequately consider the historical context in which policy is formulated. Policy outcomes under LI appear to suggest that a 'new game' is under way, when past phases of integration and existing institutions and legislation are likely to affect the outcomes of new phases of integration. Here it is contended that past bargaining outcomes could embolden EU institutions so that they can seek to strengthen their policy position, thus constraining the very actors that created them in the first place and/or gave them more legislative and delegated powers (Pierson 1996: 127; see also Schimmelfennig 2015a: 192).

Concluding observations

This book seeks to understand why and how EU defence industrial cooperation has developed from 2003–2009. In order to structure any answer to this question, this book seeks to understand how policy outcomes such as the establishment of the EDA and the adoption of the 'defence package' came about. In order to follow the policy processes leading to the establishment and adoption of these examples of EU defence industrial cooperation, this book looks at the extent to which structural factors, EU institutions, national interests and relative bargaining power affected cooperation. Before moving to the first of three example studies, it is worth recalling that structural approaches believe that defence globalisation, global competition, geopolitics and the balance of power will drive forward European cooperation. Alternatively, institutional approaches argue that EU institutions such as the European Commission, the European Defence Agency and/or the European Parliament will play a determining role in producing bargaining outcomes. Finally, the LI model understands that the most intense domestic preferences will likely reflect economic interests and that the relative power of governments serves as a pre-condition for non-agreement, exclusion or compromise. The next step in the analysis is to test these various readings of EU defence industrial cooperation against three in-depth case studies.

3 Establishing the European Defence Agency

Established in 2004, the European Defence Agency is an intergovernmental agency of the Council of the EU. Following the Thessaloniki European Council in June 2003, a Joint Action (2004/551/CFSP) establishing the Agency was unanimously agreed upon by the Council of the EU (Schmitt 2003). The Joint Action specified that the EDA's tasks include defining European capabilities and armaments cooperation initiatives, identifying operational requirements, evaluating the improvement of military capabilities and strengthening the European Defence Technological and Industrial Base (Council of the European Union 2011a). The EDA is composed of 27 participating member states (pMSs) but this number could decrease to 26 should the UK decide to leave the Agency following its decision in 2016 to leave the EU. At the time of negotiation for the EDA, the EU comprised 25 member states. The EDA has an operating budget that averages €30 million per annum. The Agency falls under the authority of the Council of the EU and a Steering Board governs the Agency on a more day-to-day basis. The Steering Board meets biannually and is composed of the ministers of defence that represent each pMS, a representative from the European Commission and the Vice-President of the European Commission/High Representative of the Union for Foreign Affairs and Security Policy (HR/VP) as chair. The HR/VP heads the Agency and a Chief Executive is responsible for the institution's daily management, policy development and public outreach activities. As stated in the Introduction, the Agency forms an integral part of the EU's defence industrial policy framework.

The Agency operates under a specific, treaty-grounded mandate. Articles 42.3–4 and 45 of the TEU ensure that the creation of, and any decisions related to, the EDA are exclusively taken by the Council of the EU. Unlike the European Commission, which uses EU legislation and the EU budget to shape the European defence market, the EDA focuses on ad hoc initiatives that aim to promote voluntary intergovernmental cooperation between the pMSs (Fiott 2015b: 545). As Bátora observes, the Agency principally operates under the logic of intergovernmental networking because 'the EDA works in a policy area of defence, where the logic of national sovereignty has been particularly strongly institutionalised' (2009: 1092). There are certain downsides to being an intergovernmental body as work programmes can only be initiated with the blessing and active participation of national governments. Many EU member states are still sceptical and suspicious of EU-level defence cooperation and this has affected the Agency's ability to oversee tangible results (ibid.: 1092). For example, '[o]f the 106 or so projects managed by the EDA since 2004 […] the vast majority have been studies into the feasibility of running capability projects' rather than concrete project outcomes (Fiott 2015b: 545).

The purpose of this chapter is to study how and why member states reached a unanimous decision in the Council of the EU to establish the EDA. In addition to the established explanations outlined in Chapter 2, this chapter will specifically test the LI model in relation to the establishment of the Agency and it hopes to tease out what role governments, firms and institutions played in forging the EDA. Here it is worth recalling how the Agency's focus on capability development, defence research and industrial matters is of vital importance to the EU defence industrial policy framework. The task at hand is to uncover how and why, if at all, the explanations mentioned earlier – structural factors, institutions, ideas and norms, national interests and/or relative bargaining power – led to the specific outcome of the creation of the EDA. In this way, it will be possible to test these diverse approaches and it will consequently be possible to comment on the explanatory power – or lack thereof – of approaches such as LI, economic patriotism (Hoeffler 2012), reactive spillover (Guay 1996) and ideational approaches (Mörth and Britz 2004; Bátora 2009). To this end, the chapter is split into two sections : the first section looks at how government, commercial and institutional actors viewed calls for the establishment of an EDA, and the second section analyses the negotiations that took place for the creation of the Agency.

A European Defence Agency: what did governments and firms want?

This section of the chapter looks at the range of government and firm preferences that were articulated in advance of the establishment of the European Defence Agency. It examines two of our four claims embedded in the explanatory approaches outlined in Chapter 2: namely, that structural pressures pushed European governments towards the establishment of the Agency; and, that national preferences are largely reflective of economic interests. Before any in-depth analysis of national and commercial preferences takes place, however, it is worth sketching the historical context in which EU member states[1] formed their national preferences and negotiated these preferences prior to the establishment of the Agency. The year 2004 was significant because the EU member states were negotiating a reform treaty commonly referred to as the 'European Constitution' – or the Treaty Establishing a Constitution for Europe. The Treaty was needed to accommodate the EU's largest-ever single enlargement in 2004, which saw ten new states join the EU – seven of which were former communist countries. Until the 'European Constitution' was formally rejected[2] following referenda in France and the Netherlands, there was a strong sense of confidence in the EU and a range of initiatives was devised to drive forward EU cooperation. For example, the 'European Constitution' foresaw the creation of the post of 'EU Foreign Minister'. The euro currency, which perhaps is the most pertinent symbol of EU cooperation, started to circulate throughout Europe and the global economy in 2002.

Perhaps more significantly for this study, 2003 saw the deployment of the EU's first operation under the Common Security and Defence Policy (CSDP) – or European Security and Defence Policy (ESDP) as it was then known – to the Former Yugoslav Republic of Macedonia in the form of an EU Police Mission in Bosnia and Herzegovina (EUPM BiH) (Howorth 2004). The creation of the CSDP correspondingly led to calls for the establishment of a dedicated agency for defence. Given that the CSDP was largely created as a response to European military failures during the crisis in the former Yugoslavia – when Europeans lacked the military capabilities and political will to respond – the move to establish an agency to improve European military capabilities seemed logical (Rynning 2011). The bilateral France–UK summit held in 1998 at St. Malo was organised to address and reflect upon Europe's military failures during the disintegration of Yugoslavia (Shepherd 2015: 66). In line with the idea that structural pressures encourage closer cooperation, Europe's failure to act during the Yugoslav crisis served as an important political catalyst for cooperation on defence. French–German efforts to establish an armaments agency through the Western European Armaments Group during the 1980s and 1990s had failed. Following the strained transatlantic relations that resulted from the United States' – plus a number of EU member states' – controversial decision to intervene in Iraq in 2003, the impulse to nurture a strategically autonomous and military capable CSDP became all the more necessary for some European states (Grevi, Helly and Keohane 2009: 13; Howorth 2013a: 11).

An agency for military capability development

Even though the idea for an armaments agency was eventually contained in the draft Treaty on the European Constitution – see Article III-311 – previous Franco-German attempts to create a defence agency were treated with suspicion by London. At the time, the UK – under a Conservative government led by Sir John Major[3] – did not look favourably on the idea (French Government 1994: 124; Matlary 2009: 65). The UK saw the proposed agency as a way to 'create a "Fortress Europe" that excluded American (and other non-European) suppliers from European defence contracts' (Keohane 2004: 2). To retain their privileged trade with the US defence market, and to maintain London's privileged defence partnership with Washington, the UK government resisted the idea of an agency on the basis that it could harm its national defence market and strategic position vis-à-vis the US. Even after the election of a relatively pro-EU Labour government in 1997 under Tony Blair's leadership, the UK's domestic preferences were on balance still unfavourable towards an agency that would focus on industrial matters. Until the establishment of the Agency in 2004, the UK government opposed the creation of an agency 'on the grounds that it could all too easily have become a sort of benefit to industry without regard to proper defence needs' (UK Parliament 2005a: 7). In this regard, the UK government appeared to be motivated by both political (i.e. the need to maintain close military ties to the US) and economic interests (i.e. keeping Europe's defence market open).

Aside from the UK's concerns about its industrial interests, Tony Blair's premiership was nevertheless vital to the establishment of the Agency (Gegout 2002; Howorth 2004: 213). Tony Blair's election to office just before Europe's failure to act in Yugoslavia crystallised his view that Europe had to become more militarily capable, both in cases when Europeans would have to act autonomously without the US and when NATO would have to act. Additionally, Prime Minister Blair's controversial decision to join the US intervention in Iraq, and the rift in transatlantic relations that the decision created, meant that the Prime Minister needed some way of re-engaging with key European partners such as France and Germany. Under Blair, the UK soon saw the Agency as a means to improve European military capabilities while also going some, albeit small, way to improving British relations with the rest of Europe post-Iraq. The UK saw the Agency as a way of applying 'top-down' pressure on those states that had hitherto been reluctant to invest in defence capabilities – what is commonly referred to as the 'free-rider' problem (UK Parliament 2003; Howorth 2013b; Major and Mölling 2013). As one former official of the UK MoD remarked during an interview, 'Prime Minister Blair wanted to develop European military capabilities under an "EU flag" because he thought that the EU could stimulate action that would have been of benefit to Europe and NATO'[4] (see also UK Parliament 2004, 2005b: 11; Howorth 2007: 77).

Yet while UK preferences had aligned with many other European states on the issue of military capability development, London was still interested in ensuring that industrial matters and joint procurement would stay off the proposed agency's work agenda. The government was keen to see the Agency play a role in rationalising existing multinational capability programmes such as the Eurofighter jet and the A400M transport aircraft, not least because this could lower the costs of these weapons systems for the UK and avoid any further duplication with competing programmes (Keohane 2004: 2). What the UK government was not prepared to endorse, however, was an agency that would promote armaments and industrial cooperation with a *préférence européenne* or 'Buy European' bias permeating its work programmes. As one former UK minister explained at the time,

> our view is that the European Defence Agency will make a major contribution to the development of real capabilities [...] we do not need another procurement agency; what we need is an agency that will be focused on capacity to deliver.
>
> (UK Parliament 2005c, 2005b: 10)

Despite seeing a need to react to structural pressures such as strained relations with the US through the EU, the UK government was loathe to endorse a new institution that could work counter to its economic interests as well.

Military capabilities yes, but industrial matters too

The UK's quest to ensure that industrial and armaments issues stayed off the proposed Agency's agenda did not mirror French interests. While the French MoD concurred with the British desire to see more capable European militaries, other parts of the French government saw the proposed agency as a way to push industrial and procurement issues to the EU level so as to deal with a waning economy of scale in the French and European defence markets (Bellais 2011). As one former official of the EDA stated during an interview, 'in Paris it was apparent that while the Chief of the Defence Staff spoke about a capability-driven agency both the DGA [*direction générale de l'armement*] and foreign ministry were overwhelmingly interested in industrial issues'.[5] In particular, the DGA, which is an agency of the French MoD responsible for procurement and defence industrial policy, saw the establishment of a European defence agency as a way to simultaneously further Europeanise its own defence industrial policies and those of other EU member states. As one exchange with a senior DGA official revealed, 'for France it was logical that a defence agency, which was established to support the CSDP, should focus on capability development, industrial policy, European procurement and defence research'.[6] In line with both LI and economic patriotism, economic interests appeared to play an important role, although in this case they aimed at creating the Agency rather than stifling it.

Behind France's preference for an agency that would focus on European procurement and industrial matters was the belief that the CSDP should lead to a meaningful EDTIB and EDEM. As the French MoD stated at the time, the EDA could lead to the 'communal acquisition of defence equipment and actions that would reinforce the European defence industrial and technological base' (French Parliament 2003a). Perhaps more than any other European state, France had long held the idea that 'procurement and manufacture of arms [...] are crucial to independence in defence and foreign policy' (Mawdsley 2015: 143; see also Treacher 2001). In this regard, the problem for France was convincing its fellow EU member states of the need for an agency that would operate under a 'Buy European' ethos. When, for example, the French Foreign Ministry argued that the Agency's major rationale should be to help member states 'preserve their defence industrial base by proposing European equipment projects' it was not clear whose interests France really had in mind (Keohane 2004: 2–3). UK officials were aware that one 'could easily interchange the words "European" and "France" whenever Paris mentioned the EDTIB'.[7]

Yet a theoretically salient challenge for the UK in ensuring a capability-driven agency was the position of several other EU member states and defence firms. Both LI and economic patriotism claim that economic interests will drive forward European defence cooperation, but there is evidence that UK firms also saw a need to focus on military capabilities. For example, the UK's leading industry association has long held that while the EDA's focus on defence research is laudable its work in this area does not make sense without tangible capability programmes (ADS Group 2014: 1). However, some UK registered firms took a different view to the government and in many ways were aligned with French preferences. For example, the UK subsidiary of Italian firm Finmeccanica stated that the Agency could help 'create a more competitive environment by focusing industrial consortia on the type of military capability that nations need' (UK Parliament 2012: 19). Even the pan-European Airbus Group – then named EADS – which has a substantial slice of its production and workforce in the UK, clearly stated in its 2004 annual report that the EDA should 'lead to more pan-European, and better coordinated, procurement, with larger production runs' (EADS 2004: 38). Notwithstanding the fact that these UK-based pan-European firms had an interest in an agency that could boost European collaboration and sales, their own preferences were at odds with the UK government.

As if to bolster this point, BAE Systems – the jewel in the UK's defence industrial crown and a company where the government holds a 'golden share'[8] – also publicly backed a defence agency that would focus on a range of defence industrial issues, and thus beyond just capability development. On 28 April 2003 the then CEO of BAE Systems, Mike Turner, co-authored an article with his counterparts Philippe Camus and Rainer Hertrich – then co-CEOs of EADS, and Denis Ranque – then CEO of Thales, calling for strong political commitment to the Agency. The article, entitled 'Time to Act', appeared in leading news journals in various European countries and it argued that European governments should move beyond the LoI framework and OCCAR towards a European Defence Agency because this 'would take on massive strategic importance for the future of the European defence industry' (Defense-Aerospace 2003).[9] Citing the US-led military interventions in Afghanistan and Iraq, the CEOs stated that such events 'demonstrated the need for Europe to enhance its defence' (Defense-Aerospace 2003). As one industry representative stated during an interview, 'major European firms wanted an agency that would be responsible for joint procurement, defence research and industrial policies'.[10]

More in keeping with the notion that structural pressures drive forward EU defence industrial cooperation was the close alignment between the preferences of the Italian government and Italian industry. Significantly, in the period directly preceding the establishment of the EDA, not only did Italy hold the EU presidency (June–December 2003) but the Italian defence market was undergoing a process of consolidation (Gasparini 2004: 21). For example, Europe's main missile producer – MBDA – was established in 2001 following a merger between BAE (UK), Mantra (France) and Finmeccanica (Italy) (Caruso and Locatelli 2011: 12). As the 2000 Anglo-Italian merger between Finmeccanica and GKN further attests, companies such as Finmeccanica wanted to consolidate its business and to acquire key European firms. Following the merger of Finmeccanica and GKN's respective helicopter divisions, which created AgustaWestland – one of Europe's leading helicopter producers – Finmeccanica further consolidated its European position by acquiring the company in 2004. For Italy, the international competitiveness of Italian defence firms went together with European cooperation (Missiroli 2001; Caruso and Locatelli 2011: 14; Darnis 2011). While firms such as Finmeccanica have engaged in EU-level defence efforts based on economic calculation, for the Italian government European cooperation was of vital strategic importance for its defence policy because it responded to numerous international factors such as increased competition (Caruso and Locatelli 2011: 14; see also Missiroli 2001; Politi 2004).

The Italian government had invested in the idea of an EDA for several reasons. The first was that institutions such as the EDA and the broader institutionalisation of European defence cooperation reflected Italy's long-held preference for EU member states to work together on defence (Gilli, Ungaro and Marrone 2015: 36; see also Giovachini 2004). The creation of the CSDP and the eventual establishment of the EDA suited Italy's preferences regarding European defence. More interestingly perhaps, the Italian government recognised that other attempts at European cooperation through the LoI framework and OCCAR had not been successful. As was noted at the time, 'only the future will show if OCCAR will form the nucleus of a precursor to a European Armaments Agency, and the creation of such an agency cannot be underestimated given the problems associated with the existing organisation' (Nones, Di Paola and Ruggeri 2003: 18). Even though Italy was a founding member of the LoI group and OCCAR, the Italian MoD and industry saw the EDA as a way to involve all EU member states and the European Commission in defence industrial cooperation and to enhance cooperation in areas such as defence research (Comelli, Di Camillo and Gasparini 2004: 50; Politi 2004; AIAD 2005: 19).

Several other EU member states also wanted the proposed agency to have a wider remit than initially proposed by the UK government, but, interestingly, only because it would allow room for the Agency to focus on their specific defence industrial interests. For example, in wanting to ensure that defence research was an important part of the proposed agency's focus, Germany shared French preferences for an agency that would help 'maintain a capable and competitive industrial base in core technological and armaments areas' (German Government 2006: 39). Given Germany's historical reticence 'to take advantage of the opportunities for cross-national defence capability cooperation and defence industrial collaboration', sections of the German government and industry saw the proposed agency as a way to promote defence research collaboration[11] (Dyson 2015: 156). Defence research and niche technology areas such as optics and avionics are critical to Germany's defence industrial base (Thoma *et al.* 2011). By grafting defence industrial and research matters onto the Agency's mandate, Germany could use European cooperation to promote its economic interests by amplifying existing federal funding on defence R&D and enhancing Germany's high-tech industries (Heidenkamp, Louth and Taylor 2013: 75–76).

Despite being leading supporters of the CSDP and having been one of the first states to float the idea of a European armaments agency, a number of Germany's federal ministries and firms were cautious about the EDA. As one former official of the German MoD remarked during an interview, 'while the chancellery was generally supportive of the idea the ministry of defence was initially suspicious of an EU bureaucracy on defence'.[12] Even some sections of German industry had misgivings at first, with one representative stating that 'we had to see if the Agency would help our business before committing to it because we were not naturally open to more bureaucratic procedures and institutions'.[13] Despite these reservations, and notwithstanding the potential benefits for its defence research and SMEs, Berlin had specific political reasons for agreeing to the need for an agency. Germany had not been pleased that, having played a key role in establishing OCCAR and pushing for the establishment of a European armaments agency (Gallhöfer 2013: 95), the UK and France had excluded Germany by bilaterally agreeing to European initiatives at St. Malo and Le Touquet.[14] As one former UK official noted, 'the Franco-British St. Malo Summit annoyed Germany because they were excluded from what they perceived to be a common European issue'.[15] The EDA therefore represented an opportunity for Germany to Europeanise defence industrial cooperation.

For its part, the Swedish government viewed the EDA as a way to further enhance European efforts for interoperability and equipment standardisation (Svensson 2006: 59). Keeping in mind Sweden's neutrality and its non-membership of NATO, the proposed agency represented a way for Sweden to strengthen military cooperation with fellow EU member states. Not only was EU cooperation more acceptable to the Swedish public than possible NATO membership, but also the proposed aims of the Agency suited Sweden's post-Cold War strategy of nurturing international cooperation. The government also realised that in the past 'multinational cooperation on defence capabilities had been hampered by the problem of agreeing to a common set of objectives and strategies, especially in those countries with sizeable national industries' (Oredsson and Winnerstig 2005: 14). The proposed agency was thus seen as a way to use a new governance structure and policy framework to try and enhance defence cooperation. Furthermore, Sweden's defence industry was supportive of the proposed agency because they saw it as a way to make Europe's markets more competitive and open (Englesson 2006; Castellacci, Fevolden and Lundmark 2014: 1230). As one interviewee stated, 'Swedish industry has long been supportive of any European measure that leads to a competitive defence market and a level playing field between the major industrial states'.[16]

Finland was perhaps rather more outspoken about the potential economic benefits that might result from European cooperation. Like France, Finland had a preference for pushing industrial policy questions to the EU level. At the time the Finnish government not only politically lent its support to the establishment of the EDA, but it stated that 'Finland is aiming to enhance the competitiveness of the Finnish defence industry within the EU framework and within clearly defined rules' (Finland Prime Minister's Office 2004: 80). For Finland, the EDA offered a way of lowering the costs of defence procurement while also supporting the Finnish defence sector.[17] As was put rather candidly in a government report at the time,

> [t]he defence establishment is investigating options for European cooperation in maintaining and updating defence materiel, so that the Finnish defence industry's requirements are also taken into account. New opportunities for this will emerge with the creation of the EU's new European Defence Agency.
>
> (Ibid.: 130)

Much like France, therefore, Finland saw an opportunity to push defence industrial matters to the EU level and to secure opportunities for its own national DTIB.

Mixed preferences and misgivings

The UK government was not alone in preferring the Agency to focus on military capability development. Belgian preferences almost mirrored London's and the Federal Government sought to establish an agency that would help Belgium adapt militarily to the post-Cold War period. This era was marked by crisis management operations and the Belgian MoD believed that the Agency could help Europe develop 'much more agile forces, able to deploy rapidly over long distances' with strategic enablers such as 'strategic air and maritime transport' and 'deployable force headquarters and strategic intelligence and communications' (Biscop and Coelmont 2013: 79; see also Belgian Government 2003, 2014). Belgium's enthusiasm for a defence agency mainly focused on military capability development derived from the country's support for the CSDP. As evidenced by Belgium's prominent political role during its 2001 EU presidency and its role in pushing for military capability development at the Helsinki (December 1999) and Göteborg European Councils (June 2001), Belgium saw an opportunity to make Europe more militarily capable and further Europeanise its own defence forces (Belgian Government 2003: 12, 2014). Belgium's focus on military capability development was not, however, simply related to the fact that CSDP could only realistically work with more capable European militaries (Belgian Government 2014). Belgium was also keen to keep industrial matters off the proposed agency's agenda because of its own national industrial interests. The country employed approximately 10,000 direct/indirect jobs in the defence sector in 2015 (de France, Mampaey and Zandee 2016: 2) and so, like many other European countries, Belgium was not overly keen to see defence industrial policy pushed to the EU level.

In contrast, most Central and Eastern European countries looked favourably on the proposed defence agency, because many saw it as a way of supporting their nascent defence industries. Even though many of these countries were still yet to formally become EU member states, countries such as the Czech Republic and the Baltic States favoured a more industrially focused agency to develop defence research relationships and to promote niche technologies (Kolín 2015: 10). This position was understandable given that '[t]he military capabilities of most accession states were in a different league [that is, inferior] from those of many EU member states' (Howorth 2007: 77). This is not to say that they did so without due regard for their national industrial interests. For example, despite the Hungarian government's long neglect of its domestic defence industry, Budapest saw the EDA as a way of encouraging inward investment into Hungary's DTIB and, consequently, to show its new-found solidarity with its domestic defence industry (Behr and Siwiecki 2004: 28). In this way, Hungary's later decision to join the EDA's 'Code of Conduct on Defence Procurement' in 2005 was a way of accepting broad liberal practices and procurement transparency while also boosting Hungary's domestic defence market (Kiss 2014: 135–136).

However, perhaps the one country that most closely mirrored British preferences was Poland. While Poland was in a similar position to most former Warsaw Pact countries, it did not embrace the idea of an agency focused on industrial and armaments matters. Instead, it saw the Agency as a potential threat to its defence industry rather than an opportunity. This was because it perceived both the proposed agency and the European Commission as liberalising forces that would open the Polish defence market to increased and potentially harmful international competition (ibid.: 329 and 386). Poland's domestic preferences at the time appear to confirm the argument that economic interests play the most important role in preference formation, although there was pressure on Warsaw to play the 'good European' given its then pending accession to the EU and the fact that it backed the Iraq War. From the very beginning the Polish government was clear that any involvement in the CSDP and the EDA should be 'shaped by the development of its own defence market and concern about the effects of liberalisation' (Zamelek 2013: 2; see also Markowski and Hall 2005). Poland's defence industrial strategy in the post-Cold War era has been focused on closing its technology gap with Western Europe and the United States, while not unduly harming its domestic industry (Behr and Siwiecki 2004: 33 and 36; Markowski and Hall 2005). Poland would only accept to include industrial matters under the purview of the proposed agency so long as it would give their industry a chance to compete with more developed defence markets[18] (see also Zamelek 2013: 5).

The Spanish government and industry took a similar view to Poland. Even though Javier Solana – a pro-EU Spaniard – was the first head of the EDA, Spain took a more nuanced view of the proposed agency. While it generally lent its support to the idea of a dedicated agency on defence (Spanish Government 2004: 9; Alfonso-Meiriño 2010), the notion that the single internal market in defence would now be bolstered by both the European Commission and the EDA was considered 'both an opportunity and a threat' for Spain's industrial defence and security sector (Cosidó 2005). On the one hand, Spain understood that it is 'undeniable that the creation of the Agency could give a new boost to the harmonisation of requirements', but, on the other hand, Spain shared Poland's desire 'to try to safeguard its industrial and defence interests in the increasingly multilateral framework it has helped create' (Cosidó 2005; see also Yustos Cordobés 2010: 216). As one Spanish industrialist stated during an exchange, 'the Agency represented an opportunity to calm the European Commission's promotion of competition and liberalisation in defence but only to the extent that the Agency does not itself start to intrude in the affairs of member states'.[19] Despite these misgivings, however, Spain was interested in ensuring reconciliation in Europe after the Iraq War, which it had joined.

This overview (see Table 3.1 below) of various national preferences towards the proposed agency has shown that before any unanimous decision on a Council Joint Action were possible, member states needed to arrive at agreement on the balance between whether the Agency should predominantly focus on military capability development or defence industrial issues. One group of member states that coalesced around the UK wanted to keep defence industrial matters off the EDA's agenda, whereas other states grouped around France saw an opportunity to push defence industrial policy issues to the EU level. In many ways, the preceding analysis has confirmed Hoeffler's (2012) central thesis that European defence cooperation reflects the interests of certain states and their respective industrial preferences. One may also draw from Guay's (1996) notion of 'reactive spillover' to show that the preferences of many member states were a response to increasing costs, international competition and the need to cooperate to achieve some form of Pareto optimality. While these are valid arguments, they fail to explain both how and why member states ultimately decided on the policy remit of the Agency. In this sense, understanding preferences on their own is not sufficient if one is to understand how these various preferences were negotiated and how compromise was achieved. With a view to explaining how and why the member states agreed to establish the EDA, the next section examines the relative bargaining power of member states and what role non-agreement, exclusion or compromise played during negotiations.

A bargain and an agency

Now that one has a better understanding of the domestic preferences of several EU member states and firms towards the proposed establishment of the EDA before 2004, it is necessary to examine how compromise between the various national positions was achieved. To this end, this section of the chapter analyses how relative bargaining power was exercised during negotiations and to what

Table 3.1 Domestic preferences and the EDA

	BE	*DE*	*ES*	*FI*	*FR*	*IT*	*PL*	*SE*	*UK*
'Buy European'					✗		✗		✗
Capability Development	✓			✓	✓	✓		✓	✓
Defence Research		✓		✓	✓	✓		✓	✗
Industrial Policy		✓	✗	✓	✓	✓	✗	✓	✗
Interoperability	✓		✓	✓				✓	
Joint Procurement		✓		✓	✓	✓			✗
Post-Iraq Cooperation			✓			✓	✓		✓

Source: author's own.

extent the threat of exclusion and non-agreement played a role in securing compromise. It should be recalled that, under the liberal intergovernmental model, power is not defined exclusively in material terms, even though market size is clearly a factor in producing policy outcomes. It should not be expected that EU member states with the largest defence markets would be willing to agree to EU-level policy and legislation that would adversely affect the health of their respective national DTIBs or governments' control over them. Rather, LI defines power as the combination of a range of factors that enables a state or group of states to condition what type of policy outcome emerges from intergovernmental negotiations (Moravcsik 1993b: 485 and 498–499).

Negotiations for the establishment of the defence agency were purposefully an intergovernmental affair. Initially, work to establish the EDA was carried forward by an 'ad hoc preparation group' that was created by the Committee of Permanent Representatives (COREPER) in September 2003 (Howorth 2004: 498; Schmitt 2004; UK Parliament 2004). This work eventually led to the explicit acknowledgement that only the 'Council, acting by a qualified majority, shall adopt a decision defining the Agency's statute, seat and operational rules' (see Article 28D of the Lisbon Treaty). Thus, changes to the mandate and structure of the EDA were, and remain, the sole prerogative of the member states. It is, however, also worth noting the significance of establishing an 'agency' as the institutional vehicle to manage the constellation of national and commercial preferences that existed. In this regard, Ekelund interestingly notes that, while the early 2000s was a period when 'several agencies were created in the EU', the sensitivities surrounding defence cooperation meant that the Agency was not established as an agency of the European Commission – as had been done for most other EU agencies (2015: 18).

Europeanisation as a bargaining tool

One of the key factors involved during the negotiations for the EDA was France's ability to Europeanise the issue of defence cooperation. While several European governments were interested in a capability-driven agency (Simón 2014: 122), it was France that wanted the EDA to focus on industrial policy and joint procurement (Mawdsley 2015: 139). It was clear during the negotiation phase that 'there was a tension between the French focus on armaments cooperation and the British insistence on capability development'.[20] It was no secret that the French government insisted on a strong EU institution that could drive forward European defence cooperation in all its forms (Advisory Council on International Affairs 2012: 17). For France, the proposed agency could lead to joint – read European – procurement programmes and these could in turn potentially benefit European – read French – industry.[21] The French government could push for a greater Europeanisation of defence cooperation because of historical circumstances and because of the experiences of past intergovernmental defence initiatives (Lundmark 2004). Given Finland, Germany, Hungary, Italy and Sweden's similar desire to be fully engaged with defence industrial issues at the EU level, any British strategy of excluding certain member states so as to establish an agency outside of the formal structures of the EU would be resisted by key member states such as France and Germany.

During the bargaining phase, the 'exclusion' of certain EU member states was not seen as a credible bargaining tactic. If anything, the French, German and Italian governments argued that the EDA was a way of overcoming the types of bilateral and/or multilateral arrangements that existed between only a handful of EU member states. As we have seen, Germany was already disappointed that it had been excluded from the establishment of the CSDP at St. Malo, and Italy had misgivings about the effectiveness of existing non-EU frameworks such as the LoI group and/or OCCAR (Mottier *et al.* 2009: 75). Even the Dutch government, which saw itself as a defence industrial player that had been generally treated as a junior partner in OCCAR and completely excluded from the LoI group, saw the proposed Agency as a way to give it a far greater say in EU defence industrial policy.[22] From the outset, the whole point about the EDA was that it would be inclusive of all EU member states – with, of course, the exception of Denmark because of its defence policy opt-outs. Following Italy's reflections on OCCAR and the LoI it was hoped that the EDA could represent a novel form of governance that could instil EU-wide cooperation. Thus, the relative bargaining power of France, Germany, Italy and several other European governments ensured that 'exclusion' could not credibly occur. This bargaining power was only amplified when key European primes (including from the UK) called for the Agency to be ambitious and far-reaching in its policy objectives.[23]

In seeking to Europeanise defence cooperation, France was keen to link the idea of the proposed defence agency with the momentum created by the 'European Constitution'. Within this strategy was the implicit sense that future European defence industrial cooperation had to be embedded in the EU, especially since the CSDP already symbolised an EU-wide commitment to defence operations. Despite France's close military ties to the UK, Paris used the 'Convention on the Future of Europe' – the body responsible for drafting the TCE, which, significantly, was presided over by former French President Valéry Giscard d'Estaing – to ensure that defence industrial policy, defence research and even military planning would be pushed to the EU level. In this respect, France wanted to link the issue of the European Convention with closer defence industrial cooperation. An important individual in France's strategy at the time was Michel Barnier, the then French Foreign Minister (2004–2005), a former European Commissioner (1999–2004) and the current EU chief negotiator for the UK exiting the EU (2016–present). Barnier represented France in the Convention on the Future of Europe's working group on defence (Eilstrup Sangiovanni 2003: 194),[24] and, consequently, he served as an interface between French defence interests and the Convention team (Irondelle 2008: 159). Having such intimate relations between Paris and the Convention team ensured that what France proposed would be a European initiative.[25] This was a vital strategy for France because, following the Iraq War, President Jacques Chirac wanted European 'autonomy' in defence to keep NATO and the US at arms-length (Cogan 2001: 128; see also Hofmann 2011: 107).

Yet France's strategy of folding the idea of the Agency into the work on the 'European Constitution' was not entirely successful. As if to anticipate the results of the Dutch and French referenda on the 'European Constitution', many EU member states did not want to embed the EDA negotiation process into the discussions of the 'Convention on the Future of Europe'. That is, agreement on the EDA was ultimately not dependent on ratification of the 'European Constitution'. In fact, under the guidance of the then Greek presidency of the Council of the EU the member states eventually settled on a Joint Action at the Thessaloniki European Council in June 2003 (Karampekios 2015: 42) that was signed before the Dutch and French votes even took place (Schmitt 2003; European Parliament 2005). In this way, the proposed EDA would go on to survive the rejection of the 'Constitution' and work would continue under Italy's 2003 EU presidency (Giovachini 2004). As Trybus remarks, the member states were 'not prepared to leave this crucial aspect of the common defence policy to the uncertainty of the implementation process of the Constitutional Treaty' (2005: 327). Here the Italian EU presidency played a vital role in ensuring the swift adoption of the Joint Action, and they also ensured that the Joint Action did not have to go through 'any detailed discussion at ministerial level' as part of the work on the 'European Constitution' (Gasparini 2004; Politi 2004). Discussing EDA-related matters in a parallel format not only side-stepped the various and sometimes confusing agendas emerging out of the Convention on the Future of Europe, but adopting a Joint Action meant that the European Parliament and European Commission did not have to be formally consulted either (UK Parliament 2005a: 2).

However, the term 'Europeanisation' should not automatically denote enhanced EU cooperation. For some member states the establishment of the EDA, although an important symbol of EU defence cooperation, represented a means of balancing against the European Commission's increasing supranational role in defence industrial policy and its desire to play an enhanced role in defence policy (Fiott 2015b; see also De Vore 2015b). It is worth noting that in its 1996 communication on defence the European Commission urged member states to give it a mandate for defence capability and industrial policy. Given the failure to establish a European armaments agency under the auspices of the WEAG during the 1980s and 1990s, the European Commission announced in 1996 that: 'the Commission should consider its possible contribution to establishing this agency and to defining its tasks and carrying out its activities' (European Commission 1996: 1; Fiott 2015b: 547). States such as Spain, which wanted to stave off the liberalising agenda of the European Commission and some other EU member states, ultimately viewed the EDA as a way to tame the integrationist impulses of the Commission.

It was therefore necessary to reconcile the preferences of those member states that wanted to use the EDA to curtail the nascent role of the European Commission in the defence sector, and those states that wanted the Commission and the EDA to play a greater role in regulating and supporting the European defence market. The compromise that was designed to ensure a balance of preferences was that, while the EDA would be an intergovernmental agency, the European Commission would be associated with its work in specific ways. Under Article 24 of the Joint Action establishing the Agency, the European Commission was made a non-voting member of the EDA Steering Board, and the Commission was openly invited 'to participate in agency projects and programmes on an ad hoc basis as part of the project steering committees' (Fiott 2015b: 549). Such a compromise was vital to the work of the EDA. One former senior EDA official explained during an interview that Agency staff 'were well aware of the possible friction that could be caused with the European Commission, so the Agency did everything it could to avoid possible tensions'[26] (see De Vore, 2015b; Fiott 2015b). Agency staff worked to this end by reaching out to key personnel at the Commission and trying to ensure complementarity between both institutions.[27]

Nevertheless, those EU member states that wanted the EDA to comprehensively focus on various aspects of defence cooperation used the momentum initiated by the creation of the CSDP to ensure that issues such as joint procurement ended up on the EDA's agenda. On this front, the UK government found itself in a difficult bargaining position. While both London and Paris had forged the CSDP based on 'exclusionary' strategies – both the St. Malo (1998) and Le Touquet (2003) summits were bilateral in nature – the UK would not have been able to influence military capability development initiatives within the EDA without a Europeanised approach[28] (Keohane 2004: 2; Trybus 2006: 667; Mawdsley 2015: 147). The UK government could hardly have called for greater European capability development through an exclusive club of states. After all, the LoI and OCCAR had manifestly failed to help London achieve its aim of boosting military capabilities in Europe in the past. Given the strong desire for an agency with a more comprehensive remit in countries such as France and Italy, the UK government was faced with a difficult choice: force 'non-agreement' by not agreeing to the Joint Action and risk not meeting its European military capability development objectives and reconciliation after the Iraq War, or 'compromise' and run the risk of defence industrial issues and joint procurement firmly making it on the agenda of the EDA.

The UK government did not find it easy to push back against French preferences for a more comprehensive EDA.[29] Given that the idea for a defence agency was inextricably linked with the broader politics of the 'European Constitution' and the prior establishment of the CSDP, the UK government recognised that failure to establish the Agency would send a divisive signal precisely at the time when Europe was already split over the Iraq War – especially given Britain's support for the war (Hyde-Price 2004: 323). It should be recalled that it was the Iraq War that convinced German Chancellor Gerhard Schröder to embrace the idea of a strategically autonomous EU (Simón 2014: 143). Additionally, Italy equally sought to mend the intra-EU rift caused by the Iraq War – it had supported the US-led intervention too – and it did so by pushing for a new EU institution on defence during its tenure as the EU president to link the two issues (July–December 2003).[30] In a sense, therefore, for the British the EDA's significance went beyond a simple discussion about the Agency's *raison d'être* because it also served to supposedly heal relations in European politics following the Iraq War. For the UK government, the need to overcome European division over the Iraq War, which was critical for the health of the NATO alliance too, far outweighed the costs associated with establishing the EDA and this is why London sought to link the two issues.

Ambiguity of aims and the 'power of the purse'

Yet if the UK government had no option but to seek a compromise rather than walk away from negotiations, or opt for a more exclusive grouping of states, this is not to say that London did not attempt to tame the degree of Europeanisation sought by states such as France, Italy and Sweden. It was soon recognised by the UK government that the range of domestic preferences feeding into negotiations could be used as a bargaining strategy. By ensuring that the Agency would deal with a broad array of tasks it would be possible to dilute the reach and ambitions of the EDA. Thus, to steer the Agency away from exclusively dealing with issues such as joint procurement and defence research, the UK pushed even harder for the Agency to be allotted a broad set of tasks and to avoid setting specific duties. As one minister confirmed in the UK Parliament at the time,

> [w]e have not got into the absolute detail yet because we did not want to proceed without too much prescription for fear of frightening people off. We want to get the broad agreement in principle first and then go down [a] detailed route.
>
> (UK Parliament 2005d: 36)

In conjunction with the intergovernmental nature of the EDA, the UK government could meet its main objectives of slowing the pace of defence Europeanisation, getting EU-wide acknowledgement of the need to develop capabilities and moving to heal the divisions caused in Europe by the Iraq War.

To lock in the UK government's preferences during the negotiations it was necessary to go beyond political statements and rhetoric and to craft an organisational structure that would ensure a certain degree of ambiguity in the EDA's taskings and staff representation. A vehicle for achieving this aim was the team assembled to establish the EDA – the 'Agency Establishment Team' (AET). The AET, which was created by the Council in November 2003, was a crucial actor and it had the task of ensuring that the Agency was fully operational by 31 December 2004. The AET was principally charged with drawing up a comprehensive plan for the EDA's organisational structure, methods and working procedures, budgetary and staffing arrangements and a programme of work (Council of the European Union 2003b: 21). Yet the AET's work, and the need to decide on senior staff appointments at the Agency, meant that there was a 'fierce turf battle' between Paris and London over the direction and governance of the Agency[31] (Howorth 2007: 110). In this respect, the UK's objective of ensuring that the EDA should focus only on military capability development had to give way to a strategy centred on ensuring that the EDA would not serve France's ambitious preferences.

Having in place a staff structure that would reflect and embed the compromise found between national preferences when unanimously agreeing to the Joint Action was vitally important for all sides in the negotiation. Not only was the EDA's first Chief Executive a UK national (Nick Witney – a seconded senior official from the UK MoD), but he was supported by a German Deputy Chief Executive (Hilmar Linnenkamp – seconded from the German MoD) and four directors for research and technology (Bertrand de Cordoue – from the French Ministry of Economy, Finance and Industry); capabilities (Pierre Hougardy – from the Belgian Joint Staff); armaments (Carlo Magrassi – from the Italian MoD); and industry and the market (Ulf Hammarström – from the Swedish Permanent Representation to the EU and NATO). These individuals not only reflected a geographical balance between the key EU member states but they also had little choice but to 'take on as much [sic] tasks as possible in order to ensure that the EDA was taken seriously'.[32] The EDA, still in its infancy at the time, could ill-afford to lose the interest of all EU member states from the very beginning by not catering to their national preferences. It is for this reason that the Agency's work programme focused on a broad array of subjects such as interoperability, procurement, capability development, technologies and industrial policy (Heuninckx 2009: 140; Dyson and Konstadinides 2013: 38).

However, contributing to the ambiguity of the EDA's aims and ensuring a staff structure that reflected member state interests was not enough to ensure an acceptable compromise between the member states. As important was restraining the Agency by ensuring that it would function on a relatively small operational budget. Here the UK was surprisingly supported by Germany. While Germany had a direct preference in ensuring that the Agency would focus on defence research and development, Berlin recognised that the EDA ran the risk of becoming an overly bloated bureaucracy. Keeping the Agency's operational costs in check was important for Germany because the country has traditionally been the EDA's largest financial contributor.[33] For example, of the €20 million in member state contributions in 2005 Germany contributed €4.3 million or 21.46 per cent of the total share (German Parliament 2005: 4; European Defence Agency 2006c: 3). While Germany of course had no objection to other states making additional financial contributions to the EDA, it insisted on a mechanism to regularly review the EDA's budget to ensure control over costs (German Parliament 2005: 2).

In tandem with the UK, Germany used its financial power to ensure that the Agency would not accrue new prerogatives once established,[34] not increase its operational budget and/or not become a large bureaucracy (Dyson 2015: 158).[35] In this regard, the German MoD was initially adamant that 'the Agency should only require 10 to 30 staff' because it 'wanted a nimble Agency able to network between Europe's ministries of defence'.[36] In contrast, at one point in time

France thought that the Agency should have a staffing level of approximately 500 experts with an operational budget of around €150 million.[37] Even though the German Federal Government has stood at odds with German MEPs[38] on the matter – MEPs who have repeatedly called for greater budgetary resources for the Agency (European Parliament 2005, 2013) – the government was eventually prepared to allow the Agency to employ 80 individual experts to begin with (Frenzel 2004). As one of the major creditors of the Agency, Germany insisted on a nimble entity and this simultaneously met the UK government's ambition of restraining France's drive towards greater Europeanisation in defence cooperation.

One of the paradoxes of the compromise achieved between member states was the impact it had on industry. Major European industrial actors could see that disagreement over the ultimate rationale of the Agency would dilute political commitment to the initiative and lead to an unclear work programme.[39] On 15 June 2004, the CEOs of BAE Systems, EADS and Thales penned yet another letter for simultaneous publication in *Le Figaro*, *Frankfurter Allgemeine Zeitung*, the *Financial Times* and the *Independent* calling on European governments to make a success of the European Defence Agency. The letter is worth mentioning here for it reflects the real sense of frustration held by the most senior executives of Europe's major defence producers. The CEOs used their public statement to reiterate that the creation of the European Defence Agency was essential to European security and to the defence industrial base in Europe, so, they exhorted, the '[c]reation of the Agency should be a landmark event' (Defense-Aerospace 2004). The CEOs recognised that the Agency could quickly become a fig leaf for a lack of action by the member states, and it is for this reason that the CEOs pressed European governments to make 'firm commitments to fully support the Agency' with projects and funding (ibid., 2004). Despite being firm supporters of the EDA at the time, major defence companies were confronted with an Agency in 2004 that did not entirely live up to their ambitious preferences or expectations (Cross 2015).

Concluding observations

How does the preceding analysis help us to answer the dual research question guiding this book? The first salient observation is that structural pressures played an important role in setting the context in which the EDA was established. The changing security and political environment in Europe certainly coloured the domestic preferences that surfaced in relation to the proposal for a European Defence Agency (Aben 1992; Bitzinger 2009; Kiss 2014). Following the end of the Cold War and the eventual enlargement of NATO and the EU to include former Warsaw Pact countries, the need for a dedicated defence agency was seen by some member states as a way to respond to shifts in the geopolitical structure of Europe and globally, and to changes to the global defence supply chain. In particular, countries such as the UK and Italy were keen to use the EDA as a way to heal the rift that had been caused by the Iraq War. Specifically for the

UK, the drive to use the EDA to boost military capability development rather than industrial issues reflected its long-standing aversion to EU initiatives that could be seen to divert attention away from the transatlantic relationship. For the UK, the EDA symbolised an opportunity to heal transatlantic relations at a time when they had hit a low, but, should countries such as France, Germany and Italy manage to place industrial issues on the Agency's agenda, it potentially represented a challenge to UK industry and London's strategic interests with regard to the UK–US relationship.

The various political rationales behind the creation and *raison d'être* of the Agency would appear to be more compelling than purely economic forms of structural pressures, although a number of member states such as Finland, France, Germany, Hungary, Italy and Sweden clearly saw the Agency as a way to benefit their respective national DTIBs. What is clear from testing the idea that economic rather than politico-strategic factors drive or halt defence cooperation, is that it is extremely difficult to compartmentalise economic and political preferences when studying the establishment of the EDA. Thus, states such as Belgium, Poland, Spain and the UK were less keen to see industrial matters form part of the EDA's remit, but each one of these states had their own respective rationale for doing so. The UK, for example, believed that the EDA was necessary for the sake of EU unity and EU–US relations but it equally did not want any undue pressure on its defence market. In contrast, countries such as Belgium saw the EDA as a way to afford the EU more strategic autonomy in defence but it was equally cautious about the Agency playing a role in industrial matters because it wanted to safeguard its national industry. On this basis, it was possible to achieve a unanimous decision to establish the EDA: some member states saw the EDA as a way to further open up the European defence market and to enhance Europe's strategic autonomy (a number of firms followed this rationale), whereas others wanted to establish the EDA in order to control the pace of defence industrial cooperation at the EU level.

Institutionalist explanations would suggest that the establishment of the Agency arguably represented a drive to establish economies of scale and to achieve Pareto optimality (Guay and Callum 2002; Hartley 2011). This does not appear to have entirely been the case, however. In fact, a number of member states such as Poland and Spain were actively against the idea of creating some form of Pareto optimality through the EDA precisely because they believed that it would have meant harming their respective national defence industrial bases. Thus, even though economic arguments such as the need to ensure economies of scale in Europe are still salient, the political reasons for establishing the Agency (e.g. the Iraq War, transatlantic relations, safeguarding national defence industries) undermine a purely economic explanation for the creation of the EDA – it is clearly not just about efficiency through the creation of institutions. In fact, when one looks at the ambiguity over the Agency's tasks and its low level of operational funding one can see the imprint of the contested economic and political preferences held by the EU member states. This would appear to take the LI model beyond a pure focus on economic preferences, even though a number of firms such as BAE Systems, Thales and Airbus saw the Agency as a way to consolidate demand and open up markets in Europe.

This institutional ambiguity could be seen as an endorsement of ideational or sociological approaches to understanding European defence industrial cooperation. When one looks at the various competing rationales for the EDA, one could say that the Agency was being used to embed or help produce new norms, ideas and practices (Skowronek 1982; Mörth and Britz 2004; Bátora 2009; Schmidt 2010). However, for a theoretical branch that prides itself on uncovering embedded power relations and meaning in institutions, it is remarkable how little ideational and institutional approaches can say about how power was articulated during negotiations for the establishment of the EDA. True, negotiations for the establishment of the Agency do reflect a power struggle between states and a contestation over ideologies, but the case of the EDA shows that there were clear differences of political and economic interest between the member states. As an *ex-post facto* explanation, ideational or sociological approaches may be useful in uncovering conflict over meaning and norms but these approaches tell us very little about the nature of member state preferences before the establishment of the Agency.

In this sense, what is clear from the establishment of the EDA is that Hoeffler's assumption that certain EU member states project their interests to the EU level to protect their national defence market has an obvious place in explaining the establishment of the Agency (Hoeffler 2012: 436). Hoeffler's approach appears to challenge the neo-functionalist logic that the EU is on a path of continuous and increasing levels of cooperation. On the contrary, what is clear is that EU member states appeared to embed their respective national preferences into the working practices of the Agency to ensure that they could control the activities of the EDA and thereby secure these national preferences. In this sense, the EDA has been shown to reflect aspects of both cooperation and conflict between the member states. Far from Guay's (1996) argument that structural pressures would lead to supranational responses to the defence sector, the birth of the EDA points to some of the member states' desire to ensure that defence industrial policy would not spillover into the European Commission's industrial and Single Market policies (as indeed foreseen by Lovering 1999). In fact, those member states who argued for a clear distinction between military capability development and industrial policy would not have easily achieved this objective in a supranational setting because the negotiating setting would have been different.

Overall, what has been observed is that, while structural pressures provided the context in which the Agency could be established, the birth of the institution was by no means automatic. Nevertheless, based on these structural pressures, every member state sought to establish the Agency as a way to advance both their economic and political preferences. Here, it has been confirmed that such preferences were not only economic in nature. Political interests, such as the need to ensure EU unity and to repair transatlantic relations, challenge the hypothesis that economic preferences are – alone – the major driver of European cooperation. This is significant because it means that the EDA was founded, and is potentially still affected, by the original bargain reached between member states. Some governments saw the Agency as an important symbol of EU unity and a way to institutionalise the drive towards further capability development. Others saw the Agency as a way to Europeanise demand and markets in Europe. Either way, in the compromise found between the member states in the run-up to the Agency's establishment in 2004, each government could claim to have served their respective domestic preferences without any due harm to their respective DTIBs.

Accordingly, the importance of understanding the bargaining process between member states is clear. Before the EDA could be established, a major compromise between France and the UK was required, but Germany also had an important role to play in wielding its financial power. What is interesting is that non-agreement and exclusion appeared to be unrealistic options for the member states because, while other frameworks such as OCCAR and LoI were by their very nature exclusionary, the EDA was a way to overcome inefficiencies and exclusion. Neither the UK nor France could project their respective interests on an EU-wide basis without the involvement of the then EU25. Had the UK walked away from negotiations, then it would have been difficult for London to reconcile its differences with fellow governments over the Iraq War. Only through bargaining and the eventual intergovernmental control of the EDA (buttressed by establishing the Agency via a Joint Action), a low operational budget and influence over key staff positions were member states able to ensure their collective preferences were met.

Notes

1 Excluding Denmark, which does not participate in the EU's defence initiatives.
2 In the vote, Dutch voters rejected the constitution by 61.6 per cent (with a turnout of 62.8 per cent) and France by 55 per cent (with a turnout of 69 per cent).
3 Conservative Party scepticism towards the EDA resurfaced during the tenure of the coalition government of 2010–2015, with the then Parliamentary Under-Secretary of State for Defence stating that the Conservative Party 'had planned to withdraw from the European Defence Agency because [they] did not think that it served the interests of the British taxpayer' (UK Parliament 2012: 224).
4 Interview with a former official from the UK Ministry of Defence, 2 June 2016.
5 Interview with a former official from the European Defence Agency, 31 May 2016.
6 Interview with an official from the French Ministry of Defence, 30 September 2015.
7 Interviews with officials from the UK Ministry of Defence, 24 March 2014 and 10 January 2015 and the European Defence Agency, 1 June 2016.
8 The UK government holds one share – termed the 'golden share' – in BAE Systems plc., which gives the UK Prime Minister, the Secretary of State for Defence and the Cabinet Secretary control over any decisions the company takes with regard to mergers and the appointment of senior officials.
9 Several interviews revealed that some sectors of industry did want to see OCCAR and LoI phase into the EDA and 'they were disappointed when this did not happen' (interviews with officials from the German Ministry of Defence, 4 April 2013, and the European Defence Agency, 25 June 2013).

10 Interviews with executives from Finmeccanica, 28 November 2014, MBDA, 26 May 2015 and an official from the European Defence Agency, 13 June 2016.

11 Interview with an official from the German Ministry of Foreign Affairs, 28 January 2014.

12 Interview with a former official from the German Ministry of Defence, 2 May 2016.

13 Interview with a former official from the German Ministry of Defence, 2 May 2016 and an official from the European Parliament, 7 June 2016.

14 Interview with officials from the UK Foreign and Commonwealth Office, 15 January 2014, the European Defence Agency, 1 June 2016, and the European Parliament, 7 June 2016.

15 Interview with a former official from the UK Ministry of Defence, 2 June 2016.

16 Interview with a former official from the European Defence Agency, 31 May 2016, and an official from the Swedish Armed Forces, 15 February 2013.

17 Interview with two officials from the Finnish Ministry of Defence, 19 February 2013.

18 Interview with an official from the European Commission, 4 April 2013, and a representative from the Polish Chamber of National Defence Manufacturers, 17 June 2015.

19 Interview with an executive from ASD Europe, 18 March 2013.

20 Interviews with officials from the European Commission, 31 May 2016, and an executive from ASD Europe, 1 June 2015.

21 Interviews with an official from the UK Foreign and Commonwealth Office, 15 January 2014, the European Commission, 19 March 2014, and the European Defence Agency, 1 June 2016.

22 Interviews with an official from the European Commission, 31 May 2016, and an executive from ASD Europe, 1 June 2015.

23 Interviews with executives from the Italian Federation of Aviation Associations, 25 May 2015 and Airbus Group, 15 June 2015 and 17 June 2016.

24 From 1999 to 2004 Michel Barnier was European Commissioner for Regional Policy and the Reform of European Institutions. After serving as a minister in Jacques Chirac's government until 2009, he was elected as a Member of the European Parliament (2009–2010) before being appointed as European Commissioner for the Internal Market and Services (2010–2014). Barnier currently serves as President Jean-Claude Juncker's special adviser on security and defence at the European Commission and is his chief negotiator in charge of the preparation and conduct of the negotiations with the UK under Article 50 of the TEU.

25 Interviews with officials from the European Defence Agency, 10 January 2015 and 19 October 2015 and the European Parliament, 28 August 2015.

26 Interviews with former officials from the European Defence Agency, 31 May 2016 and 2 June 2016.

27 During a number of interviews with former EDA officials it was pointed out that an important interlocutor in maintaining healthy EDA–Commission relations was Mr. Paul Weissenberg – the former Deputy Director General at DG Enterprise, European Commission. According to the interviewees he was a pragmatic and constructive individual. One interviewee even stated that most of the inter-institutional friction at the time of the Agency's establishment did not really occur between the EDA and the Commission, but rather between the EDA and Commission on the one hand, and the EU Military Committee (EUMC) on the other. According to the interviewee the EUMC saw the EDA as a threat because until the establishment of the EDA 'the Committee had failed to collectively improve Europe's defence capabilities' (interviews with a former official from the German Ministry of Defence, 2 May 2016 and interviews with officials from the European Union Military Staff, 4 May 2016, European Commission, 31 May 2016 and the European Parliament, 7 June 2016).

28 Interviews with officials from the UK Foreign and Commonwealth Office, 15 January 2014, and the UK Ministry of Defence, 24 March 2014.

29 Interviews with officials from the UK Ministry of Defence, 10 January 2015, and the European Defence Agency, 1 June 2016.
30 Interview with an official from the European Commission, 31 May 2016.
31 Interview with a former official from the European Defence Agency, 31 May 2016.
32 Interviews with a former official from the European Defence Agency, 31 May 2016, and officials from the European Commission, 31 May 2016, an executive from ASD Europe, 1 June 2015, and the European Parliament, 7 June 2016.
33 It is important to remember that financial contributions to the EDA's operational budget were, and still are, calculated on the basis of Gross National Income.
34 Tellingly, perhaps, one interviewee stated that he found it odd that, while most member states would send diplomats or defence officials to early meetings of the EDA, Germany would insist on sending lawyers until they were comfortable with the working practices of the Agency (interview with an official from the European Commission, 31 May 2016).
35 Interview with an official from the European Parliament, 7 June 2016.
36 Interview with an official from the European Parliament, 7 June 2016.
37 Interview with a former official from the European Defence Agency, 31 May 2016.
38 See, for example, the 2013 report drafted by MEP Michael Gahler (EPP-ED) on the EDTIB, which calls for greater financial support for the EDA (European Parliament 2013: 19).
39 Interviews with executives from the Italian Federation of Aviation Associations, 26 May 2015, the French Group for Defence Industries, 26 May 2015, and Airbus Group, 29 September 2015.

4 Adopting the defence transfers directive

Adopted on 6 May 2009 after an 18-month legislative process that formally began on 5 December 2007 with a Commission proposal, the EU directive on intra-Community transfers of defence equipment (2009/43/EC) – henceforth the 'defence transfers directive' – aims to harmonise export control systems for intra-EU trade in defence equipment. As had been made clear already, the defence transfers directive was adopted alongside a directive on defence procurement – see Chapter 5 – together forming the so-called EU 'defence package'.[1] The main objective of the defence transfers directive is to stimulate cross-border trade in defence equipment and to reduce the administrative costs associated with licensing, which, in turn, should lead to an increased supplier base in defence goods and increased security of supply in the EU (Trybus 2005: 253; Europe Economics 2009: 92; Masson *et al.* 2015: 45). Prior to the adoption of the transfers directive, one study estimated that of the 21,533 licences issued over the 2007–2008 period – amounting to some €9 billion worth of defence equipment transfers – the EU member states incurred a cost of over €400 million. Prior to the adoption of the directive, these costs were a direct result of the inefficiencies associated with the existence of individual national licensing systems (European Commission 2012b, 2007b).

The brunt of these costs would be borne by firms having to deal with a range of government bodies in every transit and end-user state – usually in a different language and with varying licensing standards (Trybus 2014: 143–144).[2] Such costs were seen as a distinct disadvantage to SMEs because, while primes could use their financial capital to manage cross-border transactions by employing skilled lawyers and translators, SMEs simply did not have the resources to develop cross-border trade in the same manner. As the European Commission noted in its 2007 *Strategy for a Stronger and More Competitive European Defence Industry* (COM(2007) 764 final),

> [b]y significantly reducing licence application costs, and by allowing system integrators to open their supply chains in more predictable conditions, the new rules will increase opportunities for competitive [SMEs] to supply components or sub-systems thereby contributing to making the European market more dynamic.
>
> (European Commission 2007a: 6)

Put more simply, the directive was seen as a way to 'facilitate transfers by eliminating unnecessary paperwork' (European Commission 2007a: 6; ASD Europe 2007).

There was also a strategic rationale behind the defence transfers directive. While there was general agreement among European governments that arms exports to non-EU third countries had to be stringently monitored, applying customs duties and licensing requirements within the EU was regarded as a disproportionate measure given that most EU member states are military allies in the CSDP and NATO. It followed that liberalising trade in defence equipment in the internal market would be an effective way of enhancing security of supply among European militaries (Andersson 2012; Fiott 2014b). Very few licences for intra-EU transfers had ever been denied, but the administrative costs and processes associated with these licences slowed the speed at which transfers between militaries could be made (Unisys 2005: 6 and 94; European Commission 2007b). While European governments had been seriously pondering the merits of closer cooperation on arms exports since at least the 1980s (Western European Union 1984: 6), the creation of the CSDP implied that EU member states were committing 'themselves to endeavour to meet requests from fellow Member States for goods and services during an emergency, crisis or armed conflict' (Andersson 2012: 111). For this purpose, the transfers directive was an ideal way of easing trade in defence equipment between European militaries (Mölling 2008: 52; Edwards 2011: 3; Briani *et al.* 2013: 8 and 17).

Based on an EU Common Military List (CML) that details relevant defence goods, the transfers directive seeks to harmonise defence equipment licensing in the EU through a three-tier licensing system: (1) a *global licence* permits transfers of multiple pieces of defence equipment to multiple EU member states for a three-year, renewable, period; (2) a *general licence* permits transfers of multiple pieces of defence equipment to a single EU member state for a five-year period; and (3) an *individual licence* permits transfers of a single piece of equipment to a single EU member state of a limited and pre-determined duration. Before any of these licences are issued the supplier must be registered with a national authority. The main purpose of registration is to verify whether the piece of defence equipment is itemised on the EU's CML, to ensure that the supplier and recipient are in good standing, to establish whether there is a dedicated senior executive within the company to oversee proper licensing, etc. On this basis, once a licence has been issued in one member state there is no need to seek separate licences in each transit and recipient state (Trybus 2014: 150–151). Although not obligatory, the defence transfers directive also states (see Article 9.8) that certified suppliers should be publicly listed on the European Commission-run online CERTIDER[3] system to increase transparency.

The initial proposal (in 2007) for, and eventual adoption of (in 2009), the defence transfers directive reflects an interesting element of the EU defence industrial policy framework. As will be recalled, one of the key aims of the policy framework is to create a more efficient European defence market. Even though many analysts and policymakers believe it is too early to judge the success of the directive,[4] the transfers directive represents a step towards creating such a market space in the EU by encouraging greater intra-EU trade. Yet, the defence transfers directive raises many questions. For example, one needs to understand why the member states should suddenly adopt the directive in 2009 given years of reticence before this time. It is also important to understand why secondary legislation was the appropriate vehicle to realise greater intra-EU defence trade. Equally important is grappling with the fact that so many smaller member states adopted the directive even though they theoretically stood to lose the most from greater defence market liberalisation. Finally, by weighing-up the empirical evidence presented below with various theoretical approaches it is necessary to understand what role government, firm and institutional interests played during the negotiations for the transfers directive.

This chapter aims to study the national preferences and bargaining processes that led to the adoption of the defence transfers directive. The aim is to apply the LI model and to uncover how, if at all, national preferences and the relative bargaining power of governments helped forge the defence transfers directive. Accordingly, it should be possible to ascertain whether domestic preferences reflected the powerful economic interests of defence firms. It should equally be possible to show how the relative bargaining power of governments – through either 'non-agreement', 'exclusion' or 'compromise' – influenced the decision to adopt the directive. Furthermore, this chapter will reveal the degree to which EU institutions such as the European Commission and European Parliament determined the outcome of the directive. Finally, this chapter will compare liberal intergovernmentalism with the competing explanations provided by ideational approaches, reactive spillover (Guay 1996), economic patriotism (Hoeffler 2012) and judicial politics (Blauberger and Weiss 2013; Weiss and Blauberger 2016). To this end, the chapter is organised in two main sections: the first section looks at the rationale behind the transfers directive and government and commercial views towards it; and, the second section analyses how and why member states eventually decided to adopt the directive. The chapter ends with some reflections on the explanatory implications of the investigation below.

Defence transfers, governments and firms

The issue of intra-EU transfers of defence equipment had long been on the member states' agenda. In 1997, the Commission sent the Council a draft Common Position containing a specific proposal for a defence transfers directive (European Commission 1997: 6). This proposal surfaced following a year-long evaluation in 1996 by member states on the potential costs and benefits of such a directive (European Commission 1996; Masson 2008: 26). The Council's 'Ad hoc Working Party on European Armaments Policy' (POLARM) had noted that only 3–4 per cent of the total defence market was disappointingly based on intra-EU trade (Council of the European Union 1997: 5). The Council of the EU viewed this period as of crucial importance to the health of the EDTIB and EDEM. For example, POLARM released a policy document in 1996 entitled

Definition of Specific Characteristics of the Defence-Related Sector, which COREPER endorsed on 10 December 1996. The document recognised the challenge posed by declining defence budgets in Europe and the fact that the US defence market had undergone 'a vast process of consolidation' leading to greater international competition for Europe (Council of the European Union 1997; Masson 2008: 29).

Despite the importance of this document, the European Commission's specific proposal for a defence transfers directive did not gain traction at the time and this continued to be the case even after 2003 when Germany put forward an official motion for a transfers directive in POLARM (European Commission 2006b: 2–4). This is especially surprising given that the member states were also negotiating the establishment of the EDA; this was a period in which EU integration in defence matters was being supported by several large EU member states, such as France and the UK. Yet, as the Commission noted at the time, steps 'to establish a free-trade area for defence equipment' were not yet attractive because numerous governments wanted to maintain national controls following the terror threat posed by 11 September 2001, and they did not want to agree to a new piece of legislation before the outcome and possible repercussions of the proposed 'European Constitution' were known (European Commission 2006b: 4). However, Germany's initiative did lead to a period of consultation and an impact assessment of the proposed directive was undertaken by the Commission in 2003 (European Commission 2003: 3 and 14). For its part, the newly created EDA also recognised the 'absurd effects' of intra-EU obstacles to defence transfers and it wholeheartedly supported the idea for a directive (2007: 5). This was an argument that was largely supported by European industry too (ASD Europe 2007).[5]

Responding to the economic crisis

In order for the transfers directive to be adopted by the Council of the EU and the European Parliament following the European Commission's legislative initial proposal on 5 December 2007, it was necessary for national and commercial preferences to somehow align. The directive was adopted using the ordinary legislative procedure (or co-decision) and it was adopted after the first reading in the European Parliament on 16 December 2008. The Directorate-General for Enterprise and Industry (DG ENTR as it was known from 2004–2010) led the Commission's work under the political guidance of Commissioner Günter Verheugen. In this regard, it is interesting and relevant to note that before the European Parliament's plenary vote on the directive on 16 December 2008, a major push for the directive occurred during France's 2008 EU presidency (July–December 2008). In order to navigate the proposed directive through debates, legislative amendments and votes in the Council (on 25 February 2008 through the Competitiveness Council configuration, COMPET) and the European Parliament (on 7 October 2008 through the committee on the Internal Market and Consumer Protection, IMCO), France played a key role. France still held the EU presidency of the Council of the EU when the European Parliament voted in plenary (545 for; 66 against; 44 abstentions) to adopt the directive.

France had a national interest in pursuing the directive as it had long been acknowledged that the country's national arms export regime needed reform – a national regime originally put in place in 1938. The push for reform only began in 1994 (Slocombe 1992; Labbé 1994: 202; Conze 1995: 48; Hébert 2006; Béraud-Sudreau 2014). The previous French system relied on a heavily regulated process governed by the Prime Minister, who had to give 'prior approval' for all transfers (*agrément préalable*, AP), and a special interministerial commission for exports of war materiel (CIEEMG). This level of bureaucracy was deemed to weigh heavily on France's ability to export goods (Ruello 2006). Some estimates have stated that in 2009 the CIEEMG received approximately 14,000 authorisation requests but it only issued 7,090 authorisations – known as AEMGs – even though the French government and industry would still have to bear the costs and time processing all 14,000 requests (French Government 2010a: 44 and 48). By using its EU council presidency to help adopt the transfers directive, France would replace the AP and AEMGs with a harmonised set of licences shared by all EU member states.

It is for this reason that the government-commissioned 'Fromion Report' stated in 2006 that 'France had a responsibility to engage with the development of intra-Community procedures' (2006: 73–76). Quite apart from the need to reform its own transfer licence regime, and as if to give expression to the role of structural pressures, 2008 was a year in which the eurozone crisis was in motion, defence budgets were declining and EADS (now Airbus Group) – the French, German and Spanish-owned firm – suffered significant job losses and a scaling-back of production (Hollinger and Wiesmann 2008). French industry demanded that the government take immediate action at the EU level to cushion the effects of the economic crisis of 2008 (French Government 2010b: 44 and 48, 2013b: 83; Foucault 2012: 25; Safran 2013: 202; Béraud-Sudreau 2014: 10). There were numerous calls from French industry and politicians for a streamlined EU regime that would simultaneously assist with domestic reforms to its export regime and put in place a level playing field for intra-EU defence transfers (Beffa 2005: 8; Guillou *et al.* 2009: 2; French Government 2013b: 120).[6]

Since the economic crisis was also affecting the German defence industry, and it was Germany that first proposed the defence transfers directive, it should occasion little surprise to learn of Berlin's support for the transfers directive. German preferences in favour of the directive re-emerged during the economic crisis of 2008. One should consider that the defence sector is of vital importance to the German economy as a whole. In 2012, the German security and defence industry generated approximately €21.4 billion in direct and indirect sales, secured approximately 317,000 direct and indirect jobs in the sector and it reached an annual job growth rate of 4.1 per cent – surpassing the German economy as a whole, which registered an average 0.9 per cent in 2012 (Ostwald, Schubert and Knippel 2012: 38). Furthermore, one should bear in mind that in 2012 approximately 70 per cent of German security and defence industry production output was exported internationally (ibid.). In many respects, Germany's push for a defence transfers directive was conditioned by the fact that the economic crisis and resulting decrease in demand for defence equipment in the EU required a European response (Brune *et al.* 2010; Dickow and Buch 2012). Moreover, Germany understood that a directive might not only allow the *Bundeswehr*[7] to save money and receive defence technologies quicker, but it also recognised that it would make it easier for German firms to cooperate in European capability programmes (German Government 2014b: 2).

The Federation of German Security and Defence Industries (BDSV) agreed with this position and it also pushed for the directive in order to forge an 'efficient and competitive European defence and technology base' (BDSV 2013). When the initial legislative proposal for a transfers directive was made in 2007 the BDSV and other industry organisations were generally pleased (Ostwald, Schubert and Knippel 2012). Despite the fact that Germany's defence firms have significant interlinkages with the commercial sector (Lock and Voβ 1996: 92; Kausal *et al.* 1999: 31), thus giving them some scope to offset falling demand in the defence sector with commercial sales, German firms generally supported the Federal Government. As the BDSV noted, '[t]he German defence industry would not be able to ensure its capacity, its internationally accepted standards, the protection of soldiers, their contribution to the industrial development and capabilities of Germany without exports' (BDSV 2013). The Federal Government recognised that the proposed directive represented an opportunity to boost the competitiveness of German defence firms in Europe (Mampaey *et al.* 2014: 11; Masson *et al.* 2015: 53).

The UK took a different perspective to Berlin and Paris regarding the economic rationale for the defence transfers directive. One should bear in mind that the European market represents a smaller share of total UK defence exports. According to SIPRI[8] the estimated cumulative total of arms transfers made by EU member states from 1990 to 2014 was \$173.2 billion and of this amount \$38.8 billion – or approximately 22 per cent – accounted for transfers within the EU (Stockholm International Peace Research Institute 2015). Of Germany's total arms exports of \$44.9 billion over the 1990–2014 period, 34 per cent accounted for intra-EU transfers; of France's \$41.9 billion, 14 per cent accounted for intra-EU transfers; and of the UK's \$33.4 billion worth of exports, 11 per cent went to the EU market (ibid.). With a low level of intra-EU defence equipment transfers the UK is more dependent on global sales. For example, UK Trade & Investment (UKTI) calculates that in 2014 the UK had a 16 per cent share of global defence exports, France held 6 per cent and Germany 3 per cent – the US had a share of 39 per cent – (UK Government 2015: 6). In more recent years, the British defence sector has registered most of its growth through export markets in the Middle East, India, Brazil and South East Asia (ADS Group 2012: 8 and 11).

The reaction of UK industry was therefore rather mixed. On the one hand, some firms viewed the transfers directive as a positive piece of legislation that 'should improve the performance of the European defence market' (ADS Group 2014: 2). Many UK-based firms such as BAE Systems and Thales UK also saw the proposed directive as a way to overcome the past problems associated with intergovernmental initiatives, and they recognised that '[t]he introduction of internal market disciplines and the eventual enforcement of EU legislation' would be vital to creating a more efficient European defence market (BAE Systems 2014: 1; Thales Group 2014: 1; see also Airbus Group 2014: 2). On the other hand, some industry groups called on the UK government to strike the right balance 'between the benefits of open markets and the retention of national industrial defence capability' (Society of British Aerospace Companies 2007). This was a view echoed by one of the UK's largest trade unions, which urged the government to resist liberalising reforms because of a fear of resulting job losses in the UK defence sector (Unite 2013: 7). More crucial perhaps was the concern that EU-level initiatives could interfere with the UK's privileged defence industrial relations with the US (Society of British Aerospace Companies 2007).

Preferences in other EU member states eventually coalesced around the idea for a transfers directive too, especially given the constraints imposed by the economic crisis of 2008. This was certainly the case among some of the countries in the Letter of Intent group. While France, Germany and the UK were cautiously supportive of the idea for a transfers directive, states such as Italy, Spain and Sweden also saw the economic benefits of adopting the transfers directive. The Spanish government was in favour of the transfers directive as a way of boosting the competitiveness of Spanish defence firms, should it lead to 'more flexible control mechanisms for [their] companies' (Spanish Government 2007: 17; see also Masson *et al.* 2010: 24). Despite Sweden's long-held preference to develop a harmonised transfer list exclusively between the Letter of Intent countries, the Swedish government was supportive of the defence transfers directive and it was under the Swedish Presidency of the EU from July to December 2009 that the directive moved from adoption to the transposition phase (Swedish Inspectorate of Strategic Products 2014: 11). Similarly to the UK, however, Sweden was interested in ensuring that the directive would not hamper or unduly affect its privileged access to the US defence market (Masson *et al.* 2010: 30).

For its part, the Italian government was generally supportive of the directive because it embedded its own national defence industrial reforms – particularly its consolidation period during the 1990s – within a broader European framework (Caruso and Locatelli 2011). The Italian government was concerned with the technicalities associated with the directive and its likely consequences for Italy's domestic regulatory and administrative procedures and structures. Much like France, Rome saw the defence transfers directive as an opportunity to reform its 'old and totally inadequate' regulations on export control (Masson *et al.* 2010: 21–22). The Italian Aerospace, Defence and Security Industry Association (AIAD) played an important role in the debate about how the Italian export regime should be reformed (Finmeccanica 2010: 88). Consequently, the government and industry were keen to move forward with the transfers directive because it was legally binding in character. For Italy, secondary legislation such as the directive was deemed to be more effective than intergovernmental initiatives such as the LoI framework, as these initiatives had fostered a slower administrative response to adopting and enforcing legislation (Nones and Marta 2007: 17).

Much like the majority of LoI countries, the Polish government and industry viewed the proposed transfers directive with cautious optimism. Despite Poland's concern that EU-level defence industrial policies were designed by and for the Letter of Intent countries (Zamelek 2013: 3), the Polish government viewed the proposal for the transfers directive as a way to create a level playing field in the EU, ensure a greater opportunity for Polish SMEs to export goods and technologies within the EU and to reduce the cost burden on its national export authority (Polish Government 2013: 5). In this regard, the Polish government and industry were locked in a challenging paradox. On the one hand, the Polish government wanted to ensure that its firms were treated in a fair and non-discriminatory fashion at the EU level and it also wanted to reduce the regulatory burden on its SMEs (Zamelek 2013: 5). On the other hand, the Polish government were weary of the fact that increased competition in the EU market may adversely affect the competitiveness of Poland's defence industry (Ulanowski 2012: 13; Terlikowski 2013: 2; Zamelek 2013: 4).

Balancing economic gain and sovereignty

Despite the general agreement for a directive by industry and government in several EU member states, numerous governments sought assurances that key parts of their ability to control exports nationally would be retained. In the case of Germany and the UK, the economic benefits of the proposed directive were welcome, but both countries agreed that a directive should not be adopted at any price. For example, the German government was concerned that the proposed directive could weaken the country's strict export policies and, consequently, supersede German law (Fiott 2016c). As one German lawmaker succinctly put it, the 'most important prerequisite for the implementation of directive 2009/43/EC is [...] that Member states retain control of their own arms export criteria' (Brandl 2011). Berlin was unwilling to see the national export authority (the Federal Office for Economic Affairs and Export Control, BAFA) lose its oversight responsibilities. It did not want to create the undesirable situation where other EU member states could re-export German defence equipment to non-EU countries with suspect human rights records (German Parliament 2011: 4, 9; Mampaey *et al.* 2014: 57). In this respect a key German preference that emerged during the 25 February 2008 debate in the COMPET was to insist on a strict divide between intra-EU and extra-EU transfers – Berlin demanded that the proposed directive relate only to intra-EU trade.

Germany's insistence on this strict division emanated from its own arms export policies. Not only are defence exports strictly monitored by the Federal Security Council (*Bundessicherheitstrat*, BSR),[9] but any decisions taken by the BSR are based on the 'Political Principles of the Federal Government for Export of War Weapons and Other Military Equipment'. The 'Political Principles', established in 1982 and updated in 2000, are a 'non-legally binding political document' that stipulate that Germany should not export arms to unstable regions and countries or where there are reasonable grounds to suspect that human rights abuses will result after the exports are made (German Government 2011: 7; Heidenkamp 2012a). Rocked by the scandal involving German firms in the development of Iraq's Weapons of Mass Destruction programme in the 1990s, successive German governments have updated 'export control legislation and strengthened the export control agency' (Holtom, Bromley and Béraud-Sudreau 2011: 17). For Germany, close and continuous monitoring of arms exports is the norm and so the European Commission's role in proposing the transfers directive was initially viewed with some degree of suspicion. For Germany, this was a constitutional question because Article 26.2[10] of the German Basic Law stipulates that only the Federal Government can give permission for the manufacture, transportation and marketing of weapons and Section 6[11] of the War Weapons Control Act (*Kriegswaffenkontrollgesetz*, KWKG) gives the Federal Government the sole discretion to deny or revoke a transfer licence at any time (German Government 2014a).

The UK was also suspicious of DG ENTR's motives when proposing the directive in 2007 (Davis *et al.* 2007; UK Government 2012a, 2012b). Industry and government were aligned in seeking assurances that the directive would not lead to greater supranational oversight for UK defence exports or a 'weakening of the UK's export control system' (UK Parliament 2008a; UK Government 2014: 2). Accordingly, one of the UK's key preferences was to ensure that any directive would not damage its privileged trade with Australia, Canada, Iceland, Japan, New Zealand, Norway, Switzerland and the United States (UK Government 2012a; Mampaey *et al.* 2014: 33; Masson *et al.* 2015: 47). The proposed directive should not jeopardise the intergovernmental nature of the LoI framework either (UK Parliament 2003). Like Germany, the UK did not want the easing of intra-EU transfers rules to make the re-export of goods to third countries any easier.[12] The UK wanted to resist a situation where the European Commission could have a final say over the government's right to reject and monitor export licences (Fiott 2016c). As one industry group that represents approximately 2,600 companies in the UK defence supply chain stated, while the defence transfers directive is welcome it should not lead to greater Commission involvement in arms exports policy (ADS Group 2014: 2).

Despite France's enthusiasm for the defence transfers directive, it too had reservations about the potential regulatory role of the European Commission. Notwithstanding calls by some French lawmakers for the French government to boldly push for the swift adoption of the directive (French Parliament 2009), foremost among the 'sovereignty safeguards' sought by the French government were reservations about how far the directive would empower the European Commission in arms exports (French Government 2010b: 20; Béraud-Sudreau 2014: 31). Much like Germany, the French government sought a clear distinction between intra- and extra-EU defence transfers to stop the European Commission from gaining powers over export licensing for transfers destined for outside of the EU. Furthermore, the French government wanted to ensure that any defence transfers directive would not make it difficult for France to export defence equipment to its overseas territories (French Parliament 2015). France's adoption and transposition of the transfers directive would be dependent on securing such sovereign safeguards (Fiott 2016c). Crucially, in its position as President of the Council of the EU, Paris had a strong voice in shaping the directive during the debate and amendment phase of the legislative process, which lasted from January to December 2008[13] (French Government 2010b: 17).[14]

Overall, therefore, national preferences were broadly aligned. European governments understood that there was a sense of economic urgency for a transfers directive because of the economic crisis, even though some governments wanted assurances that they would ultimately retain national control over exports, which thereby dampened any possible role for the Commission in the area of extra-EU export policy (see Table 4.1 below). What is clear from the position of France is that there is merit to Hoeffler's hypothesis that France wanted to Europeanise its domestic reform process to better manage 'potential conflicts arising from the combination of different territories (national, EU, or European co-operation outside the EU)' (2012: 438). Even Guay's (1996) reactive spillover theory may help one better understand how structural pressures such as the 2008 economic crisis and subsequent decreased demand for defence equipment in Europe drove governments towards the adoption of EU secondary legislation rather than an intergovernmental solution. The judicial politics approach would perhaps claim that secondary legislation was an ideal vehicle to realise these individual preferences because it would inject legal certainty while also leaving enough room for governments to address their concerns about national sovereignty (Blauberger and Weiss 2013; Weiss and Blauberger 2016).

A focus on domestic preferences has also highlighted the importance of economic and political interests in the formulation of government preferences towards the transfers directive. Interestingly, the case study has thus far revealed how much importance governments ascribed to the role of the European Commission, with several of them openly suspicious of the DG ENTR's intentions when it initially proposed legislation in 2007. This point may eventually challenge LI's claim that EU institutions will not determine outcomes, although one must analyse the bargaining process before a firm conclusion is made in this

Table 4.1 Domestic preferences and the transfers directive

	CZ	*DE*	*ES*	*FR*	*HU*	*IT*	*PL*	*SE*	*UK*
Competitiveness (inc. SMEs)	✓	✓	✓	✓	✓	✓	✓	✓	✓
Domestic Reform	✗	✗		✓		✓	✓	✗	✗
Europeanisation				✓		✓	✗		✗
European Commission		✓	✓	✓			✗		✗
Industrial Collaboration		✓		✓		✓	✓	✓	✓
Single Legal Regime	✓	✓		✓	✓	✓	✓	✓	✓

Source: author's own.

regard. A focus on domestic preferences alone does not take us far enough in understanding why the transfers directive was eventually adopted. Even though member states were generally in favour of the directive, its adoption in 2009 was not automatic. This is where a focus on relative bargaining power during negotiations for the directive during 2008 becomes illuminating. We have already seen how the economic crisis of 2008 and France's Presidency of the EU were important factors in explaining why the directive suddenly became important, but it is also necessary to explain the preconditions that allowed for the adoption of the directive in 2009. It is essential to understand the political dynamics that existed between member states during the bargaining phase.

Bargaining power and the transfers directive

As is theorised by the liberal intergovernmental model, the bargaining phase – 'step two' of the model – is characterised by the relative bargaining power of the negotiating participants. Despite the clear economic and defence industrial disparities between EU member states, under the LI model power is articulated through a government's or group of governments' ability to force compromise, to exclude participants from negotiations or to simply walk away from the bargaining process altogether. A government's ability to walk away from negotiations is heavily influenced by the costs associated with that decision. For example, a lower cost implies more margin for manoeuvre whereas a high cost would assume that a government would not walk away from negotiations but seek compromise instead. Studying the transfers directive as a form of intergovernmental bargaining may seem odd. After all, one is talking about secondary legislation that was eventually adopted through a co-decision with the Council of the EU and the European Parliament, which implies a substantial role for supranational institutions such as the Commission and the European Parliament. However, the co-decision procedure still affords member states through the Council of the EU the room to propose legislative amendments that reflect their national preferences. Furthermore, one should also bear in mind that the European Commission only initiated the legislative process for the directive on 5 December 2007 after the member states had granted implementing powers to the Commission through the 'comitology' procedure. DG ENTR obtained implementing powers from the Council's 'Committee on EU Transfers of Defence-related Products' on 23 March 2006, so even before the initial proposal for the directive in December 2007 the member states played a key role during the drafting of the initial proposal for the transfers directive.

A directive 'made in France'?

As mentioned earlier, France was in a particularly powerful position to influence the character and reach of the directive because of its role as EU President of the Council and because of its influence as one of the EU's largest defence markets. Numerous interviewees stated that the transfers directive, and the 'defence package' more broadly, became an important part of France's EU presidency programme because Paris desired to not only show French leadership on defence matters but also to showcase a substantial legislative package at the end of its presidency (Hoeffler 2012; Béraud-Sudreau 2014: 31–32, 2015b).[15] Furthermore, France's EU presidency occurred during a critical time for the EU with a great onus on France to steer the EU through the negotiations for the Lisbon Treaty. If Hoeffler is correct, the EU presidency offered France a perfect opportunity to 'upload' its economic preferences to the EU level. France was wary of the fact that, following its stint as EU President of the Council, the Czech Republic would be guiding the 'defence package' through the respective European Parliament plenary debate and vote at a time when a Eurosceptic President Václav Klaus – with constitutional powers to co-sign all legislation – was in power in Prague (Benes and Karlas 2010: 69). Although the Czech government would go on to support the proposed directive when the Council adopted the directive (Czech Government 2009: 21), there was a fear in some quarters that should the European Parliament vote down the directive in December 2008, the then Eurosceptic government in Prague would not pursue the 'defence package' back through the Council and the Parliament with as much vigour as Paris.[16]

Given France's need to reform its own national licensing regime and its willingness to Europeanise its national reform agenda, Paris exercised a sizeable amount of bargaining power during the negotiations. As far as exclusion was concerned, during both the 'comitology' and legislative phases France did threaten the European Commission and non-LoI states with exclusion should they not meet Paris's domestic preference for continued state control over the French export regime. Should Paris's preferences not be reflected in the Commission's initial legislative proposal and the subsequent versions of the proposed directive, France threatened to move negotiations for a defence transfers directive from the EU to the LoI framework (Béraud-Sudreau 2014: 31; French Government 2015: 24). Even though DG ENTR was wary of the LoI countries going it alone on defence transfers prior to its initial tabling of the directive (2006b: 4), France's brinkmanship was not credible enough because the LoI countries had manifestly failed to develop a 'global licensing system' among themselves despite initiating negotiations for one in 2000 (Idiart and Delaboudinière 2007). As was argued by the Italian government at the time, the LoI framework lacked the enforcement mechanisms needed to move beyond intergovernmental gridlock. Despite the evident drawbacks to intergovernmentalism, France – under the Presidency of Nicolas Sarkozy – used the strategy of brinkmanship to force agreement on French terms and this was a strategy used throughout its EU presidency (Lequesne and Rozenberg 2008: 17–18).

However, France could not realistically threaten exclusion and the EU represented the only plausible means of creating a legal order through which France could reform domestically without unduly affecting French industry (French Government 2015: 24). The EU offered the only institutional framework through which to allow France to reform domestically and to have common rules for all EU member states. For Paris there would have been certain disadvantages to a purely national reform agenda. First, the French government recognised that putting in place a level playing field would help reform various national regimes governing arms transfers across the EU, while also not discriminating against French industry (French Government 2010a: 24).[17] Second, having in place an EU-wide regime could reduce the costs associated with bilateral defence arrangements between European governments. For example, in the context of the French–British Lancaster House Treaties it was recognised by both countries that France's pre-transfers directive licensing regime hampered the transfer of defence equipment such as missile systems between the two countries (French Parliament 2009; French Government 2010a: 25; Béraud-Sudreau 2014). Despite the potential advantages of a transfers directive, however, the French government insisted that it would not reform its export regime through EU secondary legislation unless it could retain national control over export licensing (French Parliament 2014; Fiott 2016c).

France was, therefore, caught between the need to reform its domestic regime to support its industry to export and a recognition that the most effective way of reforming was to seek an EU-wide legislative solution. Ultimately, France's rather hollow threat of exclusion would not have met its desire to ensure a level playing field at the EU level or to further liberalise the European defence market. Furthermore, the threat of exclusion failed to take into consideration the economic preferences of other EU member states. For example, Poland had long claimed that the idea of the EDTIB was a thin veil for the interests of the LoI states, and it would have been vindicated in its view had France pushed for exclusion. In threatening exclusion at the early stages of the legislative process, France perhaps underestimated the intensity of non-LoI preferences towards secondary legislation. Despite the commonly articulated view during interviews that medium and smaller member states did not fully understand the technical implications involved in transposing the directive, there was a clear understanding that the directive would lower administrative costs and potentially boost their export potential (see Masson *et al.* 2010: 28).[18]

Without a realistic chance of excluding certain member states from a European transfers regime, France could have ensured its national sovereignty by walking away from negotiations. The costs of doing so, however, would have been high because there was no alternative mechanism for creating a level playing field at the European level. Fortunately for France, many of the other EU member states were equally interested in retaining certain national controls over export policy. In this regard, a breakthrough moment during the negotiations occurred when the European Parliament – in its role as co-legislator – agreed that national controls should be retained in certain areas. The Commission submitted the draft proposal for the directive to the European Parliament on 5 December 2007. In its October 2008 report on the transfers directive, the Parliament recognised that the proposed directive could ameliorate the duplication and inefficiencies associated with individual national licensing regimes (European Parliament 2008a). The report even recognised that the transfers directive would be beneficial to defence SMEs in smaller member states (European Parliament

2008a). However, the IMCO committee – as the responsible committee for the directive – also recognised that important sovereign safeguards needed to be retained.

The IMCO committee would go on to adopt the proposed defence transfers directive on 7 October 2008, but in its revisions to DG ENTR's proposal presented to plenary on 15 October 2008, IMCO stressed the need to maintain strict arms controls to stop any re-exportation of defence equipment to suspect non-EU countries (European Parliament 2008a). In order to ensure sufficient controls IMCO insisted: first, on the insertion of specific clauses to safeguard the member states' right to refuse to issue a licence under the directive for national security purposes (see Amendment 8, Recital 17, of the amended proposal); and second, to stress the autonomy of national authorities on setting the terms and conditions for licences (see Amendments 34, 36).[19] These points were also emphasised by the Parliament's Foreign Affairs Committee (AFET), which gave its opinion on the draft proposal on 12 September 2008.[20] The AFET and Industry, Research and Energy (ITRE) Committees also sought assurances from the Commission that the transfers directive would not lead to the re-exportation of arms to non-EU countries with suspect human rights records (European Parliament 2008b). Thus, in its role as co-legislator, IMCO sided with the Council by agreeing to retain sovereign controls over defence equipment exports – thus consequently enforcing the member states' national preferences. The European Commission would formally agree to the European Parliament's amendments on 16 December 2008, thus giving way to a plenary debate and vote on the same date.

Faced with the EU member states and European Parliament both seeking to ensure state control over export authorisation, the European Commission was encouraged to modify the proposed directive and it sent a revised version of the directive back to the Council and the Parliament in December 2008 before it was voted on by Parliament on 16 December and unanimously agree to by the Council on 23 April 2009. Most important was the Commission's revision that stipulated that, although 'the decision to authorize or deny an export is, and should remain, at the discretion of each Member State, such cooperation should only stem from the voluntary coordination of export policies' (Council of the European Union 2009: 8). Articles 4.5 and 4.9 of the transfers directive make it clear that member states 'determine the type of transfer licence' granted and they can also 'withdraw, suspend or limit the use of transfer licences they have issued at any time for reasons of protection of their essential security interests'. Article 5.4 takes this a step further by stating that national authorities still have the right to 'lay down the conditions for registration prior to first use' of the transfer licences. As if to bolster LI's hypothesis that institutions cannot force policy outcomes, the directive is thus 'general in nature and leaves much room to [sic] the member states to interpret the policy' (TNO 2009: 145).

Reform and opportunity

Yet it is not entirely wise to characterise the decision to adopt the directive as a mixture of a compromise between various economic preferences in favour of the directive and France's initial threat of exclusion. In fact, even though France was in a relatively powerful bargaining position to influence the nature and reach of the transfers directive before its adoption by Council and the Parliament, Germany and the UK could have decided to forgo giving the Commission implementing powers for a legislative proposal, which would have stopped negotiations and the legislative process in its tracks. Simply put, without the alignment of British and German preferences, France would have been forced to undertake its reforms on a national rather than an EU basis (Fiott 2016c). Germany and the UK were in a relatively powerful bargaining position prior to and after the Commission's initial legislative proposal in December 2007 because neither member state needed to overhaul their domestic export licensing regimes in the same way that France did. In fact, the German and UK national licensing regimes provided the blueprint for the European Commission's designs for an EU three-tier licensing proposal (Liberti, Matelly and Maulny 2010: 45). Germany had a three-tier licensing system composed of an individual licence (*Einzelgenehmigung*), a general licence (*Allgemeingenehmigung*) and a global licence (*Sammelgenehmigung*). The UK also operated a system of three specific transfer licences: the Open General Trade Control (OGTCL) licence, the Standard Individual Trade Control Export (SITCL) licence and the Open Individual Trade Control (OITCL) licence.

In fact, the UK and Germany had both reformed their licensing systems long before 2009. During a wave of mergers and acquisitions during the 1980s, Germany reformed its licensing policies to mirror the reforms being made to the *Bundeswehr* and Germany's defence acquisition processes (Seibertz, Stähle and Hensler 2010: 23). The need to ensure the effectiveness of Germany's export policies was underlined during the 2003 'Struck Reforms' – named after the then defence minister Peter Struck – which called for Germany to 'maintain an efficient and competitive industrial base in core areas of technology' and to do so through enhanced European cooperation (German Government 2003: 14). This point was reaffirmed in Germany's 2006 White Paper on defence (German Government 2006: 63 and 75). In the UK, New Labour was swept to power in 1997 vowing to conduct an 'ethical foreign policy' where tighter controls on arms exports would be introduced. Yet a raft of reforms had already been introduced in the mid-1980s by the then Conservative government. The so-called 'Levene Reforms' – so named after the former Chief of Defence Procurement at the UK MoD, Sir Peter Levene – identified the need for the UK defence market to become more competitive by relying on market liberalisation (Walker and Gummett 1989: 421; Smith 1990: 195; Bishop 2003a; Deakin 2010; Taylor and Louth 2012: 2; Louth 2013a: 31).

The German and UK governments' potential to walk away from negotiations was high, and this gave the two governments more influence to help craft a directive that would meet their respective preferences. For the UK, the potential to walk away from negotiations was even higher than in Germany. For example, in 2008 only 2,944 of a total 10,417 transfer licences issued by the UK government related to intra-EU trade (Liberti, Matelly and Maulny 2010: 8; see also Hartley 2014: 159). On this basis, should the proposed directive not meet British concerns about national export controls then London could have opted to scupper the directive before the Commission even put the initial proposal on the table (UK Parliament 2007, 2008c; Taylor 2011: 7). The UK government also questioned the proposed directive during the legislative phase because the Commission's legislative proposal initially wanted the directive to apply to security services as well as militaries. The Commission argued that many EU member states have paramilitary and gendarmerie forces that are not technically military in nature, but still require transfers of defence equipment such as helmets, shields, firearms, etc. While France, Italy and Spain were in favour of security services making it into the initial proposal, the British defined 'security services' as intelligence services and there was a fear that UK intelligence services could thus become subject to EU legislation (UK Parliament 2008b: 8–9). Accordingly, in February 2008 the UK government sought assurances from the Commission and fellow member states in the Council that the EU's CML would form the basis of the intra-community transfers regime, and that it would be unambiguous regarding dual-use goods and technologies. Despite initial French reservations, both the Commission and the IMCO committee eventually took the UK's concerns on board to only itemise military equipment such as firearms and automatic weapons, heavy artillery, anti-tank weapons, ammunition, torpedoes, superconductive equipment, etc. (Council of the European Union 2011b, 2014).

Although Germany had greater economic reasons than the UK to support the directive – in 2008, 6,351 licences of a total of 16,054 were granted by Germany for intra-EU transfers – the Federal Government did not want to relinquish its national export control powers (Liberti, Matelly and Maulny 2010: 8; German Parliament 2011: 4). A key element of Germany's proposed amendments to the directive in February 2008 was the Federal Government's insistence on a strict divide between intra-EU and extra-EU export controls. It should be recalled that, prior to the transfers directive, the EU had already adopted an EU *Common Position on Arms Exports Controls* (2008/944/CFSP). The existence of both the Common Position and the transfers directive represented an interesting development in EU export control policies, because while the transfers directive aimed to liberalise trade within the EU the Common Position sought to tighten export controls on extra-EU trade. Initially the adoption of the Common Position had led some member states to question why a specific defence transfers directive was needed; after all, the Common Position did not in theory prevent intra-EU transfers from being made (European Commission 2006b: 2). Yet this posed a challenge for Germany because there was an emerging blurred line between the Common Position on extra-EU transfers and the Commission's eventual oversight of intra-EU transfers. The German government argued that the Commission's involvement in export policies could water down the stringent export control principles agreed to under the Common Position (German Parliament 2011: 4).

Germany's reservations about EU export control policies were partially based on perceptions about the stringency of export control policies in several Eastern European countries.[21] For example, as one of the largest exporters from the region, the Czech Republic took some time before adopting the Common Position and it was involved in several public scandals such as the delivery of a large quantity of weapons to the UN-embargoed Democratic Republic of Congo in 2007 (Kiss 2014: 226). The position of the Eastern European countries during the negotiations for the transfers directive was important. Not only did countries such as the Czech Republic, Hungary and Poland have a vested interest in reducing the administrative burden on their respective SMEs, but the prospect of putting in place a legally binding transfers regime could help dispel some of the negative perceptions towards their export licensing standards that prevailed among certain LoI countries.[22] Although mistrust between the LoI countries and Eastern European states still prevails, it is often overlooked that, for many former Warsaw Pact countries, accession to – and a bargaining compromise on – EU regimes on arms transfers and export controls were a way of rehabilitating their reputation as arms exporters and adjusting to the new economic and defence industrial environment of the post-Cold War era (Mintál 2008: 406; Kiss 2014: 357–359).[23]

Despite the UK's ambivalence towards the transfers directive, however, the government eventually saw the directive as an opportunity to shape the internal EU defence equipment market. For the UK, a necessary precondition for adopting the directive in the Council of the EU in April 2009 was that the proposed EU regime would mirror the system already in use in the UK. As the then Secretary of State for Defence, Desmond Browne, stated: 'we did not agree with the early proposals. We argued for a set of proposals which were much more akin to the scheme that we have in this country' (UK Parliament 2008b). By foisting its own licensing regime on the EU, and threatening to walk away from negotiations if the Commission did not adopt its regime as a blueprint during the comitology phase, London sought to 'ensure that all Member States' adopt an 'equally rigorous' regime to that already in place in the UK (UK Parliament 2008c, 2008d). As the Secretary of State went on to explain: 'our licensing practices in our view were ahead of most other Member States and we are trying to get them to bring their licensing practices to where we believe ours are. That manifestly would be in our interest' (UK Parliament 2008d).

The UK's insistence on the use of its national regime as a model for the EU's transfers system was a significant pre-condition before the Commission could table its proposed directive. Without the Commission's willingness to adopt and promote the British–German licensing model in its proposal, there would likely have been little reason for Germany or the UK to continue with negotiations.[24] The Commission had a vested interest in ensuring the path of least resistance prior and during negotiations because it was a firm supporter of the directive. As many Commission officials stated during interviews,

> [the Commission] was quite strategic in looking for member state allies that could help with the adoption of the directive, and, even though France was enthusiastic about the directive, without Germany's and the UK's support it would not have been possible.[25]

Furthermore, the Commission took seriously the consequences of not agreeing to secondary legislation because it feared either a division between LoI and non-LoI countries and/or the member states' choice to deal with the issue of transfers on an intergovernmental basis through the European Defence Agency. The Commission had already stated that the EDA 'has no mandate for dealing with transfers' (European Commission 2007b).

In this respect, the Commission and the UK and German governments agreed that the only way to reform the European defence transfers market would be to harness 'the power of the internal market' (Fiott 2015b: 546). In this regard, the European Commission understood that the transfers directive – when taken in conjunction with the defence procurement directive – was needed to avert the very real risk that EU member states would invoke Article 346 TFEU (ex Article 223 EC Treaty) every time they wanted to make a transfer of defence equipment to another government. The European Commission had foreseen this problem when stating back in 1999 that no transfers regime would deliver results if member states were to always invoke Article 346 (European Commission 1999). Even though some representatives in national capitals recognised that the Commission might try to use the transfers directive to make it harder for member states to invoke Article 346 (French Parliament 2011c), the ECJ's 1999 ruling in *Commission* v. *Spain* (C-414/97) made it clear that it was neither practicable nor desirable for member states to invoke Article 346 for each licence that they wanted to keep outside of the remit of the EC Treaty (Trybus 2005: 254). As a key element of the bargaining process for the larger EU member states, the transfers directive was a way to dampen small and medium-sized states' ability to invoke Article 346 and thus block transfers. In this sense, therefore, the Commission eventually found allies in the form of the UK and German governments.

Concluding observations

What does the analysis above tell one about the explanatory approaches detailed in Chapter 2? What is again clear is that structural pressures such as the 2008 economic crisis played an important role in providing a rationale for directive 2009/43/EC. On this basis, it could be argued that the liberalising ideology that appeared to accompany the directive points to the strength of ideational explanations (see Britz 2010). However, despite the language of liberalisation one can observe that the member states still managed to retain national authority over export licensing. Politics related to national control authorisation and the role of the Commission in export policy played as significant a role as economics during the negotiations for the directive, and in reality the transfers directive has so far only marginally liberalised Europe's defence markets. In other respects, the economic crisis of 2008 could be the type of structural pressure foreseen by reactive spillover to lead to greater supranationalism in EU defence industrial cooperation. Taken at face value, the 'defence package' did perhaps grant more supranational oversight of intra-EU transfers but again EU member states maintained significant control over national export authorisations despite the adoption of the directive (Europe Economics 2009: 92; BAE Systems 2014: 2; Masson *et al.* 2015: 54 and 58).[26]

In this chapter, therefore, structural pressures cannot be used in isolation as a sole explanation for closer EU defence industrial cooperation. Neither can one easily say that the European Commission played the definitive role in pushing for the transfers directive. Judicial politics' assumption that the adoption of the directive was a direct result of the Commission's ability to threaten the member states with ECJ-driven integration while also offering member states a legal 'middle ground' to provide for legal certainty for intra-EU defence transfers can be challenged (Blauberger and Weiss 2013). While there is certainly some theoretical merit to the idea that the transfers directive offered member states legal certainty, there is little evidence to suggest that EU case law was ultimately responsible for driving the member states towards a compromise. Judicial politics ascribes too much importance to Cases 414/97 and 337/05, and it neglects important historical phenomena such as the 2008 French Presidency of the Council of the EU, the economic crisis of that same year and the fact that larger member states actually sided with DG ENTR on most aspects of the transfers directive.

In this respect, the example of the transfers directive has challenged the idea that the Commission drives forward EU cooperation. First, at no point during the legislative process did any amendment by the Council or the Parliament seek to endow the Commission with a mandate to exercise control over the export policies of member states.[27] While the Commission had a clear understanding of what it wanted to achieve with the transfers directive, it necessarily had to remain flexible as amendments to the proposed legislation emerged from both the Council and the Parliament. In fact, there is general agreement among governments and industry that the compromise achieved during 2008 has undermined the effectiveness of the transfers directive (German Government 2013: 10; Mampaey *et al.* 2014: 6–7; Swedish Inspectorate of Strategic Products 2014: 11; ASD Europe 2015; Masson *et al.* 2015: 43). This observation would appear to confirm the claim that supranational institutions are not automatically hardwired to seek ever-closer union (Bickerton, Hodson and Puetter 2015a: 712; see also Schimmelfennig 2015b: 727).

Accordingly, much like the study on the establishment of the EDA, the case of the transfers directive reveals the importance of governments, firms and national preferences once again. This is a conclusion that both the LI model and economic patriotism would expect to observe. This study has revealed how, prior to the adoption of the directive, industrial actors in France, Germany, Italy, Poland and the UK pushed their respective governments to move ahead with the harmonisation of intra-EU export licensing. In this regard, a compelling reason why the transfers directive was finally adopted can be found in the sustained push by certain EU member state governments towards that end. France's desire to reform its domestic licensing regime led the country to seek a European solution that would allow it to reform domestically while also creating a legal order at the EU level that would improve upon past intergovernmental failures. It is intriguing to observe that France and Italy were able to reform their respective national regimes in a manner that did not damage their industrial interests. The paradox, perhaps, is that in pursuing the transfers directive, Paris and Rome indirectly based their reformed national licensing regimes on the British and German models.

Much like the case of the EDA, however, it has not been easy to disentangle economic and political preferences. The claim that economic rather than political preferences drive forward EU defence industrial cooperation does not hold in the case of the transfers directive either. Accordingly, this chapter has revealed that the domestic preferences forwarded by industry were not merely economic in nature. For some companies and governments, preferences were more geared to stopping any transfer of power for export licensing to the European Commission. In this respect, while most firms and governments understood the economic logic of removing cross-border barriers to trade in defence equipment, a number of governments pursued political preferences that wanted a clearly defined line between intra-EU transfers and extra-EU transfers. Governments and firms, therefore, wanted to pursue both their respective economic and political preferences, but this would mean that the DG ENTR's initial legislative proposal would have to be amended by the Council and by the Parliament.

In this sense, secondary legislation such as the transfers directive was essential for France and others because it allowed the member states enough leeway to retain their national sovereignty while also streamlining intra-EU trade for the benefit of their industries. Thus, there is merit to the idea that 'the EU appears to be a regulatory arena aiming primarily at sustaining firms through facilitating trade, enhancing competitiveness and expanding markets' (Hoeffler 2012: 447). However, one of the major shortcomings of economic patriotism is that it does not explain what interests emerge at any given point in time or how and/or why these interests were mediated (Mair 2004; Bulmer 2008). Use of the LI model reveals how compromise between member states was achieved during the legislative process leading to the directive. While France threatened to exclude the Commission and non-LoI member states prior to the Commission's initial legislative proposal, this was not a credible threat given Paris's desire to put in place a level playing field for defence transfers. On the contrary, what appeared to initiate the legislative process for the directive was the threat that countries such as Germany and the UK – which had no overriding need to reform their respective export regimes – would simply walk away from negotiations by not agreeing to grant the Commission implementing powers. Compromise was only achieved when, first, the European Commission used the British–German export regimes as a blueprint for the EU regime, and second, once assurances were given during the legislative process that national authorities would ultimately remain in charge of export authorisation.

To conclude, by drawing on a range of theories, this chapter has sought to explain how and why the member states adopted the directive on defence transfers in 2009. The chapter has surmised that the combination of a strong French preference for domestic reform of its export regime; the European Commission's decision to use the British–German export models in its legislative proposal; and the smaller industrial states seeking legal certainty and final agreement that the directive would not empower the European Commission on export policy; all played a vital role in securing agreement. This case study shows that the most important factors behind the adoption of the directive in 2009 was the French Presidency of the EU and the prevailing economic crisis that began in 2008. However, by focusing on the important combination of domestic preferences and relative bargaining power, this case study has revealed that governments used the transfers directive to not only sustain the government–industry link that exists at the domestic level by reforming national export regimes, but to also use EU legislation to reaffirm the importance of Article 346 TFEU and to ensure that vital member state competences regarding export licensing were recognised by the Commission.

Notes

1 Recall that while the directives were jointly adopted in 2009, each directive was negotiated by different sets of national ministries (interviews with officials from the European Commission, 31 May 2015, and 31 May 2016).

2 Interviews with an official from the European Parliament, 8 January 2014, and an executive from Finmeccanica, 28 November 2014.

3 See: http://ec.europa.eu/growth/tools-databases/certider/.

4 Interviews with officials from the European Union Military Staff, 31 March 2014, the UK Export Control Organisation, 5 November 2015, the European Commission, 27 May 2016, and the European Parliament, 7 June 2016.

5 Interviews with executives from Selex ES, 26 November 2014, Avio Aero, 28 November 2014, Diehl Group, 28 November 2014, DCNS Group, 28 November 2014.

6 Interviews with officials from the French Ministry of Foreign Affairs, 2 December 2013, and the French Ministry of Defence, 8 April 2014.

7 The *Bundeswehr* is composed of the German army (*Heer*), navy (*Marine*) and Air Force (*Luftwaffe*).

8 SIPRI's Trend Indicator Value (TIV) database is used to highlight general trends over time and they are calculated on actual deliveries of weapons systems and the known unit costs of these systems. The TIV data do not reflect actual sales prices and they only apply to legal transfers of military equipment destined for use by armed forces, paramilitary forces, intelligence services, rebel forces or international organisations (Stockholm International Peace Research Institute 2015).

9 The BSR is a body composed of officials from the Federal Ministry for Economic Affairs and Energy (BMWi), the Federal Ministry of Defence (BMVg), the Federal Ministry of the Interior (BMI) and the Federal Ministry of Finance (BMF).

10 This article reads: '[w]eapons designed for warfare may be manufactured, transported or marketed only with the permission of the Federal Government. Details shall be regulated by a federal law.'

11 For example, Section 6(3.1) states: 'a licence shall be denied if there is a danger of the war weapons being used for an act detrimental to peace, especially for a war of aggression'.

12 Interviews with an official from the UK Export Control Organisation, 5 November 2015, and former official from the UK Ministry of Defence, 2 June 2016.
13 Interviews with officials from the European Defence Agency, 1 February 2016, the European Commission, 27 May 2016 and 15 June 2016, and the French Ministry of Defence, 22 June 2016.
14 'Accidents of history' such as a particular country holding the EU presidency of the Council do occur. As Kingdon (1984) states, policy processes tend to be 'messy' with policy ideas only really taking hold through luck and particular 'windows of opportunity'.
15 Interviews with officials from the European Defence Agency, 19 October 2015, the European Commission, 15 June 2016 and 31 May 2015, and the French Ministry of Defence, 8 April 2014 and 22 June 2016.
16 Interviews with officials from the French Ministry of Foreign Affairs, 2 December 2013, and the French Ministry of Defence, 8 April 2014.
17 Interview with an official from the European Defence Agency, 28 March 2014.
18 Interviews with officials from the European Commission, 31 May 2015 and 31 July 2016, the UK Export Control Organisation, 5 November 2015, and the European Defence Agency, 1 June 2016.
19 Interestingly, during one interview a European Parliament official stated that had AFET rather than IMCO taken the lead on the transfers directive proposal – rather than just give its opinion – then national safeguards may not have easily prevailed (interview with an official from the European Parliament, 7 June 2016).
20 It is noteworthy that the issue of re-exportation was raised so forcefully during the Parliament's reading of the draft proposal, and this perhaps owes much to the fact that the rapporteurs of the IMCO (MEP Heide Rühle) and AFET (MEP Angelika Beer) Committees were both German members of the Group of the Greens/European Free Alliance: a political group with strong reservations about arms exports.
21 Interview with an official from the European Commission, 31 May 2016.
22 Interviews with executives and officials from ASD Europe, 6 April 2015, the European Commission, 31 May 2015 and 31 May 2016, and the European Parliament, 28 August 2015.
23 Interviews with officials from the European Commission, 31 May 2015 and 31 May 2016, and a representative from the Association of the Defence and Security Industry of the Czech Republic, 29 June 2016.
24 Interviews with officials from the European Commission, 15 July 2015, 27 May 2016 and 31 July 2016.
25 Interviews with officials from the European Commission, 4 April 2014 and 31 May 2015.
26 Interview with an official from the French Ministry of Defence, 30 September 2015.
27 Interview with an official from the European Commission, 19 March 2014.

5 Adopting the defence procurement directive

As mentioned briefly in Chapter 1, the EU directive on defence procurement (2009/81/EC) – henceforth the 'defence procurement directive' – aims to limit member states' ability to award defence contracts on an uncompetitive and non-transparent basis. Rather than awarding defence contracts to firms on the basis of discriminatory selection criteria such as nationality (see Recital 61 and Articles 4 and 21(1) of the directive), the directive seeks to ensure, in accordance with Article 18[1] TFEU, that defence contracts are awarded on the basis of 'quality, price, technical merit, functional characteristics' and overall cost-effectiveness (Masson *et al.* 2015: 12–13; see also European Commission 2004: 7, 2007c: 19; Weiss 2014: 30). Adopted on 13 July 2009 after a 20-month legislative process that began with a Commission proposal on 5 December 2007, the defence procurement directive applies to supply and service contracts worth over €412,000 and to works contracts worth over €5.1 million – excluding VAT – and an important part of the drive towards greater transparency in awarding defence contracts is that contracts awarded under the directive should be posted on the Tenders Electronic Daily (TED) database.[2] The TED database details public contracts online to allow firms from across the EU to bid for tenders in other EU member states.

Before the defence procurement directive, two other directives – the public procurement directive (2004/18/EC) and the utilities directive (2004/17/EC) – governed the way member states could procure defence and security equipment. A specific directive on defence procurement under 2009/81/EC was favoured because 2004/18/EC was ill-suited to the award of defence contracts (Schmitt 2005a: 14–15; Kennedy-Loest and Pourbaix 2010: 400). The Commission, or Directorate-General Internal Market and Services (known as DG MARKT from 2004–2010) and Commissioner Charlie McCreevy to be more precise, recognised that it was 'not always clear which rules should apply to which defence contracts' under directive 2004/18/EC (European Commission 2005: 3). While Article 14 of the general public procurement directive stated that the directive would not 'apply to public contracts when they are declared to be secret', member states interpreted this in the widest possible sense and they applied Article 346 TFEU 'quasi automatically for the very large majority of defence equipment contracts' (Masson and Martin 2015: 13). For example, in many cases some member states even invoked Article 346 for security contracts related to equipment such as firemen's headgear and T-shirts, even though such equipment could not plausibly be deemed necessary for a state's 'essential security interests' (Trybus 2006: 674; UK Parliament 2008b).

Despite publishing a Green Paper on defence procurement in 2004,[3] and an Interpretative Communication on Article 346 in 2006,[4] the European Commission believed that a specific defence procurement directive would help clarify when EU member states could invoke Article 346, which might possibly limit the use of Article 346 for purely economic reasons (Edwards 2011: 3; Blauberger and Weiss 2013: 1123).[5] While the Commission and the ECJ were not opposed to member states using Article 346 for contracts that truly touched upon 'essential security interests', they were concerned that under the general public procurement directive member states were invoking Article 346 for economic reasons such as job protection. The Commission stated that it had no intention of using the defence-specific directive to define the member states' 'essential security interests' (European Commission 2006a: 3, 2009a: 2). However, the Commission did believe that directive 2009/81/EC would help clarify the 'grey area' between military and security procurement and reduce the opportunities for member states to invoke Article 346 (European Commission 2005: 4, 2006a: 6–7, 2007c: 14; Institut de relations internationales et stratégiques, Istituto Affari Internazionali and the University of Manchester 2010: 123–124).

Much like the transfers directive, 2009/81/EC raises interesting theoretical questions because it touches upon sensitive issues such as the application of Article 346, defence offsets and security of supply. For this reason, it is fair to say that of all the EU's defence industrial-related initiatives, the defence procurement directive has attracted the most scholarly attention. For example, in her study of the directive, Hoeffler argues that the defence procurement directive was a way for member states such as France to use EU-level governance and supranational regulations to promote their national industrial interests (2012: 436). In contrast, Blauberger and Weiss ask why the member states should choose to adopt the directive in 2009 given that most member states resisted the directive prior to this time. They also ask why even smaller member states should choose to adopt the procurement directive given that they stood to arguably lose most from greater competition in the European defence market. For Blauberger and Weiss the question is less about national economic interests and more about the European Commission being able to 'strategically [engage] in judicial politics in order to push and pull member states towards EU legislative agreement' (2013: 1134).

With a view to further developing the existing theoretical reflection on directive 2009/81/EC, this chapter looks specifically at the role played by domestic preferences and relative bargaining power during the negotiations for the defence procurement directive. Recalling the four approaches detailed in Chapter 2, this chapter looks at the importance of structural factors, EU institutions, ideational elements, national interests and bargaining power during the negotiations for the procurement directive. In looking at the role of institutions such as the European

Commission, this chapter also seeks to better understand how, if at all, EU institutions influenced the outcome of negotiations for the procurement directive. Finally, this particular study also compares the LI model to competing theoretical approaches, especially the judicial politics approach advanced by Blauberger and Weiss (2013; Weiss and Blauberger 2016). Accordingly, this chapter is structured in two main sections, with the first section looking at how member states and firms approached the proposal for a defence procurement directive, and the second section then zooming in on how these preferences were advanced by governments during the bargaining phase. The chapter concludes with some general observations about the explanatory relevance of the case of the defence procurement directive.

The need for a defence procurement directive

This section of the chapter looks at the various domestic preferences that emerged prior to the adoption of the defence procurement directive. As will be shown, while several idiosyncratic views towards the directive existed, preferences coalesced around two broad groups: one group wanted to further liberalise the European defence market, the other group wanted to be able to continue to fully protect their national defence markets. It is important to note that the idea for a defence procurement directive did not come from nowhere. First, a special group[6] of personalities on defence procurement convened during 2004–2005 to conduct much of the intellectual groundwork to outline the costs and benefits of adopting a specific defence procurement directive at the EU level. Second, much of this intellectual support fed into the ideas eventually contained in the Interpretative Communication released by the European Commission in 2006, which already floated the idea of a dedicated directive for defence contracts (Georgopoulos 2007: 21). DG MARKT would table their specific legislative proposal for the directive on 5 December 2007, and on 17 January 2008 the European Parliament assigned IMCO as the responsible committee (just as had been the case for the transfers directive).

To liberalise and standardise defence procurement

France and Germany were chief among the supporters of the proposed directive as they both wanted to harmonise procurement policies in Europe, stimulate more demand in the European defence market and clarify the rules of public procurement as they related to the defence sector (Hoeffler 2012: 435). As the President of the Council of the EU in the second half of 2008, France was in an ideal position to politically support the directive as it passed through the legislative process. France viewed the proposed directive as a way to advance its long-standing preference to liberalise the internal European defence market and to thereby enhance the competitiveness of French firms in the EU (Eliassen 2002).[7] Unlike the transfers directive, which the government used to ease its domestic reform process, France's procurement regime had been subject to reform since the 1990s. Not only did the 1994 and 1996 'White Books' on defence call for changes to France's defence market (Conze 1995: 48; Kausal *et al.* 1999: 27), but in 1997 France adopted measures to help diversify the supplier base through open tendering (Guillou *et al.* 2009: 172). In 2004 the government continued its reforms by issuing decree no. 2004–16, which called for more competitive tendering for defence contracts (French Parliament 2011a; Hoeffler 2012: 445).

Recognising that the conditions that had permitted France to maintain a DTIB from the 1960s to the 1980s were evolving (French Government 1994: 116), the government decided to consolidate French industry[8] and push for EU regulation to ensure a level playing field (French Government 1994: 120; Serfati 1997: 53; Joana and Smith 2006: 87; Guillou *et al.* 2009: 2). The timing of this renewed effort to agree to EU legislation on defence procurement was not incidental. For example, France has an opportunity to significantly influence amendments to the proposed directive through its position as President of the Council of the EU. There was a clear rationale for France to use the presidency, because, as predicted by structural explanations, the economic crisis of 2008 was hampering the competitiveness of French firms. The 2009–2014 French Military Programme Law (LPM) sought to freeze the defence budget at an average of €39 billion over this period, which was down from €45 billion in 2008 (Foucault 2012: 5; French Government 2013b: 83; European Defence Agency 2014b). It is for this reason that the Sarkozy presidency decided 'to promote a competitive defence industry in France and Europe' during its EU presidency programme (French Government 2008: 265).

While Paris had little need to completely overhaul their procurement system after the adoption of the directive, the French government did see two specific opportunities embedded in the proposal for the directive. First, the government understood that providing greater clarity over the application of Article 346 could further liberalise defence markets and end discrimination against French firms (TNO 2009: 36; French Parliament 2011a). Discrimination in European defence markets had been a long-standing issue for French firms and associations, with, for example, a number of French SMEs grouped under the 'Richelieu Committee' seeking greater market access in Europe whenever it could be achieved (Comité Richelieu 2007: 4). It was understood by France that the proposed directive would better establish ECJ jurisprudence in defence procurement, and France stressed the need for the European Commission to take offenders to Court should governments invoke Article 346 incorrectly (French Parliament 2011a). Primarily, France saw the proposed directive as a way to liberalise the defence markets of its European counterparts (French Parliament 2011c, 2012b).[9]

Second, France saw the proposed directive as a way to outlaw the use of defence offsets in the EU. Removing offsets was in France's interests because of its trade interest of exporting to the EU market, particularly for those of its SMEs that could not afford to meet the offset requirements of importing states (French Parliament 2011a; French Government 2013b: 120). With offsets in place,

France found it difficult to offer European states sufficient workshare programmes and technology transfers in the manner that international competitors such as the US did. France saw offsets as a way for EU governments to discriminate against European suppliers in favour of American counterparts. For example, France had cried foul at Poland's 2003 decision to purchase American F-16C/D Fighting Falcon jet fighters over its own Dassault Mirage 2000–5 Mark II jets. As the French Ministry of European Affairs noted at the time, the Polish decision was 'detrimental to industry and employment in the European Community and contrary to the will to create a common military defence' (French Parliament 2003b). France therefore viewed the proposed directive as a way to ensure that fellow EU member states could not discriminate against French industry.

The German government was also interested in the proposed directive because it would help create a level playing field for its SMEs and because it promised to abolish defence offsets (Ostwald, Schubert and Knippel 2012). Both objectives were vital to Germany considering the negative impact of the 2008 economic crisis (Dickow and Buch 2012). What is more, German preferences in favour of a defence procurement directive reflected the country's post-Cold War approach to procurement and industrial relations in the manufacturing and high-technology sectors (Gorton and Schmid 2000; Vail 2003; Fohlin 2007; Heeg 2014; Möller 2014: 130). While Germany remains competitive in the production of land systems and marine technologies (Seibertz, Stähle and Hensler 2010: 23), its defence industry is characterised by the dominance of private firms and the insistence that defence contracts be issued based on transparency and commercial standards (Glas 2012: 10). Given Germany's ability for rapid technological conversion from defence to the commercial sectors, and the significant interlinkages that the German defence sector has with the commercial sector, uncompetitive and discriminatory procurement practices are not favoured (Lock and Voß 1996: 92; Kausal *et al.* 1999: 31; Gotkowska 2014; Scherner, Streb and Tilly 2014).

Reform of Germany's procurement regime since the end of the Cold War had greatly coloured the Federal Government's approach to the proposed directive. Post-Cold War reforms saw industry recalibrated to deal with an era of network-centric warfare and the battlefield technology revolution (King 2011: 36; see also Lock and Voß 1994: 341, 1996: 85; Dyson 2007: 1–5 and 36). The Scharping Reforms[10] and the *Bundeswehr*'s experiences during the Kosovo crisis – Germany's first military operation since the Second World War – made clear that Germany could not undertake crisis management tasks with military capabilities that had been developed for the purposes of Cold War deterrence (Thiele 2001: 75; see also Longhurst 2000; Meiers 2001; Sarotte 2001; Murphy and Johnson 2004; Breuer 2006; Dyson 2007: 111; Thiele 2012: 9; Heidenkamp 2012b: 37). This point would take on even more relevance given Germany's decision to deploy approximately 1,800 troops as part of the 49,000-strong International Security Assistance Force (ISAF) deployed by NATO in Afghanistan in 2014. As the 2006 German White Book would make clear, the high-technology crisis management operations that the *Bundeswehr* were now engaged in 'requires an efficient and sustainable defence industry base [especially] given the limited national resources and restrained national demand' (German Government 2006: 63 and 75).

The German government was therefore highly interested in a defence procurement directive that would help meet Germany's economic and industrial interests (h_3). Even though Germany would reform its domestic procurement system in 2010 under the 'Weise Proposals'[11] by streamlining institutions (Heidenkamp 2012b: 37), the Federal Government remained consistently opposed to defence offsets. After all, given the role commercial firms such as OHB-System, Carl Zeiss, SAP, IBM and Siemens play in developing defence systems (Gotkowska 2014: 2; see also Glas 2012: 5), Germany's procurement system could hardly operate on a non-transparent basis. German-based industry associations agreed with the government on the importance of the proposed directive. Despite some displeasure with the Commission's ability to challenge defence offset practices and state subsidies in the defence sector, German industry viewed the directive as a way to instil legal discipline throughout Europe (Bundesverband der Deutschen Industrie 2013: 17). German industry saw the directive as an opportunity to enhance standardisation in procurement, which they viewed as a necessary response to the negative impact of the 2008 financial and economic crisis (Bundesverband der Deutschen Industrie 2013: 16).

Sweden also looked upon the defence procurement directive positively, although the Swedish government and industry agreed that the directive would only be truly effective if fully transposed by all EU member states (Castellacci, Fevolden and Lundmark 2014: 1231). Swedish SMEs were particularly interested in the directive's potential to open up markets in the EU and to ensure fairer access for Swedish SMEs into wider defence supply chains in Europe (Castellacci, Fevolden and Lundmark 2014: 1220). In this respect, Swedish SMEs reflected the European Commission's own understanding that the proposed directive could open the European defence supply chain (Eurocon 2010: 121). Yet the quest for greater transparency in defence tenders also raised an issue for Sweden because – along with the Czech Republic – it was among the few countries to have mandatory offsets in their procurement processes (Europe Economics 2009: 47). Accordingly, the Swedish government's preference for a directive to liberalise defence markets in Europe was tamed by its reluctance to see defence offsets fall under the proposed directive. Nevertheless, the government in Sweden – along with Italy and the UK – expressed their strong opposition to the idea that the proposed directive could be used to erect protectionist barriers for non-EU states (Yukins 2009: 7; French Parliament 2010).

The UK government shared France, Germany and Sweden's desire to liberalise the European defence market through competitive tendering and controls over the use of Article 346. Yet the UK took some time before it fully subscribed to the idea of a defence procurement directive. This was mainly due to its desire to wait and see whether the EDA's Code of Conduct on Defence Procurement – which came into force on 1 July 2006 – would be effective. The Code was not legally binding but it did prefigure some of the aims of directive 2009/81/EC, including the need to establish transparent and objective selection criteria so that contracts could be awarded based on the most economically advantageous solution (European Defence Agency 2008: 10). The Code also helped establish an Electronic Bulletin Board (EBB),[12] so that suppliers across Europe could bid for defence contracts posted by government procurement agencies. Much like the TED bulletin board that accompanied directive 2009/81/EC, the success of the EBB was dependent on government agencies using the bulletin board. The voluntary nature of the Code meant that member states were not legally bound to ensure transparency in their defence acquisitions.

The ethos behind the proposed directive was also very much in line with the UK's own defence procurement regime. UK reform on defence procurement had begun in the 1980s, and, following the 'Levene Reforms', it was understood that if the UK defence sector was to be globally competitive then it needed to ensure competitive tendering for defence equipment (Walker and Gummett 1989: 421; Smith 1990: 195; Louth 2013a: 31–32). The then Conservative government argued that the UK defence market had, up until the reforms, lacked 'competition between defence contractors' (Walker and Gummett 1989: 420). Although some scholars question whether the Levene Reforms did reduce costs and improve efficiency (Schofield 1995; Macdonald 1999), successive governments after the reforms continued the liberalisation and commercialisation of the UK's defence procurement regime (Bishop 1995; UK Parliament 1997). One estimate calculates that in recent years up to 75 per cent of all UK defence contracts have been awarded through competitive tendering (Europe Economics 2009: 134). Europe played an important role in the UK government's – then New Labour – thinking throughout the mid-1990s and 2000s for two reasons: first, under its 2002 Defence Industrial Policy the UK government had promised to treat all suppliers on an equal and non-discriminatory basis regardless of ultimate ownership – this was seen as a way to enhance European collaboration; and second, because the UK government wanted fellow European governments to follow the path it had taken on procurement liberalisation (UK Government 2003: 4, 2008e).

Industry was rather supportive of the UK government's eventual backing of the Commission's proposal for a procurement directive. Although some firms were suspicious of the European Commission's involvement in defence procurement-related matters (ADS Group 2014: 1), large sections of UK industry had clear preferences to restrict the use of Article 346 and to ban defence offsets in other EU countries (ADS Group 2014: 3; BAE Systems 2014: 9). Other parts of industry and unions took a more nuanced view, however. Parts of the National Defence Industry Associations (NDIAs) saw open tendering in UK defence procurement as a potential threat to British industry. As the Unite Union made clear, buying 'off-the-shelf' fills 'the armed services with horror and devastate[s] defence manufacturers' (Unite 2013: 7). The logic here was that open tendering could lead to an erosion of UK defence manufacturers by relying on imports of defence equipment rather than manufacturing such equipment in the UK. Despite such views, however, the UK government at the time made clear its intention to keep the UK market open and to try to use the proposed directive to liberalise other European defence markets (UK Parliament 2008e: 8).

Italy shared the desire to further liberalise the European defence market, especially because the 2008 economic crisis was having a negative effect on European defence budgets (Palloni and Lizza 2014: 2982). The Italian government believed that the proposed defence procurement directive, and the 'defence package' as a whole, would help create a single European market in defence (Di Lenna 2009: 83). This preference was particularly intense, even though the transposition of directive 2009/81/EC would have far-reaching implications for Italy's defence procurement regime and would require a great deal of domestic reform (Italian Government 2009: 14). One should recall that in 2008 the ECJ provided its judgement on the *Commission* v. *Italy* (C-337/05) regarding the procurement of Agusta and Agusta Bell helicopters by the Italian state. The Court's opinion that Italy's uncompetitive tendering for the helicopters was counter to EU law, and that Italy's invocation of Article 346 was misplaced, provided a shock to Italy and other governments across Europe (Trybus 2009: 975). In keeping with Blauberger and Weiss's (2013) assumptions, therefore, in Italy the directive was also seen to ensure legal clarity over the treatment of defence procurement under EU law.

Yet the Italian government was not simply interested in the directive for the purposes of legal clarity, because important industrial considerations were raised too. Unlike France, which had openly advocated for a 'European preference' clause to be inserted in the directive, Italy took a more nuanced – yet no less strategic – approach to the directive. Italy could not openly call for a 'fortress Europe' because it maintained close industrial ties with the United States. Leading Italian firm Finmeccanica had just acquired US-based DRS Technologies in 2008 for an estimated US$5.2 billion following the involvement of Finmeccanica in the development of the US101 medium-life helicopter and C27J Spartan military airlift aircraft procurement programmes (Marrone and Ungaro 2014: 164). Nevertheless, some quarters in Italy understood that a single European procurement regime would force Washington to deal with the EU as a whole rather than on a bilateral basis with individual member states (Briani 2009: 7). In other words, for Italy the proposed directive could enhance the EU's bargaining power in negotiations with the US for better access to the US defence market.

Even some of the EU's smaller and medium-sized member states were interested in adopting a defence procurement directive. Belgium, for example, believed that the directive could be used to ensure that the larger states would not invoke Article 346 to the detriment of non-LoI countries. Belgium's contention that the Commission should challenge larger states drew from the country's history of domestic reforms to defence procurement. While Belgium had maintained a defence offset policy since the 1950s, it was in the late 1990s and early 2000s that the Federal Government reformed the national procurement system to take into consideration Article 346 (Belgian Government 2008: 9). Following Royal Decrees on 6 February 1997 and 6 December 2001, Belgium's defence procurement system would rely first and foremost on the Belgian MoD for politico-military advice on the acquisition of equipment, rather than on the ministry of economy and, thus, economic considerations – which were explicitly banned by the ECJ (ibid.: 13). Yet Belgium was rather unique in simultaneously insisting on measures against the use of Article 346 and calling for the retention of defence offsets. Belgium questioned the idea that offsets were economically inefficient, and the Belgian government instead argued that the EU's drive to remove offsets worked counter to the global trend in offsets, which would put Belgium's national DTIB and the broader European defence market at risk (ibid.: 21 and 23).

The resistance against EU legislation on defence procurement

Despite being generally supportive of the proposed directive, countries such as France and the UK nonetheless held specific misgivings. Whereas the French government was interested in opening the European defence market, several French firms voiced concerns about the proposed directive. As was aired during one parliamentary debate, 'French arms manufacturers have recently expressed concern about the arrangements for the implementation of' the directive because 'a maximalist interpretation of the directive could lead to the obligation to open French markets to third countries, particularly the United States' (French Parliament 2010). The French government was in a challenging position because it would be difficult to argue for non-discrimination against French firms in the EU while also asking fellow European governments to actively discriminate against non-EU firms. It is for this reason that several French lawmakers backed the proposed directive on condition that the directive contained a 'European preference' in procurement. Without such a preference, lawmakers explained, the EDTIB would be weakened and companies from America would be at an advantage because US firms 'can submit offers at particularly low prices as their profits are already insured with their protected domestic market' (French Parliament 2011b; see also French Parliament 2010).

For its part, the UK government wanted to ensure that the proposed directive would not hamper the UK's defence trade with the US. London was adamant that the directive should not lead to a 'Fortress Europe' in defence (UK Parliament 1997: 24). The UK would therefore resist French efforts to use the directive to install a 'European preference' in EU defence procurement legislation. Furthermore, the UK did not want the directive to apply to contracts in sensitive areas such as nuclear submarines, warship building and cryptography (TNO 2009: 36). Much like its preferences during the negotiations for the transfers directive, the UK government wanted to ensure that the proposed defence procurement directive would only relate to defence contracts rather than the broader category of 'security contracts'. Again, while the term 'security services' in countries such as France and Italy is used to denote gendarmerie and/or paramilitary forces, in the UK the term was used to describe intelligence agencies (UK Parliament 2008e: 9). In this regard, it should be noted that under Article 14 of the general public procurement directive (2004/18/EC) all intelligence service contracts were exempted and the ECJ could not rule on UK security service-related – read intelligence-related – issues (ibid.: 9; see also UK Parliament 2008f). For the UK government to agree to 2009/81/EC, any defence-specific procurement directive would have to retain similar safeguards to those already enjoyed under 2004/18/EC.

Even segments of UK industry were concerned about the proposed defence procurement directive, especially because of the potential effects it could have on the shape of Europe's defence supply chains and the ability of leading primes to determine the size and location of their suppliers. In obliging procurement agencies and firms to procure defence equipment in the most transparent conditions possible, some of the UK's largest defence firms believed that this would curtail their ability to select their own suppliers and commercial partners. As the UK-based BAE Systems noted: while '[c]ompetition is an important tool in defence procurement [...] so too are accreditation, relationship management, track records, and continuous improvement' (2014: 10). In other words, firms like BAE Systems did not want to have to automatically select firms for the sake of transparency when this could lead to a potentially reduced quality of service. As the firm made clear, 'the programme risks of using an untried new supplier outweigh potential savings against an established incumbent' (ibid.: 10). Therefore, while the proposed directive was welcome insofar as it liberalised European defence markets, many UK-based firms did not want to see EU secondary legislation affect the supply chains they maintained.

One of the other major industrial countries that was initially opposed to the directive was Spain. One of Madrid's major fears was that the proposed directive would be used to ban defence offsets in the EU. Spain had traditionally relied upon offsets as a way to ensure the country's industrial self-sufficiency and its technological development (Countertrade & Offset 2014a: 4). Spain – much like Greece, Poland and Portugal – believed that the authority to award defence contracts is a sovereign matter, and that contracts could not always be awarded solely on the basis of 'the price and quality of equipment' (Edwards 2011: 2).[13] Spain had form in this area. Along with Hungary the Spanish government had initially decided to not be part of the EDA's Code of Conduct on Defence Procurement – even though these two countries would subscribe to the Code on 1 July 2007 (Alfonso-Meiriño 2010: 52 and 54). Madrid's argument for not subscribing to the Code was based on an objection to the principle, taking root at the EU level, that contracts should only be awarded based on the best economic offer. Spain argued that sometimes the more expensive solution was required for operational reasons (Yustos Cordobés 2010: 216). If Spain viewed the EDA's Code of Conduct with suspicion, despite its intergovernmental and voluntary nature, then the proposed directive was a source of real concern.

Spain was not alone in its preferences to retain the status quo under the general public procurement directive. Portugal was equally suspicious of the proposed directive, and Portugal was the only member state to abstain during the vote on the directive in the Council on 7 July 2009 because of severe misgivings about the directive. Much like Spain, Portugal had long-viewed defence offsets as a way to boost its defence industry and to ensure that it could import technologies from key allies such as the United States (Martí Sempere *et al.* 2009: 44).[14] Unfettered imports from the US were of importance to Portugal given the fact that the two top suppliers to the Portuguese armed services over the 2007 to 2011 period were the US – with US$162 million, and the Netherlands – US$113 million (UK Government 2013). Defence industrial relations with the US were important not only because of cooperation in NATO, but because Portugal and the US had signed a bilateral memorandum of understanding in 1980 that stressed the importance of defence trade and technology transfers between the two allies. For Lisbon, it was long acknowledged that procurement policies should promote 'the involvement of the national [DTIB] in acquisition contracts and direct offsets' (Portugal Government 2011: 12).

The Dutch government joined Spain and Portugal in insisting on the importance of defence offsets to its industry. The Hague saw no need to raise the issue of offsets in the proposed directive. In fact, the Netherlands had consistently made clear that defence offsets 'contribute to the industrial base of the Netherlands through technological advancement [and that] the first objective is the involvement of Netherlands defence-related industries and R&D institutes in the development and production of defence equipment and related services' (Netherlands Government 2007: 1).[15] The Netherlands used defence offsets as a way to proactively support their national DTIB (Rosenkötter and Fritz 2008: 21). Similarly, Norway – a non-EU member that still transposed the directive because of its membership of the European Economic Area (EEA) – also believed that the directive would alter the privileged access Norwegian firms had had vis-à-vis the Norwegian government up until the adoption of the directive. Norwegian firms such as Kongsberg and Nammo relied on a close relationship with the Norwegian government to secure national and international contracts. Should the directive lead to more open tendering then there would be a risk for Norwegian firms that foreign competitors would start securing contracts (Castellacci, Fevolden and Lundmark 2014: 1227).[16]

Many Visegrad Group countries had also traditionally relied on defence offsets to support domestic industry (Martí Sempere *et al.* 2009: 44). Poland, which by 2008 had only been an EU member state for four years, was the most vocal about the potential negative effects of the proposed directive. Since the end of the Cold War successive Polish governments had been careful to shield Polish industry from global competition by ensuring that procurement contracts favoured national firms – a strategy known as 'Polonisation' (Soloch 2015: 23). When Poland did award contracts to non-Polish suppliers it would insist on defence offsets to facilitate technology transfers to, and workshare programmes with, its firms (Europe Economics 2009: 165; Soloch 2015: 23). In fact, to improve the competitiveness of its defence sector the then Polish government decided in 2002 to consolidate its industrial sector through the creation of a state-owned conglomerate called the Bumar Group (Terlikowski 2013: 2). Yet Polish opposition to the ethos of the proposed directive also revealed the country's belief that EU legislation was being used to support the established industrial players such as the LoI countries rather than emerging industrial actors (Ulanowski 2012: 13; Terlikowski 2013: 2).

Unlike the defence transfers directive, national preferences towards the procurement directive were less closely aligned (see Table 5.1 below). Even though the economic crisis of 2008 continued to add a sense of urgency – something expected by structural approaches – not all preferences were geared to accepting the proposed directive as tabled by the Commission on 5 December 2007. While France, Germany, Italy, Sweden and the UK generally saw the need for a defence procurement directive, countries such as Belgium, the Netherlands, Poland, Portugal and Spain viewed the proposal with a degree of suspicion because of its potential to ban defence offsets. While adoption of the directive did ultimately result in changes to national procurement regimes, what is unique about the defence procurement directive was that none of the major defence industrial countries saw the directive as a way to reform their domestic regime; so, reform was not an end in itself. Again, economic patriotism is useful here but only insofar as it alerts us to member states' desire to project national interests to the EU level. There is even some merit to judicial politics' expectation that EU case law would be used to coalesce governments behind the need for legal clarity in defence procurement. This was certainly an element behind Italy's support for the directive. Yet, as this book has argued, to fully test the applicability of LI it is necessary to analyse what role relative bargaining power played during negotiations for the directive as it passed through the legislative process.

Bargaining for a defence procurement directive

This focus of the case study in this section is on ascertaining how governments exercised their relative bargaining power during negotiations for the directive. The aim is to see how, if at all, threats to abandon negotiations or to exclude certain member states featured during negotiations before a compromise was found. Unlike the transfers directive, the procurement directive was negotiated

Table 5.1 Domestic preferences and the defence procurement directive

	BE	*CZ*	*DE*	*ES*	*FR*	*IT*	*NL*	*PL*	*PT*	*SE*	*UK*
Ban Defence Offsets	✗	✗	✓	✗	✓	✗	✗	✗	✗	✗	✓
'Buy European'		✗			✓					✗	✗
Contest Article 346	✓			✗	✓			✗	✗	✓	✓
Level Playing Field	✓		✓		✓	✓	✓	✓		✓	✓
Liberalisation	✓		✓		✓	✓	✓	✗		✓	✓
Security Contracts					✓	✓					✗
Sensitive Tech					✗						✗

Source: author's own.

using the now defunct 'Regulatory Procedure with Scrutiny' procedure (pre-TFEU), which mandated the European Commission to propose legislation in close coordination with the member states and the European Parliament (European Commission 2007d). Thus, prior to officially proposing the directive on 5 December 2007, DG MARKT worked in tandem with the EDA and the Council-established 'Advisory Committee on Public Contracts', which consisted of relevant officials from member state governments, and the Council's COMPET. Once the proposed directive had been formally tabled, the co-decision procedure was used, which ultimately saw the adoption of the directive on the basis of a QMV in the Council of the EU on 7 July 2008 – except for Portugal, which abstained, all member states voted in favour of the directive – and a European Parliament plenary vote on 14 January 2009, resulting in 597 for, 69 against and 33 abstentions. Despite the eventual consensus on the directive, the adoption of the directive was preceded by complex and protracted negotiations (Schmitt 2005a: 25), and the bargaining process, which formally began on 5 December 2007 with the publication of the legislative proposal, mainly involved a focus on inserting exemptions in the directive (Blauberger and Weiss 2013: 1131).

Even though the European Commission had negotiated various public procurement directives since at least the 1970s (Gelderman, Ghijsen and Schoonen 2010: 244), bargaining for the defence procurement directive was in many ways more politically sensitive than any other public procurement directive negotiated in the past – it was certainly more sensitive than negotiations for the defence transfers directive. This was because directive 2009/81/EC touched upon sensitive issues such as defence offsets, information exchange and security of supply, and it was therefore clear that 'negotiating the defence procurement directive was something new for the Commission [because] prior to the directive [the Commission] did not have much experience in trying to balance market liberalisation and security considerations in secondary law'[17] (see Trybus 2002: 1347; Fiott 2015a: 160). Even though defence offsets 'are nowhere mentioned in the directive', they 'played an important role during negotiations' (Weiss and Blauberger 2016: 453). As we shall see, despite the pressures emanating from the 2008 economic crisis and the vibrancy of France's presidency of the Council of the EU, the issue of defence offsets would mean that bargaining for a compromise would not be at all problem free (Castellacci, Fevolden and Lundmark 2014: 1219).

'Buying European' and non-agreement

In sharing the European Commission's desire for a defence procurement directive, the French – as President of the Council of the EU – initially aimed for a maximalist interpretation of what European defence procurement and security of supply should mean. Paris was keen to use the energy of its Council Presidency to build a consensus around defence procurement in Europe and to secure French national interests in the process (French Parliament 2011a). France's initial bargaining strategy was to use the proposed directive to oblige other member states to 'Buy European' defence equipment (Gabriel and Weiner 2010: 1).[18] As described above, France believed that the pressures emanating from the 2008 economic crisis would require a collective European response to shortfalls in defence demand. By seeking to amend the Commission's initial proposal, France saw the directive as an ideal vehicle for Paris because it actively sought to avoid 'exclusion'. By seeking compromise on the directive at the EU level every member state would be legally bound to greater transparency in defence procurement, although compromise would imply that the directive would perhaps have to be less ambitious in scope than first envisaged by France and DG MARKT.

The European Parliament was sympathetic to French interests on the idea for a 'Buy European' clause, even though a German MEP chaired the principal parliamentary committee in charge of reporting and voting on the proposed directive. Under Alexander Graf Lambsdorff's (MEP – ALDE) chairmanship of the IMCO committee, it was suggested that the directive should encourage reciprocity between EU member states, so that a contract awarded to suppliers from another member state would require that member state to return the favour. This suggestion was particularly worrying to the UK government, which saw this proposal as damaging to trade with non-EU countries such as the United States (UK Parliament 2008f). Nonetheless, IMCO's report of 17 October 2008 made clear in its amendments to Recital 37 (see amendment 1) and Articles 3 (see amendment 3) and 37 (see amendment 8) that '[w]hen dealing with economic operators, contracting authorities shall take into account the need to sustain *European industrial and technological pre-eminence* where this is economically valuable and strategically important' (European Parliament 2008c; emphasis added). This amendment clearly echoed French interests, even if the European Parliament's goal was actually to safeguard the whole EDTIB.

Yet France would find it difficult to advance the idea of a specific 'Buy European' clause because of significant opposition from other EU member state governments.[19] From the outset many other member state governments and industry saw the proposed directive as a thin veil through which to protect European industry and discriminate against non-EU firms and investments.[20] This view was held by Italy, Poland, Portugal, Spain, Sweden and the UK because each had strong defence ties with the US, and they thus favoured a directive that did not discriminate against non-EU–NATO allies (French Parliament 2011a). France had to tread a fine line during the negotiations lest other member state governments conspired to vote down the proposal in the Council on 7 July 2009. It could not be assured that most states would vote in favour of the directive in the Council, particularly if it included a 'Buy European' clause. Under the pre-Lisbon Treaty voting system decisions were adopted based on a 74 per cent majority of member states' weighted votes in favour, but this majority had to represent at least 62 per cent of the total EU population. In practice this would mean that for the directive to be adopted it would require a majority of 15 member states – who represent a majority of the EU population – to vote in favour. Assuming that member states such as Belgium, Czech Republic, Greece, the Netherlands, Poland, Portugal and Spain would have voted against the directive because of concerns about a ban on defence offsets, it would not have been adopted in the Council.[21]

The French government would have to take a different route to ensure that European governments would favour European suppliers first. In this regard, while no specific 'Buy European' clause was inserted in the adopted directive, France was successful in ensuring that the directive would at least refer – however indirectly – to European industrial interests and international competition (French Parliament 2011a). While Recital 18 of the directive recognised that the 'Member States retain the power to decide whether or not their contracting authority/entity may allow economic operators from third countries to participate in contract award procedures', it also states that such decisions should be taken 'on grounds of value for money, recognizing the need for a *globally competitive European Defence Technological and Industrial Base*, the importance of open and fair markets and the *obtaining of mutual benefits*' (emphases added). This sort of language was vital for French domestic preferences, but these words also reflect the preferences of other member state governments. Recall that Belgium, the Netherlands, Poland, Portugal and Spain were making the case for their right to continue to rely on defence offsets based on maintaining a competitive EDTIB. Syntaxically, the term 'obtaining of mutual benefits' is not automatically bound to the EDTIB and it can accommodate procurement between EU and non-EU governments too. On the basis of such language, the Commission saw no objection to accepting both the Council's and Parliament's amendments to the directive on 14 January 2009.

Yet, although France would achieve an indirect reference to a 'Buy European' clause, it had to ensure that the proposed directive would not affect certain contracts. In this vein, France had to balance its domestic preferences: on the one hand, it was pushing for market liberalisation and the Europeanisation of defence procurement, but, on the other, bargaining for a far-reaching directive could have negative implications for its own defence industry. For example, along with countries such as Poland, Spain and the UK, France eventually sought to protect its right to pursue government-to-government contracts – both with EU and non-EU governments – and this was inserted under Recital 30 of the directive following the Commission's revision to the proposed directive on 14 January 2009. France's revisions to the proposed directive on 1 December 2008 in COMPET called for government-to-government contracts between EU and non-EU states to be excluded from the remit of the directive (Estrup Ippolito 2014: 257). Any directive that included government-to-government contracts could potentially hamper French international exports. It may seem contradictory for France to insist on this point given that it had argued for a 'Buy European' clause; after all, it was government-to-government contracts between, say, the US and Poland that had alarmed France in the first place. Yet, as any ambitious amendments by France to the initial proposal would have risked non-agreement in both the Council and, potentially, the Parliament, Paris had little option but to use disagreement over a 'Buy European' clause as a bargaining device to insert safeguards for its own industry.

Once it became clear during the negotiations that only a balanced directive could ensure compromise, several other EU governments sought specific exemptions too. For example, both the UK and Poland governments sought to ensure that the proposed directive would not apply to cooperative bilateral and/or multinational initiatives such as NATO, the LoI or OCCAR. The directive would go on to ensure that under specific circumstances governments could still award a contract without advertising a public tender (see Recital 28 and Articles 12 and 13). Such circumstances would include contracts that related to armaments and defence R&D cooperation under NATO (European Commission 2009b). This was an important exemption for a host of EU governments. Italy, Poland, Portugal, Spain, Sweden and the UK were all interested in ensuring that the proposed directive would not affect their defence trade relations with the US. France and the UK would also use the exemption on international projects and defence R&D to continue with their, bilateral, joint projects without falling foul of EU law and regulations (French Parliament 2011a). The fact that the directive did not eventually apply to 'multinational investment programmes and R&T projects in armaments' implied that member states could rebrand offsets so long as they were applied in the context of a collaborative investment programme (Terlikowski 2013: 2).

The UK government sought specific assurances too, especially as it related to the treatment of security contracts. In one sense the UK failed to have reference to 'security services' deleted from the proposed directive during the COMPET debate of 1 December 2008. Recital 11 of the directive specifically refers to security equipment and/or services related to police, customs and civil protection. This reference was included to ensure that countries such as France, Italy and Spain would have legal clarity regarding the procurement of sensitive equipment purchased for their paramilitary and/or gendarmerie forces. The UK did, however, manage to attain a specific exemption for the exchange of information when extremely sensitive information related to terrorism, encryption purchases, intelligence services activities are involved (see Recital 27). The UK government was therefore successful in ensuring that the directive would specifically exclude contracts related to all forms of intelligence activities, border management, counter-terrorism and/or organised crime (Masson *et al.* 2015: 13). This was a crucial exemption for the UK and without it there was an increased likeliness of non-agreement.

Yet, interestingly, what items should be covered by directive 2009/81/EC was also a question of debate in both the COMPET and IMCO. All the member states agreed that the proposed directive should apply to military equipment, logistics, training, testing and studies (European Commission 2009c: 4). However, DG MARKT used the negotiations to widen the scope of the directive beyond the '1958 List'[22] that informed the basis of Article 346. After all, the whole rationale for negotiating a specific defence procurement directive was that the existing public procurement directive (2004/18/EC) did not adequately cover security and/or dual-use equipment. In its 2006 Interpretative Communication on defence procurement the Commission had argued that while the ECJ recognises that

Article 346 refers to the military products on the '1958 List', any defence procurement directive would have to 'take into account the evolving character of technology and procurement policies' (European Commission 2006a: 5). Rather successfully, the European Commission used the initial proposal to include reference (see Recital 10 of the directive) to all equipment 'specifically designed or adapted for military purposes' without listing individual technologies in the way the '1958 List' did (European Commission 2009a: 4). This step would make it easier for the Commission to challenge those member states that planned to invoke Article 346 for security and/or dual-use equipment contracts.

Non-agreement, exclusion and defence offsets

So far it has been argued that a basis for compromise was France's inability to insert a 'Buy European' clause in the proposed directive at any point during the 20-month legislative process. However, the one issue that caused the most concern and deliberation during negotiations was how the defence procurement directive would treat defence offsets (Weiner 2012: 16). Prior to the formal proposal for the directive, three broad coalitions of governments on the issue of offsets existed. As per numerous interviews with EU officials, the three broad coalitions of governments included: the 'openly hostile' – Greece, the Netherlands, Poland, Portugal and Spain – the 'cautious but constructive' – Italy and Sweden – and the 'openly positive' – France, Germany and the UK.[23] The Polish government would lead opposition towards a ban on defence offsets. Poland had long made clear that a directive that included a ban on defence offsets would cause deeper 'differences between industries from countries with [sic] weaker defense industry and the industries in countries with [six] strong defence industry' (Ulanowski 2012: 13). In this regard, Poland argued that the EDTIB should strive to close the gap between established and emerging industrial players – this was not the notion of the EDTIB shared by France or the UK. Poland made the argument that not only would liberalisation 'wipe out the majority of the defence industries in Poland' (Terlikowski 2013: 2), but also that banning defence offsets would actually harm Europe's competitiveness because international, non-EU, competitors were openly using offsets to support their industries (Ulanowski 2012: 14; Countertrade & Offset 2014b: 4).[24]

Such warnings, while clearly catering to Poland's domestic preferences, were not brushed aside so lightly by those member states seeking an outright ban on offsets. The French government could see that non-agreement on a ban on defence offsets would be read as a failure by French industry (French Parliament 2012a). France, Germany and the UK each had to be careful that their collective insistence on a ban on defence offsets before the formal legislative proposal was tabled would not result in a complete rejection of the directive from the outset (Eriksson *et al.* 2007: 29; Rosenkötter and Fritz 2008: 21; Weiner 2012: 36). Again, should the governments of the Czech Republic, Greece, the Netherlands, Poland, Portugal and Spain fail to agree to a ban on offsets then the directive negotiations would have resulted in non-agreement. This was a particularly sensitive negotiating environment, especially as some elements of the European Parliament were also keen on an outright ban on defence offsets. Prior to the IMCO committee's vote on the proposed directive on 7 October 2008 (and this after the initial proposal had been tabled by DG MARKT), for example, in its opinion of 12 September 2008 the AFET Committee – then chaired by ex MEP Karl Von Wogau (EPP-ED) – insisted 'that the practice of offsets and juste retour has to be abolished' (European Parliament 2008d).

Ultimately, it was left to the German and UK governments to communicate to the French government and the European Commission that defence offsets should be kept out of the directive before DG MARKT could table the legislation. When it became clear that there was significant opposition to the inclusion of defence offsets, the UK government pushed for a text that 'should neither explicitly authorise nor prohibit offsets' (UK Parliament 2008f). The UK had good reason for this strategy in two respects: first, because the government realised that the Commission could still legislate on defence offsets after the adoption of the directive; and second, because it feared that non-agreement on the directive would mean a return to the EDA's Code of Conduct regime. France, Germany and the UK were vindicated in their position following the adoption of the directive. As the Commission would go on to make clear in its 2009 Guidance Note on offsets, 'offset requirements are restrictive measures which go against the basic principles of the Treaty, because they discriminate against economic operators, goods and services from other Member States and impede the free movement of goods and services' (European Commission 2009d: 5).

The failure to get an agreement on a defence offset ban was not easy for the Commission to swallow because it had long argued that offsets were counter to EU law (European Commission 2007a). The European Commission understood that securing an outright ban on defence offsets would make it much easier for it to challenge member states whenever they chose to invoke Article 346 for suspect contracts. In particular, the judgement following *Commission* v. *Spain* had made clear that the invocation of Article 346 'does not constitute a general, automatic exemption, but should be justified case by case' (European Commission 2004: 6, 2006a: 5, 2007a: 4). As the Commission made clear, it was not for the institution to define 'essential security interests' on behalf of the member states, 'nor which military equipment they procure to protect those interests' (European Commission 2006a: 9). Nevertheless, acceptance that the directive would not include a ban on defence offsets meant that the European Commission would have to engage in a dual strategy of: first, getting broad agreement on the directive so that there was some specific legal basis at the EU level for the treatment of defence procurement; and second, providing greater legal clarity through a series of Guidance Notes that were published throughout 2009 during the transposition phase.[25, 26]

The flexibility of the governments of France, Germany and the UK also emerged out of a recognition that there were significant shortcomings associated with the EDA's Code of Conduct. They realised that the Code was only politically binding and it did not legally bind participating states (Schmitt 2005a: 18).

The danger was that without the directive the member states would yet again rely on the EDA's Code of Conduct, which, while affording maximum flexibility to governments, would not have the legal power to compel member states to introduce greater transparency in defence procurement procedures (Hoeffler 2012: 445; Fiott 2015b: 549). Under its Code of Conduct the EDA had made clear that it shared the Commission's understanding that offsets were harmful, although the Agency's approach was to encourage the member states to look at offsets as an emergency measure rather than as a 'life-support' machine for ailing industries (Georgopoulos 2011: 33). Despite this, the voluntary nature of the Code did not provide those member states that sought to ban offsets the optimum vehicle through which to alter the procurement practices of other member states.

While the Code of Conduct had been initially attractive to London because it was a voluntary, intergovernmental initiative (UK Parliament 2007), it was only when the Code of Conduct failed to deliver on its objective to open markets that the UK government became more interested in the virtues of a legally binding initiative such as the directive (UK Parliament 2007, 2008d; see also Georgopoulos 2011: 41). As was recognised by the European Commission, 'a directive would only be acceptable if the Code proved ineffective' (2005: 9; see also Schmitt 2005a: 44). In this regard, the failure of the Code of Conduct to change defence procurement habits in the EU signified the limits of an intergovernmental approach to defence industrial regulation. While the EDA's Code of Conduct was not exclusionary in terms of its membership – after all, every EU member state had the opportunity to sign up to the Code – the experience of other, more exclusionary, intergovernmental efforts had failed to sufficiently liberalise defence markets in Europe. Not only was OCCAR exclusionary in nature but European governments had for decades – albeit to no avail – tried to enhance defence procurement transparency through intergovernmental initiatives such as the IEPG, the WEAG and NATO (Taylor 1991: 148).

Security of supply and non-agreement

Despite giving in on the issue of defence offsets, however, France, Germany and the UK continued to seek a directive that would open up defence markets, especially those of the non-LoI countries, during the legislative process. The recognition by these three states that a ban on offsets could not be written into the directive was a key element in forging compromise. A bargaining compromise also implied that the European Commission would also have to be flexible over the issue of defence offsets.[27] However, France and the UK and other governments had to reach a compromise on how the directive would affect security of supply in Europe. One will recall that security of supply implies that a government and/or military can import a sufficient level of defence equipment and supplies needed in wartime. Given the global nature of defence supply chains, however, several factors can conspire to choke defence equipment supplies such as criminal or improper behaviour, resource constraints or politically motivated decisions to stop the supply of a piece of equipment and/or technology. As was mentioned earlier, the establishment of the CSDP and the existence of NATO implied that EU governments should work closer together on ensuring the EU-wide supply of defence equipment. After all, this was one of the important rationales behind the proposal for the 'defence package'.

Yet security of supply was not a particularly problem-free element of the negotiations because of the different approaches to security of supply taken by governments in Europe. Some member state governments embedded security of supply criteria, such as the location of technological assets and sub-contractors in tenders and during contract negotiations, whereas others did not (European Commission 2007c: 22). The governments of France and Italy, for example, wanted a security of supply regime that would make it difficult for so-called 'Trojan Horse' investors and firms to acquire or merge with European firms and thus potentially affect national supply chains (Eurocon 2010: 134). In contrast, however, countries such as Germany, Sweden and the UK were keen to ensure that the directive would not lead to substantial regulation of defence supply chains in Europe because these countries had traditionally operated relatively 'open' supply chains that were accessible by third-party suppliers (ibid.: 119). The directive would have to embody a compromise of these two broad positions before adoption was certain.

The French government would use deliberations over security of supply to yet again raise the issue of a 'European preference' in procurement, but it also had a keen interest in ensuring that its primes – or *maîtres d'oeuvres* – would not be unduly affected by EU regulation (French Parliament 2011a). Thus, in one respect the French government lobbied for a minimum threshold for sub-contracts under the directive during the 25 February 2008 COMPET debate in the Council. Accordingly, it was argued that the directive should stipulate that for all defence contracts awarded, at least 30 per cent of the contract value should be tendered on an EU-wide basis. In other words, this would oblige governments to offer part of the tender to other EU-based firms. This call would not only assist SMEs to engage with procurement authorities across the EU (Europe Economics 2009: 7), but it would de facto imply that EU-based procurement agencies would – for part of the contract at least – favour European SMEs. In another respect, however, France was keen to ensure the central position of its primes because this was a key way to ensure that French SMEs would principally benefit from DGA contracts. Primes had long held the notion that they had the sole right – rather than governments or institutions – to manage supply chains, but this was convenient for many governments too because primes would tend to include national-based SMEs in their contracts rather than those of competitors (ibid.: 17–18).

The UK government was openly opposed to the idea of writing a 30 per cent minimum threshold for defence contracts into the directive. Agreeing to such a threshold would have meant that the directive 'would offend the basic principle of prime contractor responsibility for its supply chain' and it would 'degrade the economic efficiency of the contract' because it would oblige firms to seek other

EU-based suppliers (UK Government 2010: 13). While London would fail to have reference to the 30 per cent threshold completely removed from the draft proposal in February 2008, it could secure wording under Article 21(4) of the directive that would give member states the option to transpose the 30 per cent rule on subcontracting or not (European Commission 2009e: 5). It should occasion no surprise to learn that the UK exercised its right to not transpose the 30 per cent sub-contracting rule. Yet the UK government also needed to balance the liberalisation of defence markets in Europe with the protection of its industry. The directive (see Article 23) still stipulated that 'Security of Supply requirements must not be formulated in a way that only national suppliers can fulfil them' (European Commission 2009g: 3). Beyond the '30 per cent rule' the UK would still have an obligation to ensure transparent tendering.

Those governments with large primes were keen to ensure that the proposed directive would not reduce primes' ability to shape the defence market, even though monopsonistic behaviour had been identified as a major reason to adopt the defence procurement in the first place. Disagreement between France and the UK over the thresholds to which the proposed directive would apply would be reflected in the divergent positions of these two countries towards security of supply. For example, while the adopted directive set the threshold for supply and service contracts – those most likely to involve SMEs – at €412,000,[28] the French government had initially pushed for a threshold amount of €1 million in December 2008 which was the amount that had already been set under the EDA's Code of Conduct (UK Parliament 2008b; Martí Sempere *et al.* 2009: 22). By doing so, the French government would be able to ensure that non-French defence SMEs would find it difficult to bid for defence contracts in France because they would not have the financial or human capital to bid for large defence contracts. In contrast, the UK government insisted on a much lower threshold of €250,000 for service contracts to allow its SMEs to compete at the lower value end of defence supply contracts (UK Parliament 2008b). Without agreement between France and the UK to somehow reduce the proposed French threshold by almost €600,000, compromise would have been difficult.

Compromise and the negotiated procedure

When the proposed 'Buy European' clause, the planned ban on defence offsets and disagreement over security of supply are taken together, it is a wonder that EU member state governments could reach a compromise at all. A final piece of the bargaining puzzle was required to allow member states to agree to a minimum legal standard for defence procurement while also securing their respective domestic preferences. That final piece was the agreement between member states to use the 'negotiated procedure' for the award of defence contracts (see Recital 40). In public procurement three types of procedure exist: 'open', which permits all suppliers to bid for tenders; 'restricted', which places restrictions on certain suppliers; and 'negotiated', whereby procurement agencies can engage in negotiations with suppliers before a tender is formally made public (Gelderman, Ghijsen and Schoonen 2010: 244). More specifically to defence contracts, the negotiated procedure allows national procurement agencies to avoid publishing technical specifications in advance of a tender, even though it 'must provide more information after having selected several potential suppliers' (Weiss 2014: 31).

Compromise was greatly facilitated by agreement on the use of the negotiated procedure because it allowed governments in France, Germany, Italy, Poland, Portugal, Spain, Sweden and the UK to insert safeguards for their respective defence industries. It should be noted that the UK and France had long operated the negotiated procedure in their own procurement regimes (European Commission 2007c: 21). Much like the transfers directive, where the German and UK models provided the blueprint for the EU's own transfer regime, the negotiated procedure model would serve as a convenient policy mechanism that would allow the member states to continue to address issues of information exchange and security of supply without the automatic risk of infringement proceedings (Trybus 2013; Heuninckx 2015). One of the main reasons why the member states agreed on the negotiated procedure prior to the formal legislative proposal related to purely operational considerations. It was noted before the negotiations that very few, if any, of the member states were in a position to stockpile weapons and ammunition because of cost considerations. They therefore required a procurement system that would allow governments to 'surge' production in times of crisis and this could not always be done in the most transparent manner for reasons of time, cost and information exchange (Schmitt 2005a: 31; Heuninckx 2015: 330).

Aside from technical considerations, however, the negotiated procedure mainly served political ends. For France, the failure to achieve an explicit 'European preference' in the text implied that compromise over the directive (however basic in intent and cautious in application) was required to: (1) empower the Commission to open up markets to French trade and SMEs; (2) safeguard French industrial interests by not subjecting firms to obstacles to trade; and (3) show that the 2008 French EU presidency of the Council was a success. Agreement on the use of the negotiated procedure would give the DGA and French industry flexibility when awarding defence contracts. It is for this reason that the head of the French defence procurement office at the DGA, Laurent Collet-Billon, stated at the time that it was important for the French government to use the EU presidency to incorporate France's favoured defence procurement method of the negotiated procedure (French Parliament 2011a). Despite initially wanting an ambitious directive, Paris was satisfied that the formal adoption of the directive on 13 July 2009 would 'provide an effective basis to ensure the preservation of [French] interests' (ibid.).

For other governments such as Belgium, Italy, the Netherlands, Poland and Spain the negotiated procedure was welcome, but there was wider recognition that the directive would do little, at least in the short term, to end the practice of defence offsets. The failure to ban offsets was a loss for Germany and the UK, who had joined France in pushing for the offset ban. For the UK government, the failure to be bolder on defence offsets would hamper the European Commission's ability to challenge member states on the invocation of Article 346. While the governments of Italy, Portugal, Spain and others in the EU were cautious of the impact of defence-related rulings by the ECJ during the 2000s, some governments such as the UK took a rather bullish attitude when reasoning that ECJ rulings would take time to be concluded and would not automatically effect UK industry (UK Parliament 2007; Rosenkötter and Fritz 2008: 8). With this mindset in place, it was hoped that directive 2009/81/EC could lead to a liberalised European defence market. As it stood, however, the negotiated procedure was the only real practical means of ensuring that governments could retain their right to control their procurement regimes while also allowing for a minimum level of EU-wide regulation on procurement (as was already prefigured by some astute observers, see Schmitt 2005a: 30).

Concluding observations

How does the case of the defence procurement directive advance our analysis of how and why governments engage in European defence industrial cooperation? Much like the cases of the EDA and the transfers directive, structural pressures in the form of the 2008 economic crisis yet again appear to have provided a significant impetus for closer cooperation. However, structural pressures affected European defence industrial cooperation in specific ways. For example, any hint that the 2008 economic crisis gave heed to a liberalising agenda at the EU level (Joana and Smith 2006; Britz 2010; Schmidt 2010) can be challenged. There is little evidence to suggest that any liberalising agenda – despite the use of language such as 'reduce costs in the defence sector' in the directive – successfully superseded the political/sovereign preferences of member states and some firms. As has been demonstrated, the defence procurement directive only partially opened the European defence market. In fact, this is one of the major reasons why a directive rather than a regulation was proposed by DG MARKT in the first place. A directive gave governments much more room to adapt national procedures and to insist that the specificities of their own markets were taken into consideration during the revisions of the proposed directive and during the transposition phase (Gelderman, Ghijsen and Schoonen 2010: 260).

As was the case with the transfers directive, member state governments were collectively interested in a legal framework that would permit them to not only balance economic and political considerations, but to also ensure that the relevance of governments in the defence sector was maintained (and potentially bolstered). Here, institutionalist explanations would suggest that the adoption of the defence procurement directive was an attempt to create economies of scale and Pareto optimality. As with the other two case studies, however, this does not appear to be the case because a number of opt-outs for specific national preferences were negotiated, arguably delimiting the effectiveness of the directive. Again, apart from the economic rationale for the defence procurement directive, political considerations ensured that Pareto optimality was not achieved. Here, the defence procurement directive could also be seen as an instance of Hoeffler's argument that certain EU member states project their interests to the EU level to protect their national defence market. Just like the examples of the EDA and the transfers directive, however, while Hoeffler's approach challenges the neo-functionalist logic that the EU is on a path of continuous and increasing levels of cooperation, it fails to explain how the member states as a collective designed and bargained for the directive.

Similarly to the case of the transfers directive, directive 2009/81/EC did not confer any new powers on the Commission for defence procurement beyond its existent duty to launch infringement proceedings for Article 346 violations. In fact, the analysis has shown that any ambitious agenda the Commission may have had prior to the legislative proposal in December 2007 was curtailed once the member state governments decided to stop any EU oversight for defence offsets in the directive. The negotiating governments did not want to agree to any directive that would further question their right to invoke Article 346 whenever they deemed it necessary. If anything, most member states used Directive 2009/81/EC to reaffirm their right to invoke Article 346 TFEU. This directly challenges Blauberger and Weiss's claim that the Commission played a crucial role in the adoption of the directive (2013: 1122). While it is true that the Commission was in a position to influence the scope of the directive, amendments proposed by the Council and Parliament effectively curtailed the Commission's desire to ban defence offsets. This would again point to the limits of Guay's structural argument because several member state governments actively fought to ensure that there would be no spillover from national to Commission competences on defence procurement via the directive.

Political and economic preferences yet again played a key role before and during the legislative process for the directive. The difficulties associated with disentangling economic and political preferences were felt most acutely during the negotiations for the defence procurement directive. The preceding analysis on domestic preferences and the negotiations clearly show how member state governments wanted to secure a directive that would suit their political and economic preferences. In the case of countries such as France it is clear that a strategy to Europeanise their national interests was in play, but it was not possible for France – even as President of the Council of the EU – to infuse the directive with a 'European preference'. Furthermore, while many firms in France, Germany, the UK, etc. actively sought greater market access in the EU through the defence procurement directive, several firms in Poland, Portugal, Spain, etc. shared their government's opinion that a ban on defence offsets would be negative for business. Before the directive could be adopted by both the Council and the Parliament, economic and political imperatives needed to be balanced.

While the legislative process lent itself to compromise, a bargain between EU member state governments was required. Compromise was achieved for several reasons, including France's eventual tempering of its insistence for a full ban on defence offsets and a 'Buy European' clause. Paris understood that without compromise there was the possibility that a group of other governments could have blocked the proposed directive in the Council of the EU both before the Commission made its initial proposal in December 2007 and during the COMPET debates in February and December 2008. One could therefore argue that the threat of non-agreement was a key driver behind compromise; as was the ability of a group of states with relatively smaller DTIBs to resist the LoI group's desire to ban offsets. Despite having many of their initial preferences watered down during negotiations France, Germany, Italy and the UK still wanted to give defence procurement a legal basis at the EU level. Exclusion never realistically played a role during the negotiations because some governments – in particular the UK – recognised that a return to an intergovernmental, voluntary, approach to defence procurement would be largely ineffective.

Notes

1 'Within the scope of application of the Treaties, and without prejudice to any special provisions contained therein, any discrimination on grounds of nationality shall be prohibited.'
2 See: http://ted.europa.eu/TED/main/HomePage.do.
3 The Green Paper was published on 23 September 2004 under document number COM(2004) 608 final.
4 The Interpretative Communication was published on 7 December 2006 under document number COM(2006) 779 final.
5 Interviews with executives from the ASD Europe, 6 April 2015, Airbus Group, 15 June 2015, and officials from the European Commission, 27 May 2016 and 31 May 2016.
6 This special group of personalities was chaired by Dr. Burkard Schmitt, who was then a senior researcher at the European Union Institute for Security Studies (EUISS), Paris. Schmitt played a key role in devising and articulating many of the ideas contained in the EU's 'defence package'. Schmitt would later join the European Commission to actively implement many of the ideas he had developed while at the EUISS.
7 Interview with an official from the French Ministry of Defence, 22 June 2016.
8 France's industrial consolidation took place in the 1990s/2000s with the creation of Airbus Group (then EADS) (which was established after the merger of *Aérospatiale-Matra* (France), *Construcciones Aeronàuticas SA* (Spain) and *DaimlerChrysler Aerospace* (Germany) in 1999); *Thales* (established in 2000 through the merger of *Thomson-CSF* (France) and *Racal Electronics plc.* (UK)); *Safran* (established in 2005 through the merger of *SNECMA* (France) and *SAGEM* (France)); and *DCNS* (established in 2007 through the merger of *DCN* (France) and *Armaris-Thales* (France)).
9 Interviews with officials from the French Ministry of Foreign Affairs, 2 December 2013, and the French Ministry of Defence, 8 April 2014 and 30 September 2015.
10 Named after the then German defence minister Rudolf Scharping.
11 Named after the head of the German Federal Employment Agency, Frank-Jürgen Weise.
12 See: www.eda.europa.eu/procurement-gateway.
13 Interview with an official from the Greek Ministry of Defence, 7 April 2014.
14 Interviews with executives from Selex ES, 26 November 2014, and ASD Europe, 6 April 2015.
15 Interview with an official from the Netherlands Ministry of Defence, 27 May 2013.
16 Interviews with officials from the Norwegian Ministry of Defence, 17 November 2015.

17 Interview with an official from the European Commission, 31 May 2016.
18 Interviews with officials from the French Ministry of Foreign Affairs, 2 December 2013 and the French Ministry of Defence, 8 April 2014.
19 Interview with an executive from Dassault, 8 June 2016.
20 Interview with an executive from ASD Europe, 5 July 2016.
21 The pre-November 2014 voting weights were as follows: 29 votes (France, Germany, Italy and the UK); 27 (Poland and Spain); 14 (Romania); 13 (the Netherlands); 12 (Belgium, Czech Republic, Greece, Hungary and Portugal); 10 (Austria, Bulgaria and Sweden); 7 (Denmark, Ireland, Lithuania, Slovakia and Finland); 4 (Cyprus, Estonia, Latvia, Luxembourg and Slovenia); and 3 (Malta). Had the Czech Republic, Greece, the Netherlands, Poland, Portugal and Spain voted against the directive it would have resulted in 242 votes in favour with 103 against – the minimum threshold being 225 votes in favour – and it would not have met the 74 per cent majority threshold even though the 62 per cent threshold was met. Incidentally, had the directive been voted with the same voting patterns but under the post-Lisbon QMV formula the directive would have passed the 55 per cent majority threshold for minimum member states required and it would have passed the 65 per cent population threshold.
22 The so-called '1958 List' (or Council Decision 255/58 of 15 April 1958) lists a range of military equipment that can reasonably be exempted from EU law under Article 346. Such equipment includes nuclear arms, tanks, toxic agents, warships, aircraft, etc.
23 Interviews with officials from the European Commission, 4 April 2014, 27 May 2016 and 31 May 2016.
24 Interviews with officials from the European Defence Agency, 28 February 2013 and 2 October 2013.
25 Interview with an official from the European Commission, 31 May 2016.
26 These included the Guidance Notes on 'Specific Defence Exclusions' (2009b), 'Subcontracting' (2009e), 'Field of Application' (2009a), 'Offsets' (2009d), 'Research and Development' (2009f), 'Security of Information' (2009c) and 'Security of Supply' (2009g).
27 Interviews with officials from the European Commission, 4 April 2014, 27 May 2016 and 31 May 2016.
28 The threshold amount for 'works contracts' stood at €5,150,000 at the time of the adoption of the directive.

Conclusion

This book has shown why and how governments, firms and EU institutions developed the EU defence industrial policy framework from 2003 to 2009, and concludes that structural factors played an important role in the push towards the establishment of the EDA and the adoption of the 'defence package'. However, EU institutions did not play a determining role in forging policy outcomes. This book has also argued that political as well as economic preferences played a chief motivating factor behind the establishment of the EDA and the adoption of the 'defence package'. Not all economic or political preferences automatically favoured closer EU cooperation on defence industrial issues, but where economic preferences did align this made potential compromise on policy initiatives and new institutions more likely. This book has argued that the EU is regarded as an attractive venue for European defence industrial cooperation because it allows governments the opportunity to amplify national interests and to ensure that the traditional link between governments and firms is maintained in a context of defence globalisation.

Yet, alone, the combination of international stimuli, EU institutions and preferences are not enough to explain how the EU defence industrial policy framework was developed over the 2003–2009 period. One of the important ways in which this book advances our understanding of EU defence industrial politics is by drawing on the importance afforded by LI to relative bargaining power. Without the ability of some governments to keep issues such as defence offsets or export authorisation on or off the legislative agenda it would not be possible to find compromise at the EU level. Market power does not appear to be a reliable guide to whether one set of national preferences come to the fore or not. Here, the EU's decision-making processes are key because compromise is hardwired into negotiations at the EU level. As the case of the EDA revealed, bargaining in the Council of the EU for a Joint Action to establish the Agency encouraged member state governments to settle on an accommodation of multiple preferences. Even where the co-decision procedure was employed, member state governments became engaged in a legislative process that favoured compromise. Interestingly, as far as the 'defence package' is concerned once the legislative process began it was extremely difficult for any one government to secure all of their political and economic preferences.

EU defence industrial cooperation: why …?

A more in-depth answer to the question of *why* governments, firms and EU institutions have developed the EU defence industrial policy framework can be articulated in three interlinked parts.

First, governments developed the policy framework to use EU institutional and legal structures to reassert their control over national markets and defence firms and to maintain and enhance their role in managing defence market interdependence and globalisation. Each of the example studies in this book reveals the importance of structural pressures on the defence market in Europe – these pressures at least provide the impetus for intergovernmental and/or supranational responses at the EU level. As has been made clear, regardless of the market size of individual states in the EU, member state governments are responding to defence globalisation, interdependence and the strategic imperative to retain sovereign control over their national DTIBs by using EU structures to enhance their ability to respond to the preferences of domestic economic actors and to boost national sovereignty and national strategic autonomy. In this regard, the argument that structural pressures lead to closer defence industrial cooperation at the EU level appear to bear out. Increased market competition, the rising costs of defence technologies, geopolitical shifts, the global balance of power, the globalisation of defence supply chains and a collective decrease in defence spending provided a suitable incentive for closer defence industrial cooperation between European governments during the period under investigation. As was discussed earlier, the defence sector is increasingly globalised in nature and the need to develop and produce a range of defence and dual-use technologies not only implies the need for global supply chains, but that there exists a higher level of political and economic interdependence between states and firms.

Each of the case studies examined in this book show how structural pressures influenced the policymaking process. As we have seen, the establishment of the EDA was regarded by many defence firms and governments as an effective way of managing issues such as military capability development, defence research, joint procurement and industrial policy. The steps taken from 2003–2004 to create the Agency occurred in a broader political and historical context of closer EU integration. At the time, certain governments in Europe wanted to use EU integration as a way to distance the continent from US actions and policies. In contrast, those governments that had sided with the US during the Iraq War saw the establishment of the EDA as a way to seek reconciliation between governments. Accordingly, these governments sought to link the Iraq War with EU defence industrial cooperation. In a context where the EU had created an ESDP and was working towards a 'European Constitution', the establishment of a defence agency seemed like a logical response to international pressures. As far as the two defence directives are concerned, we have seen how the fallout from the 2008 economic crisis added great impetus and a sense of urgency for the swift adoption of the two pieces of EU secondary legislation. Countries such as France and Italy were keen to reform domestic defence procurement and export licensing structures to make them 'fit for purpose' for the new economic context that befell Europe after 2008.

Furthermore, the creation of the CSDP has raised certain expectations about why and how far European governments should cooperate on defence industrial issues. It should be recognised that the political basis for the EU defence industrial policy framework to emerge has been the creation of the CSDP, which, in its own right, was established as a reaction to structural factors such as the fallout from the end of communism in the Balkans, and Europe's changing relationship with the US following the 11 September 2001 terror attacks and the subsequent US-led military interventions in Afghanistan and Iraq. The emergence of the EU defence industrial policy framework and enhanced EU cooperation on defence industrial issues in the post-Cold War era has accompanied sometimes uncomfortable and politically loaded discussions about European strategic autonomy, security of supply and the EU's capacity as a military actor. Nevertheless, it has been shown in several instances throughout this book that governments have attempted to link EU-level cooperation on defence industrial issues with the CSDP or other issues to arrive at a bargaining compromise. This was most certainly an element of the negotiations for the EDA.

The interplay between structural pressures and how European governments respond to them has been a key feature of the analysis in this book. Despite international factors such as the Iraq War and/or the 2008 economic crisis, for example, countries such as Germany and the UK adopted a 'wait and see' approach to the EDA and the 'defence package'. For countries such as France and Italy, however, the adoption of the 'defence package' did represent an important vehicle through which to respond to the economic crisis and increased international competition. In particular, France took a similar line during the establishment of the EDA too. However, other European governments did not share this approach. As can be observed during the adoption of the defence procurement directive, governments in Belgium, the Netherlands, Poland, Portugal and Spain did not agree with the notion that an EU ban on defence offsets was the best response to international pressures such as increased competition. In fact, in the case of Poland and Spain the argument was made that defence offsets – although counter to EU law – were a more effective response to structural pressures than EU legislation, because offsets secured Workshare programmes which could lead to valuable technology transfers and employment.

Therefore, governments respond to international stimuli in different and often contradictory ways. Sometimes EU-level cooperation is a way to manage structural pressures, other times the EU policy framework is viewed as a hindrance. This conclusion reveals something important about interdependence between EU states in the defence sector, because it appears that some states are more dependent on each other and the EU than others. Here market size is not necessarily the determining factor in whether a state is dependent on other states and/or the EU. For example, countries such as France and Italy – as leading industrial states in Europe – saw the EU as a manager of interdependence, although Germany and the UK had a much more nuanced approach to EU cooperation despite being of approximately the same market size. This point should not lead to any misunderstanding: the size of a state's defence market will undoubtedly afford a government a greater opportunity to forego EU cooperation. Nevertheless, based on the three case studies in this book, market size does not appear to be a consistent factor in whether a government decides to cooperate at the EU level or simply go it alone. The case studies are replete with examples of relatively smaller member states resisting EU cooperation even though, theoretically, they could equally have been at the forefront of pushing for greater EU cooperation. This adds weight to the idea that for some states the EU is an effective way to manage defence globalisation beyond their national borders, whereas for other states the EU is seen as an accelerator of globalisation and market liberalisation.

In this sense, the EU defence industrial policy framework is an effective way of balancing national sovereignty and market openness in an international and highly institutionalised context. The specific nature of EU structures (its institutions and decision-making processes – that is, the legislative process and the role of the Council of the EU) allows governments to amplify their ability to balance market liberalisation and national sovereignty within an interdependent economic setting. It is for this reason that an intergovernmental – rather than supranational – institution such as the EDA was created to partially deal with defence industrial issues. Likewise, the relative flexibility afforded by directives – rather than regulations – gave governments the opportunity to factor in national specificities during the transposition phase of both the defence procurement and transfers directives. Relatedly, governments rely on the EU's institutional framework to show domestic firms that governments are the pre-eminent representatives and protectors of economic interests. As each of the case studies reveal, while a number of governments and firms looked to the EU level as a way to open up the defence market in Europe a host of other governments were keen to ensure that the European Commission would not expand its oversight over defence offsets and export policy.

For those smaller and medium-sized governments that are more acutely exposed to international competition and want to protect national industry, the EU offers a framework through which to devise legislation and policy that does not automatically discriminate against smaller and medium-sized countries. In many ways, the push towards EU legislation and institutions derives from a genuine fear on the part of smaller and medium-sized countries that they will be excluded from multinational defence industrial initiatives. Exclusion would hardly serve their domestic preferences because firms would forego vital economic opportunities and governments would be unable to frame and shape national responses to market liberalisation and defence globalisation. The EU allows those governments with a relatively smaller defence market to craft responses to international stimuli that would be nearly impossible on a purely national basis. Furthermore, those governments that want to protect national industry are weary of exclusion because they may miss the opportunity to craft policy that has a direct bearing on their ability to invoke Article 346. The case study on the defence procurement directive (see Chapter 5) shows active engagement by smaller and medium-sized countries to ensure their treaty-based rights are honoured.

For those governments that seek greater market liberalisation, however, the EU framework provides sanctioning and compliance mechanisms. While some governments are more interdependent in the European defence market than others, certain governments use EU structures to create the basic conditions for market liberalisation in an EU market setting. The 'defence package' is a valid example of how these governments achieved a level (albeit basic) of regulatory harmonisation and legal certainty. Neither the EDA nor the 'defence package' diminish national sovereignty; instead they permitted many member states to reassert their sovereign control over national DTIBs. This situation was actively pursued by governments. EU institutions and legislation relevant to the defence industrial sector allow governments to reassert their control as the arbiters of domestic preferences. It is for this reason that in this book there has been scant evidence to suggest that unalloyed economic preferences determine policy outcomes. Were this to be the case, then one could assume that many firms would completely embrace market liberalisation and globalisation and thereby loosen their links to governments. Such a situation could see firms move out of the defence sector altogether or see them move country to where demand is the greatest – in turn, this would rob governments of industrial capacity, a technology and skills base, and strategic autonomy.

Second, defence firms helped develop the EU defence industrial policy framework in order to use EU institutional and legal structures to either further liberalise the European defence market or to ensure that governments remained the ultimate arbiter and representative of domestic economic preferences. Much like governments, during the three example studies several European defence firms viewed the EU as a framework through which to promote and adopt legislation and institutions that would ensure a level playing field in the European defence market. Approaching EU-level cooperation from a purely commercial perspective, many firms view what the EU can achieve in maximalist terms – that is, the EU can open up markets in countries that have traditionally maintained closed defence economies, yet only on the understanding that EU institutions do not fundamentally alter the relationship between governments and firms at the national level. For some larger firms, however, the EU policy framework is a way to overcome being nationally rooted and answerable to a single government. Accordingly, the EU is seen as a means to foster more intense cross-border trade and to recast the traditional government–firm relationship.

Yet for defence firms without a pan-European reach the EU policy framework guarantees that governments and firms can maintain close links. In this respect, those defence firms that were in favour of closer EU cooperation did so on the understanding that their governments could reclaim the ability to protect national economic interests in the face of increased international competition. As a way of maintaining the traditionally close relationship between governments and firms, intergovernmental bargaining at the EU level represented a way to ensure that domestic preferences were represented at an international level and that exclusionary initiatives by select groupings of governments would not cause any undue harm to national markets. For example, many governments view the 'defence package' as a set of legislative tools that can be used to liberalise the European defence market. However, other firms and governments viewed them as a way to emphasise the specificities of the defence market, reiterate the pre-eminence of Article 346 and ensure that governments retained sole responsibility for national DTIBs. Therefore, the respective roles of the European Commission and the EDA were scrutinised extremely closely during the domestic preference formation phase in each case study.

Finally, institutions such as the European Commission helped develop the EU defence industrial policy framework to advance EU cooperation, enhance their knowledge of domestic preferences, to boost their credibility and neutrality as a policy actor vis-à-vis governments and to ensure that any new policy initiatives would be consistent with the EU treaties. Again, institutions such as the Commission did not play a determining role in producing policy outcomes, but involvement in the bargaining process was a way to ensure that the Commission could learn more about the constellation of domestic preferences that existed towards EU-level defence industrial cooperation. Whereas institutions such as the European Parliament could have little claim to being neutral and unbiased (e.g. favouring closer EU integration or not), throughout the 'defence package' negotiating process the Commission necessarily had to accommodate various domestic preferences in its role as executive. There is little to no evidence in this book to show that the European Commission devised legislative proposals that sat in stark contrast to the constellation of preferences that existed prior to the adoption of the 'defence package'. As the experience of the defence procurement directive showed, for example, even though there was a treaty-based obligation to outlaw defence offsets, the Commission purposefully acquiesced to excise mention of defence offsets from the directive to secure a compromise.

Thus, the idea that EU institutions such as the European Commission, the EDA and/or the European Parliament drive forward EU defence industrial cooperation is only partially verified. There is ample evidence to suggest that, while the European Commission devised and proposed legislation (Schmitt 2005b), there are limits to the roles institutions play in driving forward EU cooperation. This may seem like a counter-intuitive argument to make given the importance of the European Commission and the European Parliament in the legislative process. After all, in proposing pieces of legislation the Commission not only liaises with relevant Council working groups beforehand, but it also works with the Council and the relevant committees in the European Parliament to take legislation through to adoption. The studies in this book on both the defence transfers (Chapter 4) and procurement directives (Chapter 5) attest to the importance of the Commission and the Parliament in the legislative process. However, what the two studies also reveal is that there is no point at which the Commission is successful in overriding either the Parliament or the Council in amendments made to the initial legislative proposals. The Commission instead remains pragmatic and in most, if not all, cases the relevant DGs acquiesce to member states' preferences by providing an adequate balance between economic and political preferences and the preferences of larger and medium-to-smaller-sized member states.

Yet, the conclusion that EU institutions do not drive forward EU defence industrial cooperation should not undermine the importance of institutions such as the Commission during negotiations for defence industrial policy. As the studies have revealed, the role of the Commission was not only closely scrutinised by numerous governments, but capitals seemed to assume that any EU-level defence industrial initiative must somehow automatically equate to a loss of national sovereignty over defence industrial issues. This would appear to challenge the claim that EU institutions do not drive cooperation, because the European Commission did become a direct factor during the calculation of domestic (political) preferences. More specifically, while member state governments wanted to protect core elements of national sovereignty such as defence offsets, export licensing and government-to-government contracting, many governments justified doing so in relation to what they perceived to be the Commission's presumed strategy of wanting to accrue greater powers over the defence sector.

The perception that some member state governments have towards institutions such as the European Commission in the domain of defence industrial policy is rather paradoxical. Indeed, governments may have afforded the European Commission more importance than even the LI model is willing to concede. The example studies in this book provide ample evidence that the European Commission was not directly responsible for policy outcomes, however, much of the energy expended during intergovernmental negotiations by governments was nonetheless directed towards ensuring that the European Commission's mandate for defence industrial matters did not expand beyond its current mandate/s. Interestingly, in the cases of the defence directives, many governments pursued a concerted strategy of curtailing the role of the Commission in relation to their domestic preferences. If, as LI predicts, institutions are not that important during policy formation, then this is a puzzling situation. If an institution such as the Commission becomes a major object of interest during negotiations as well as a policy initiator then this provides a valuable insight into how and why member states agree to negotiate at the EU level in the first place. In this respect, one may reasonably argue that institutions such as the Commission constitute a 'preference' in their own right because they are perceived to potentially have influence over national defence markets and the overall structure of the EU's Single Market.

For example, a number of member state governments preferred negotiating and adopting defence industrial policy at the EU level because they feared exclusion. In contrast to negotiating defence industrial policy in NATO's structures, OCCAR or the LoI framework, some EU member states saw real value in negotiating through the EU. As many scholars have pointed out, the EU offers its member states a relatively high level 'of regulatory expertise, coherence and sanctioning authority' (Damro 2012: 688; see also Meunier and Nicolaïdis 2006). However, the three studies above suggest that some governments engaged with EU-level initiatives to actively slow or halt transfers of power to the relevant EU institutions. The study of the establishment of the EDA shows how the institutionalisation of defence industrial cooperation through the Agency allowed member states to not only control what did or did not end up on the EU's defence industrial policy agenda, but it gave the member states an intergovernmental entity – underpinned by a Joint Action – that could be used to tame the mores of the European Commission and supranationalism if needed (Fiott 2015b). In this way, there exists an interdependence between past intergovernmental bargains – that is, the establishment of the EDA – and ones that come later in history – that is, the 'defence package'.

EU defence industrial cooperation: how ...?

In turning to the *how* part of the research question, it is worth considering the specific nature of bargaining and negotiation at the EU level. Before this, however, it is necessary to recap the importance of economic and political preferences in the policy process. Without the existence of individual government and firm preferences there would be no need to initiate intergovernmental negotiations. In this regard, this book has challenged the claim that intense national preferences reflect the economic interests of defence firms rather than the politico-strategic preferences of governments or armed forces. Under the liberal intergovernmental model it is claimed that governments are more likely to favour and represent economic rather than security or sovereignty-linked preferences.

Accordingly, the defence firm preferences presented in each of the case studies reveals that economic preferences can work either towards greater European cooperation or against it. For those firms that had an economic interest in favour of EU-level legislation and institutions there was clear evidence of governments articulating the economic interests of these defence firms. Recall, for example, those very public pronouncements by the CEOs of Airbus, BAE Systems and Thales during the establishment of the EDA. In this respect, there has been evidence during the case studies of large conglomerate firms going 'above the heads' of governments to try to directly influence EU policy. Some large firms can be said to have increasingly tenuous ties to any single government meaning that they can afford and seek to influence policy that has an EU-wide impact. However, these positions were met by several defence firms pushing their governments towards adopting a more sceptical approach to EU legislation and institutions. The logic here is that greater EU-level cooperation would challenge traditional government–firm links in some countries and this would adversely affect business. As far as defence firms are concerned, economic preferences pushed either towards greater European cooperation or against it.

However, the three case studies presented in this book challenge the notion that only firm preferences matter or that these preferences are wholly economic in nature. There is ample evidence in these case studies to show that governments and political preferences played an equally important role during negotiations for new legislation and institutions. For example, while France has traditionally been *dirigiste* in its defence industrial policies (Gordon and Meunier 2001; Levy 2008), during the negotiations for the EU's 'defence package', Paris emerged as one of the chief supporters of market liberalisation in Europe as a way to extend its defence markets in Europe. This drive towards liberalisation did not entirely exist in the period prior to the establishment of the EDA (2003–2004), but France managed to realign its domestic preferences to lead and take advantage of market liberalising EU secondary legislation (2007–2009). In contrast, while Poland was supportive of EU efforts for closer defence industrial cooperation at the advent of the 2000s because it was on course to become an EU member state, by the close of the decade it had serious reservations about how far EU defence industrial cooperation should amount to an EU-wide liberalisation drive. While these preferences take on an economic hue, their political qualities are unmistakable.

In this regard, liberal intergovernmentalism is incorrect to view governments as mere 'arbiters' of domestic preferences and 'negotiators' during the bargaining phase. All three studies show that governments do much more than simply arbitrate preferences. Governments have their own preferences to advance. This is not to say that economic preferences are not important drivers of domestic preferences, but it does show that governments temper intense economic preferences with concerns related to national sovereignty and security. For example, even though governments such as Germany and the UK were faced with intense economic preferences in favour of an ambitious work agenda for the Agency, both governments sought to retain political control over the institution by insisting on specific work priorities, a suitable staffing structure and budgetary control over the EDA's operational resources. The governments in Germany and the UK were not wholly against the establishment of the Agency, but they understood that without certain safeguards defence firms and the EDA could strike up a relationship that would diminish sovereign control over the pace of EU integration in the defence sector. This same behaviour was also present during the negotiations for the defence transfers and defence procurement directives.

In this respect, it is challenging to surgically separate economic preferences from concerns about national sovereignty, for these seemingly separate sets of economic and political preferences are symbiotically linked. None of the case studies in this book show that economic preferences completely determined policy outcomes, and, in the cases where economic preferences did triumph, there was still a strong element of national sovereign control associated to policy outcomes. For example, many firms and governments were successful in avoiding specific mention of defence offsets in the defence procurement directive. The simultaneous payoff was that firms could still enjoy Workshare programmes with foreign – non-EU – buyers to retain orders and technology transfers, and individual governments could still regulate national defence markets by taking strategic decisions on what defence equipment they would procure. Such a situation has a direct policy and legal consequence, for any legal challenge of a national invocation of Article 346 TFEU is precisely based on the premise that national sovereignty-related preferences and economic preferences can be separated. While there may be a legal case to separate these types of preferences, this book has revealed that the links between governments and firms – especially in the way that these actors each use the other to secure specific political ends – means that Article 346 is likely to remain an obstacle to the creation of a genuine single market in defence.

An inability to separate economic and political preferences feeds into the bargaining process. In this regard, this book has revealed that relative bargaining power – or the ability to force either exclusion, compromise or to abandon negotiations altogether – does condition whether EU cooperation is possible or not. This claim forces one to move beyond a simple focus on domestic preferences towards a recognition of, and engagement with, a 'constellation of preferences' and the political dynamic that this constellation produces. The constellation of preferences and how they are managed by EU member state governments through the EU's decision-making process is a critical component of any explanation as to *how* the EU defence industrial policy framework has been developed. Understanding how a constellation of preferences emerges and what it represents is also a key component in unlocking how the member state governments balance economic and political interests and state sovereignty and market openness. In essence, the constellation of preferences makes it possible to ascertain how governments attempt to narrow the gap between the perceived 'winners and losers' from EU defence industrial cooperation (Hartley 2011: 132).

We have seen how countries such as France, Germany, Italy, Sweden and the UK all (individually) pushed for greater liberalisation of the European defence market based on their domestic economic preferences, yet this constellation of preferences did not automatically result in the creation of the EDA or the adoption of the EU's 'defence package'. Instead, intergovernmental bargaining played a vitally important role not only in managing the constellation of domestic preferences across the EU, but also in finding a compromise on policy outcomes that would be acceptable to most member state governments. Relative bargaining power did play a vital role in how governments, firms and institutions developed the EU defence industrial policy framework over the 2003–2009 period. Not only did relative bargaining power raise the threat of exclusion for several governments – which thus incentivised cooperation – but it also led to a compromise between governments. In the case of the EDA, and as predicted by the LI model, issue linkage between the Iraq War and the need for European reconciliation played an important role in forging compromise.

The three example studies in this book have shown that negotiations for policy initiatives – whether settled by a joint action by the Council or the ordinary legislative procedure (co-decision) – effectively allowed both larger and smaller member states to secure their most important national preferences (even if in many cases these preferences did not initially quite align). So, while countries such as France saw the EDA as a way to instil a 'Buy European' mentality at the EU level, smaller member states saw the Agency as a mechanism to ensure that they would not be excluded from defence industrial policy initiatives developed at the European level. In terms of the transfers directive, France clearly used the negotiations to help reform its domestic export regime but, by adopting the directive, countries such as the Czech Republic and Hungary improved the ability of their firms to export on the European market. As far as the defence procurement directive is concerned, although many governments were cautious about the directive lest it shepherd in a ban on defence offsets, most governments saw it as a suitable legislative device through which to open larger defence markets and to crystallise the principle of non-discrimination in EU law on defence procurement. In many respects, therefore, the three case studies point to the validity of LI's claim that bargaining can help governments secure domestic preferences that would otherwise not have been achievable (Moravcsik 1993: 485).

In this sense, the three case studies reveal something interesting about how relative power functions during negotiations for EU defence industrial policy. The analysis in this book has revealed that in an EU setting it is not necessarily the size of one's defence market that makes the difference during negotiations. While there is evidence to suggest that France, Germany and the UK could have all walked away from negotiations on the EDA and the 'defence package' they ultimately did not do so, even though the relative size of their respective defence markets could have cushioned to some extent the negative effects of non-agreement. In an EU context, governments wishing to secure outcomes through negotiations therefore cannot simply rely on the size of their defence market. The studies in this book have revealed that larger and smaller member states alike do not simply abandon negotiations – even if they can cushion the losses from non-agreement. If most member states do not believe a certain policy outcome would be desirable then negotiations may not occur, but each of the case studies in this book highlights that the prevailing political and economic structural pressures of the 2003 to 2009 period, and the specific decision-making processes of EU policy and law, made it difficult for member states to simply avoid negotiations. In this sense, one can observe that in each of the three example studies analysed there is at least a pre-disposition towards initiating negotiations.

Despite the rather hollow threat of walking away from negotiations, however, the three case studies do point to the important catalytic role played by the threat of exclusion. For several governments, the threat of exclusion was a broadside to their sovereignty. In fact, working through the EU was an attractive option because it presumed that the principles of non-discrimination and non-exclusion would guide the policy process and any negotiated outcomes. Smaller and medium-sized member states were suspicious of exclusionary fora such as OCCAR and the LoI, and so the EU served as a means by which member states could stand toe-to-toe with one another regardless of market size. In each of the case studies one can see countries such as Belgium, Finland, the Netherlands and Poland regularly making – and succeeding to make – the point that EU defence industrial policy cannot be exclusionary. This was not only because it would be difficult for larger member states to reap the benefits of market liberalisation without the full cohort of member states on board, but because it is odd to exclude member states from defence industrial policy when the CSDP and, more importantly, the Single Market are both written into the EU treaties as inclusive initiatives. Furthermore, for many of the larger member states it was also apparent that while exclusionary fora such as OCCAR and the LoI agreement were preferable for procurement programmes, they are not well-suited to managing the European defence market overall.

Theoretical implications

It is worth considering the explanatory implications of the answers provided to the research question. In contrast to competing theoretical explanations of why and how EU governments cooperate in the defence sector, this book has forwarded compelling evidence to suggest that, unlike other approaches, liberal intergovernmentalism is a model that views EU-level cooperation as a way for governments to not only secure domestic economic and political preferences but to also reassert government control over national DTIBs and defence markets in the context of defence globalisation and interdependence. In this way, liberal intergovernmentalism suggests that EU-level policy outcomes are designed to ensure that governments remain relevant to their defence firms in a market environment where firms are more mobile and increasingly less inclined to remain symbiotically linked to governments. In this respect, LI appears correct to augur that institutions such as the European Commission play a specific, yet non-decisive, role for policy outcomes. The studies in Chapters 3, 4 and 5 also show that supranational institutions are not necessarily hard-wired to seek ever-closer union (Bickerton, Hodson and Puetter 2015b: 712; see also Schimmelfennig 2015b: 727).

Despite the strengths of liberal intergovernmentalism, however, it is worth considering some of the explanatory specificities that have emerged during this book. First, any insistence on the prime importance of economic preferences does not carry well into studies of the defence sector. True, this book has shown how governments have aggregated and represented the preferences of the defence industry in each country, but only to a certain degree. What has been interesting to observe is that governments can and do intervene to recalibrate the economic preferences they are purported to represent. They do so when political or strategic preferences arise. In some cases, defence firms even share the political preferences of governments, which would strongly suggest that in the defence sector firms are not simply economic agents. As stressed by Moravcsik and Schimmelfennig, the specific nature of policy domains will determine how important economic interests are when compared to security and/or geopolitical concerns (2009: 70). Interestingly, the case studies reveal that in the defence sector one is not dealing with a dichotomy between economic and political preferences per se but rather a bargain between the two within and between states.

Second, the three example studies in this book reveal that the LI model does not appear to be able to take full account of historical phenomena or the sometimes 'messy' nature of policymaking. One of the hallmarks of liberal intergovernmentalism is its parsimonious, 'three-step', conceptual structure. Yet, in many of the case studies analysed in this book, historical phenomena had a decisive effect on policymaking and certain governments sought issue linkage on this basis. While no theory can account for a phenomenon such as the timing of the French presidency of the Council of the EU, there is a danger that LI's compartmentalisation of political processes blinds the researcher and/or analyst to instances where actors can influence all parts of the policy process. Here one can recall that while EU institutions such as the European Commission are not considered important for 'step one' of the LI model, this book has indicated that such institutions played an intriguing role during – and in fact became the direct object of – the preference formation phase.

It is true that liberal intergovernmentalism proceeds without any accommodation or explanation for random phenomena that occur during the bargaining process. Scholars such as Kingdon (1984) and Pierson (1996) have both pointed to the rather 'messy' nature of policymaking and the fact that each negotiation cannot be analysed in an historical vacuum. The establishment of the EDA occurred after decades of attempted collaborative efforts within the Western European Union. The 'defence package' was adopted in 2009 but efforts designed to liberalise the European defence market were around before this time. To treat each negotiation for a policy initiative as some sort of 'new game' without its attendant historical baggage and the specific EU institutional context in which each negotiation takes place is to provide a de-contextualised account. One also must recognise that serendipitous occurrences, such as the French presidency of the Council of the EU in 2008 and the economic crisis of the same year, can greatly impact the policy process by adding a sense of urgency or by conditioning the ultimate objective of policy initiatives. Historical events such as crises and a change in government may provide 'windows of opportunity' that can feed directly into national calculations about whether to seek compromise at the EU level.

Third, while one can usefully treat political processes as rational games it is important not to lose sight of the importance of historical circumstance and the implications of political bargains. One must avoid seeing intergovernmental bargains as mere 'one shot games'. Individual sets of negotiations emerge from a specific historical context. The idea for an EDA did not simply emerge in 2003 and neither did the 'defence package' suddenly surface in 2008. Before intergovernmental negotiations formally begin between governments, there is a political and historical legacy and process of keeping a policy idea either on or off the political agenda. This is the specific, and valid, point raised by historical institutionalism. Likewise, once a policy outcome emerges out of intergovernmental bargaining it should not be viewed as some static result that is not open to future shifts in policy. Negotiated outcomes are in fact subject to a constant deliberative process that requires renewed collective agreement (Bickerton, Hodson and

Puetter 2015a: 712). As Blauberger and Weiss correctly recognise, 'political struggles' between governments and institutions are likely to continue in the future (2013: 1135). Governments will continue to assert their control of the defence sector, but firms and institutions will contest or embrace governments in important ways.

Where this book has therefore added to the ongoing debate about the nature of EU defence industrial cooperation is by shedding light on the intricate relationship between governments and firms in an EU setting. Whereas theories such as reactive spillover, judicial politics and economic patriotism point to issues such as structural pressures, ECJ-driven integration or economic interests, this book has argued that EU-level efforts are driven by the desire of both governments and firms to redefine and manage their relationship in a context of defence globalisation and broader EU integration processes. Thus, economic preferences are important, but in seeking to secure these preferences the EU institutional framework allows governments to simultaneously reaffirm their position as the ultimate arbiter and promoter of domestic preferences. In this sense, EU-level bargains allow governments to reassert control over national DTIBs in a context where defence globalisation and broader geopolitical forces threaten to irreparably alter the traditional links that exist between governments and firms. Despite its shortcomings, liberal intergovernmentalism has been a useful theoretical model and each of the case studies reveals that the LI model does have salience when explaining 'everyday' policy decisions.

Our study of LI in relation to EU defence industrial cooperation also has implications for the emerging debate on 'new intergovernmentalism'. Indeed, Bickerton, Hodson and Puetter (2015a, 2015b, 2015c) argue that, since the Maastricht Treaty in 1992, EU cooperation has been marked by an intensification of cooperation at the EU level, but not with any requisite transfer of power from the member states to supranational institutions such as the European Commission. What follows from their claim is that EU cooperation is certainly intensifying, but through greater intergovernmentalism rather than supranationalism. Such an argument challenges the main tenets of LI in one important respect, that under LI supranational institutions are designed to lock in and oversee intergovernmental bargains. Under new intergovernmentalism, however, it is argued that supranational institutions such as the Commission are actively avoided by member states in favour of *de novo* agencies and bodies in order to reassert the power of the European Council and Council of the EU.

This book has made the case that structural factors partially explain why EU member states are willing to engage in EU-level defence industrial policymaking. For new intergovernmentalism, major shifts in the political economy of Europe have supposedly led to a move from supranationalism to intergovernmentalism. New intergovernmentalism augurs that greater Euroscepticism and a more general crisis of representative politics in national systems have led governments to reassert themselves within the EU policymaking system (Bickerton, Hodson and Puetter 2015a: 710). As far as the defence sector is concerned, such arguments are relevant because major shifts in the nature of the defence market in Europe (i.e. especially as they relate to globalisation and the relationship between governments and firms) have made EU policy and solutions more relevant. As we have seen in this book, EU solutions to major changes in the European defence market have been negotiated to help governments bargain preferences in an interdependent context and to retain control over national DTIBs and markets.

This book has revealed how the EU member state governments have, on many occasions, sought to balance against supranational actors by creating intergovernmental bodies such as the EDA and adopting particular legislative packages such as directives 2009/43/EC and 2009/81/EC. In particular, the establishment of the EDA in 2004 would seem to support the argument forwarded by new intergovernmentalism that *de novo* bodies are favoured in the post-Maastricht era by member states. The adoption of the 'defence package' would also underline the new intergovernmentalist focus on deliberation and consensus between governments as a hallmark of EU cooperation in the post-Maastricht period. Indeed, both of the defence directives were preceded by months of negotiation and compromise. This book has revealed that at least in the case of EU defence industrial cooperation a chief reason behind the creation of new institutions and soft law was the fear that the Commission would gain new powers in defence industrial policy. Furthermore, many states believed that the privileged link that governments had with defence firms would be irreparably broken by greater supranational involvement in policymaking.

Yet criticism of new intergovernmentalism also warrants attention in the context of the focus of this book. Schimmelfennig (2015b) has argued that new intergovernmentalism is not new because intergovernmentalism has always existed in the EU (pre- and post-Maastricht). From the negotiations for the eurozone to the French veto against British entry into the European Community membership in 1975, it is pointed out that 'the anecdotal evidence does not speak compellingly in favour of a "new" or "softer" post-Maastricht intergovernmentalism' (Schimmelfennig 2015b). Furthermore, it is shown that although there has been a clear shift in the political economy and domestic politics of Europe in the post-Maastricht period, new intergovernmentalism does not as yet comprehensively link these shifts to policy outcomes in the way that LI does (Schimmelfennig 2015b: 728). Finally, other scholars argue that one cannot really say with certainty that the Commission and other supranational institutions are irrelevant to EU policymaking because they still occupy an essential role in the EU's legislative processes (Nugent and Rhinard 2016).

This book has shown how, at least in the domain of defence industrial policymaking, the Commission exercises an important triple role: first, as one preference among many that EU governments take into consideration when formulating national positions; second, depending on the bargaining process (i.e. QMV or the Ordinary Legislative Procedure), it is an essential arbiter of the constellation of national preferences; and finally, it contributes to ensuring an information-rich environment during negotiations by engaging in discussions in Council working groups, producing guidance communications and documents and initially drafting legislation. Accordingly, the idea advanced by new intergovernmentalism that increased deliberation and consensus has led to a decline in the Commission's role and an increase in the relevance of the Council overlooks the fact that the EU policy process is by its very nature consensus-based and deliberative despite the bargaining setting (Schimmelfennig 2015b: 725; Nugent and Rhinard 2016). In each of the example studies in this book, there was not one instance where consensus and deliberation did not play a role, although the type of bargaining process selected (i.e. QMV or the Ordinary Legislative Procedure) did affect the type and extent of policy outcomes.

Based on the analysis in this book, it is clear that both LI and new intergovernmentalism suffer from explanatory weaknesses. In the case of LI, it has been shown how a parsimonious explanatory model risks oversimplifying the policy process. Acknowledging the fact that all theory is supposed to simplify to some extent, this book has shown how in defence industrial policymaking preference formation, bargaining and policy outcomes cannot be neatly compartmentalised. Likewise, new intergovernmentalism looks to create a parsimonious division between intergovernmentalism and supranationalism. Of course, a study of the defence sector may actually be seen as a perfect case study for new intergovernmentalism as it is a policy domain that has so far resisted a greater degree of supranationalism. As the two example studies on the 'defence package' show, however, the relationship between governments and EU institutions is not so neatly captured by existing theories. Indeed, when negotiating the two directives certain governments made it their explicit objective to partner with the European Commission to secure their national preferences.

The theoretical discussion contained in this book also opens up a broader discussion about the applicability of LI to other aspects of EU defence cooperation. In particular, there is obvious scope to apply LI to more recent instances of cooperation such as Permanent Structured Cooperation and the European Defence Fund. With regard to PESCO, a focused case study on how this initiative was bargained between member states and EU institutions would be of benefit to academic discussions. In particular, analysing the national preferences and how they aligned behind PESCO could give scholars an indication of why PESCO was deemed necessary at this particular point in time. The case of the EDF is also interesting because here there is clearly a role for the European Commission, which would raise questions for LI and new intergovernmentalism in terms of the role of established EU institutions versus *de novo* bodies.

Policy implications

The theoretical conclusions contained in this book also raise some important policy-related questions. The most obvious conclusion is that EU member state governments do not really appear to want to create a consolidated EDTIB as part of broader EU defence policy. To the extent that EU member states do appear to support the idea of an EDTIB, this book has shown that at least from 2003 to 2009 they have done so in order to advance their own national economic and political interests. What is beneficial about channelling European defence industrial cooperation through EU institutions is that national preferences are dampened and altered and a compromise between states is achieved. On a broad level, this compromise is required if the larger firms in a handful of EU member states are not to completely dominate the European defence market. However, compromise also implies that various initiatives taken at the EU level will not hold the political force required to fundamentally alter the nature of the European defence market. It should not occasion any surprise to learn of the limits of the EDA or the 'defence package', for governments used the EU decision-making process to manufacture institutions and legislation that would institutionally and legally embed the constellation of national preferences.

Of course, this situation drastically reduces the room that EU institutions such as the European Commission have to create a genuine single European market for defence. One of the obvious responses to the prevailing intergovernmental logic in defence is to increase the role of supranational institutions. Thus, one could argue that a supranational response to industrial cooperation and capability development could be found. There are obvious limits to what the EDA – as an intergovernmental agency – can achieve when it is entirely beholden to EU member state governments for initiatives and progress. Another obvious response to the underwhelming effect of the 'defence package' would be to move from secondary law such as directives to regulations. The logic here would be that the fact that directives need to be transposed into national law provides EU member state governments with more room to adapt legislation. A regulation would have direct effect in the member states and thus supranational oversight and governance would be far more effective. Yet such solutions do not pay clear enough attention to the important political dynamics that contribute to EU defence industrial cooperation. No single EU member state is willing at present to empower institutions such as the European Commission with supranational authority over national DTIBs. What is more, such a situation would assume that institutions such as the European Commission are able to think and act in a strategic manner about the European defence market and defence more broadly. During our study of the 2003–2009 period, little suggests that the EU member states are willing to transfer their defence planning, capability development priorities and supply chain management to the EU level.

Such grand schemes may not even be necessary, however, as shifting structural factors are yet again leading to responses at the EU level. For example, the next 5–10 years of EU-level defence industrial cooperation are likely to be coloured by the UK's 2016 decision to leave the EU and the role that could be played by EU funding for defence research and capability programmes. With the UK's departure from the EU there can be little doubt that there will be an impact on Europe's defence sector. As the three example studies in this book show, the UK has played a pivotal role in pushing for policy outcomes that have favoured open defence markets, transparent procurement processes, a ban on defence offsets and non-discrimination against non-EU states such as the United States. Along with several other EU states such as Poland, Portugal, Spain and Sweden, the UK has attempted to tame the pace and nature of EU defence industrial cooperation. The future of the EDTIB without the UK rightly raises numerous questions. Whether one should continue to include UK industry in the EDTIB is the most obvious one. Here, a less certain issue will be what happens to the liberalising agenda of certain member states. While countries such as Germany and Sweden may continue to support managed liberalisation, one of the stalwarts behind keeping Europe's defence market open looks likely to have a greatly diminished role in, and say over, the future direction of EU defence industrial policy. In terms of any future defence industrial policy initiatives, one might wonder what the constellation of preferences in the EU will look like minus the UK.

The absence of the UK should not automatically lead to the idea that a 'Buy European' act or 'European Preference' will now emerge. It is perhaps tempting to assume that with the UK outside of the EU, it will be possible for the remaining EU member states to erect a sort of 'Fortress Europe'. However, the empirical investigation offered in this book has highlighted that the fault line between market liberalisation and protectionism runs through all EU member states. The UK was not alone in opposing protectionist tendencies from emerging in EU defence industrial policy, but with the UK's departure it does – at least in theory – become easier for a protectionist ethos to gain ground. Much will depend on how the UK's departure from the EU will affect defence policy. It is no secret that with the UK's departure the EU will be less capable in military terms, and one of the major initiators of the CSDP will no longer be able to directly affect the future direction of this policy. Defining a new EU level of ambition on defence will be vital if the right sorts of signals to industry are to be made in the future, although governments will find it difficult to willingly agree to policy that questions their link to national DTIBs.

Let us recall that the (partial) impetus for an EDTIB emerged on the back of the creation of the CSDP. This is not to say that the EDTIB cannot survive without the CSDP. Industry has never placed much importance in the CSDP as a vehicle through which European industry can make up shortfalls in demand and defence spending incurred at the national level. To put it rather frankly, the CSDP has evolved into a largely civilian enterprise that can hardly be expected to whet the appetite of Europe's defence industry; especially when NATO has been emboldened after Russia's seizure of Crimea and demand for weapons technologies in the Middle East and the Asia-Pacific is on the rise. Yet this is not to say that the CSDP is unimportant, for it is the only policy mechanism through which EU member state governments can collectively discuss the EU's military level of ambition and appropriate level of strategic autonomy. Without the CSDP it is difficult for the EU to have a serious common discussion about the capabilities it requires in the future and what industry can do to support EU defence. Serious questions will now justifiably be asked about the future of CSDP considering the UK's departure from the EU.

The dawning of new forms of cooperation?

In this respect, it is important to see how the remaining members of the EU have reacted to the UK's decision to leave the Union. A flurry of initiatives and statements has been released to this effect, all designed to capitalise on a 'window of opportunity' that has opened since 23 June 2016. Indeed, on 26 June 2016 the then foreign ministers of France and Germany, Jean-Marc Ayrault and Frank-Walter Steinmeier respectively, released a joint paper (2016) calling for a 'European Security Compact' which would, among other things, help Europe support an innovative defence industry. In September 2016, the then Italian foreign and defence ministers – Paolo Gentiloni and Roberta Pinotti respectively – called for a 'Schengen for Defence'[1] which would aim to spearhead defence and defence industrial cooperation among a core grouping of European states either through Permanent Structured Cooperation or outside the EU treaty framework altogether, if necessary (Gentiloni 2016). As if to compete with these suggestions, even the then former German finance minister – Wolfgang Schäuble – argued that the EU should have a joint 'defence budget' (Wagstyl 2016).

Not to be outdone, within only a few days of the UK referendum result the HR/VP Federica Mogherini published the 2016 EU Global Strategy. Apart from its clear plea for European unity, the Global Strategy reiterated that a 'sustainable, innovative and competitive European defence industry is essential for Europe's strategic autonomy and for a credible CSDP' (European Union Global Strategy 2016: 46). The IPSD that followed on from the EU Global Strategy in November 2016 took this sobriquet much further. The IPSD called no less for a wider EU 'Innovation Initiative' to be developed that would manage disruptive technologies; it confirmed that the EDA would revise the EU's Capability Development Plan in 2018 and it called for an alignment of member state defence R&T efforts and defence planning through a CARD. The European Parliament also contributed to the debate with a report calling for a 'European Defence Union' in which Europeans would work to develop a single drone industry and strategies to encourage the joint development of defence equipment (European Parliament 2016). Based solely on these documents, the EU institutions and some member states seemed to be prepared to take a quantum leap forward on defence.

Such initiatives are to be expected in the wake of a history-making event such as 'Brexit', but one would do well to question whether these initiatives will break the pattern and style of cooperation described in this book. What was evident from the three case studies in this book is that governments have a clear interest in preserving the pre-eminence of the bargaining process and ensuring that EU efforts do not question their privileged relationships with defence firms or their ability to plan for national defence. Governments understand how to 'play' the bargaining game within the Council and during the co-decision process, as this allows governments to manage the pace of EU cooperation while also reaffirming their importance vis-à-vis national defence firms. As we have seen with the establishment of the EDA and the adoption of the 'defence package', cooperation does not necessarily entail closer integration. This may lead one to question whether EU integration in the defence sector is possible without a dramatic change in the 'rules' of the bargaining process that have been used to negotiate EU defence industrial policy thus far. A question is whether, since 'Brexit', the remaining EU member state governments are interested in altering the policymaking process at the EU level.

Here it is worth considering new EU defence initiatives such as the CARD and PESCO and whether they signal a step change in EU defence industrial cooperation. Initially conceived of as a 'European semester on defence' (to mirror the EU's economic policy equivalent), the CARD is designed to ensure that individual national defence plans are coordinated at the EU level. EU member states recognised that there is a need to 'deepen defence cooperation and ensure more optimal use, including coherence, of defence spending plans' (Council of the European Union, 2016b). Under CARD, the idea is for national defence planners to share information with fellow EU member states on their budgetary planning cycles and future capability/technology plans. Despite this ambitious idea, however, CARD will remain voluntary in nature and guided by the EDA. One has to ask whether a voluntary scheme that is managed by an intergovernmental agency will lead to a comprehensive leap forward in EU defence cooperation. Based on the experiences outlined in this book, the CARD reflects a trade-off between the need to cooperate at the EU level but to do so by protecting national sovereignty.

Furthermore, the political dynamics involved in PESCO do not deviate from the logic of intergovernmentalism that has been so prevalent over the 2003–2009 period. Accordingly, in December 2017, 25 member states joined PESCO and they accepted to adhere to 20 binding commitments and to join a first wave of 17 capability projects. The aim of PESCO is to raise defence spending in a concerted manner, develop military capabilities jointly, and make their military assets available for operations. However, whereas joining PESCO is voluntary, the binding commitments and projects will be subject to regular assessment by the HR/VP with the support of the EDA and the EEAS. Compared with previous EU efforts in the defence domain, the added value of PESCO comes from the combination of the nature of commitments that member states will make, the accountability that the framework creates for member states and the permanence of the framework. Nevertheless, PESCO does not fundamentally alter the principally intergovernmental nature of defence industrial cooperation at the EU level.

A 'game changer'?

However, one of the more promising policy initiatives to have been tabled since 'Brexit' has been the European Commission's 'European Defence Fund'. This idea relates to the use of financial incentives as a catalyst for closer EU defence cooperation. The fund will be divided between interlocking funding 'windows'. A 'research window' will see the European Commission make available 100 per cent of the eligible costs for collaborative European defence research programmes. Financial support to the tune of €90 million will initially be provided by the EU budget under a Preparatory Action on Defence Research (PADR) from 2017 to 2020. In the post-2020 period the Commission hopes to establish an EDRP worth an estimated €500 million per year as part of the next Multiannual Financial Framework. The 'research window' will be accompanied by a 'capability window', which will focus on the joint development and procurement of defence capabilities. Under this window, the Commission would fund approximately 20 per cent of the eligible costs of production with the remaining 80 per cent coming from pooled national contributions. This co-financing will amount to €500 million over 2019–2020 and from 2020 onwards this amount could climb to €1 billion per year. These incentives are clearly designed to move beyond a strictly intergovernmental approach to defence cooperation in the EU and they may add to the nature of EU defence industrial cooperation (as it has thus far been understood in this book) in interesting ways.

First, direct EU funding for defence research and capability development raises questions about how the EU can and will balance a desire for greater autarky in defence while also ensuring an efficient market (Moravcsik 1991: 23). For example, co-financing defence projects will give institutions such as the Commission and EDA an increased voice over what capabilities are prioritised and developed. In effect, this forces these institutions into new terrain because they have hitherto not had to think seriously about military strategy (i.e. why do you need a piece of defence equipment and for what type of conflict). Furthermore, funding defence research and joint capability programmes out of the EU budget means that the European Commission, Council and the Parliament will face a challenge that is all too familiar to governments but not perhaps to EU institutions – that is, how many 'guns' and how much 'butter' does the EU want? This dilemma may force EU institutions to become far more strategic than is presently the case.

The role that financial incentives could well play in the next stage of EU defence industrial cooperation invites a branch of theoretical reflection on EU defence industrial cooperation. Existing theories do not consider what role financial incentives could play in augmenting the formation of domestic preferences, altering the nature of intergovernmental bargaining and/or enhancing the role of EU institutions. Liberal intergovernmentalism is, for one, blind to the effect of financial incentives. In this regard, there exist whole branches of scholarly research on the positive and negative effects of financial incentives on policy processes and agent behaviour (see Crumm 1995; Gneezy, Meier and Rey-Biel 2011; Bowles and Polanía-Reyes 2012). One of the important reasons why future research should consider the relevance of financial incentives is that it points to much more policy innovation on the part of EU institutions such as the European Commission. It is as though the Commission has recognised that financial incentives may overcome the tentative and sometimes reluctant approaches to EU defence industrial cooperation taken by the EU member states.

While financial incentives may add an interesting dynamic to intergovernmental cooperation on defence industrial matters, however, one should not overestimate the extent to which governments will want to increasingly rely on EU funding in the defence sector. The introduction of financial incentives may eventually question the delicate link that governments have to domestic firms, so one must proceed with caution because by using resources from the EU budget the European Commission is effectively creating economic demand. This is especially so in the domain of defence research where the Commission will become the EU's fourth largest investor in defence research behind France, Germany and the UK. One should ask whether each member state government will feel comfortable with the Commission playing this type of role. Yet there are already many mechanisms by which governments can control the use of financial incentives. One should recall that the EU budget is based on national financial contributions – the budget is not some bottomless treasure trove, but is built on the already limited financial resources of the member states. In this respect, while financial incentives should be studied as an increasingly interesting element of EU defence industrial cooperation, one should proceed on the understanding that governments will not want these initiatives to imperil their privileged links to industry or their ability to control national DTIBs.

This book has made the case that EU defence industrial policy processes have been designed to reinforce national DTIBs and to bolster the link between governments and national industry. Given the pressures that relate to defence globalisation, EU policy and legislation have effectively allowed governments to reaffirm and enhance their relevance in the defence sector and in the eyes of their firms. Whether this situation is of benefit to the EU is unclear, although a political process that leads to the emboldening of national governments does not necessarily lead to a sustainable defence industry in Europe. One often hears that Europe's defence market is fragmented, and this reflects a continued impulse on the part of governments to ensure national – rather than European – strategic autonomy. This logic may not appear wise in a market context in which economies of scale are important and where being able to afford sophisticated defence technologies relies on a level of investment that is increasingly difficult to achieve on a purely national basis. The period studied in this book has shown how governments are not ready to embrace a higher level of liberalisation or EU-level regulation. Governments do not yet want to radically alter the privileged relationship they have with defence firms.

Note

1 This title is not designed to confuse the reader. The Schengen Zone of course refers to the free movement of people, but Italy used the 'Schengen for Defence' concept to denote the fact that Schengen had originally been established outside the formal structures of the EU but was then steadily migrated under EU structures. Italy's proposal suggests a similar path for European defence cooperation.

Bibliography

Aalto, E. (2008) 'Interpretations of Article 296', in D. Keohane (ed.) *Towards a European Defence Market*, Chaillot Paper, No. 113 (Paris: EU Institute for Security Studies): 13–49. See: www.iss.europa.eu/uploads/media/cp113.pdf.

Aben, J. (1992) *Économie politique de la defence* (Paris: Éditions Cujas).

Aberbach, J.D. and Rockman, B.A. (2002) 'Conducting and Coding Elite Interviews', *Political Science and Politics*, 35(4): 669–672.

Adams, W. (1968) 'The Military-Industrial Complex and the New Industrial State', *The American Economic Review*, 58(2): 652–665.

ADS Group (2014) 'ADS Response to the Call for Evidence on the Government's Review of the Balance of Competences between the United Kingdom and the European Union'. See: www.gov.uk/government/uploads/system/uploads/attachment_data/file/224229/evidence-ads.pdf.

ADS Group (2012) 'UK Aerospace Survey 2012'. See: www.weaf.co.uk/filemanager/userfiles/files/AerospaceSurvey_web_2012-v6.pdf.

Advisory Council on International Affairs (2012) 'European Defence Cooperation: Sovereignty and the Capacity to Act', No. 78. See: http://aiv-advies.nl/6cv/publications/advisory-reports/european-defence-cooperation-sovereignty-and-the-capacity-to-act.

AIAD (2005) 'Relazione Esercizio 2004'. See: www.vita.it/static/upload/attach/news/57807.pdf.

Airbus Group (2016) 'Shareholding Structure'. See: www.airbusgroup.com/int/en/investors-shareholders/Share-information.html#chapter-01.

Airbus Group (2014) 'Airbus Group Submission on EU-UK Balance of Competences'. See: www.gov.uk/government/uploads/system/uploads/attachment_data/file/332665/free-movement-of-services-competence-review-evidence-public-responses.pdf.

Airbus Group (2013) 'Annual Report 2013'. See: www.airbusgroup.com/dam/assets/airbusgroup/int/en/investor-relations/documents/2014/Closings/Airbus-Group-Financial-Statements-2013/Airbus%20Group%20Financial%20Statements%202013%20(short%20notes).pdf.

Airbus Group (2000) 'Annual Report 2000'. See: www.airbusgroup.com/dam/assets/airbusgroup/int/en/investor-relations/documents/2000/annual-report/en/EADS-annual-report-2000/EADS%20annual%20report%202000.pdf.

Aldrich, R.J. (2004) 'Transatlantic Intelligence and Security Cooperation', *International Affairs*, 80(4): 731–753.

Alexander, M. and Garden, T. (2001) 'The Arithmetic of Defence Policy', *International Affairs*, 77(3): 509–529.

Alfonso-Meiriño, A. (2010) 'The Establishment of the European Defence Agency', in Spanish Ministry of Defence (ed.) *European Defence Agency: Past, Present and Future* (Madrid: Ministry of Defence): 19–60. See: www.portalcultura.mde.es/Galerias/publicaciones/fichero/European_Defence.pdf.

Alic, J.A. (1986) 'The Federal Role in Commercial Technology Development', *Technovation*, 4(4): 253–267.

Allin, D.H. (2016) 'Donald Trump's America', *Survival: Global Politics and Strategy*, 58(2): 221–228.

Al-Yousif, Y.K. (2002) 'Defense Spending and Economic Growth: Some Empirical Evidence from the Arab Gulf Region', *Defence and Peace Economics*, 13(3): 187–197.

Andersson, H.E. (2016) 'Liberal Intergovernmentalism, Spillover and Supranational Immigration Policy', *Cooperation and Conflict*, 51(1): 38–54.

Andersson, J.J. (2012) 'Defence Industry and Technology: The Base for a More Capable Europe', in S. Biscop and R.G. Whitman (eds.) *The Routledge Handbook of European Security* (Oxon/New York: Routledge): 105–114.

Anthony, I. (1998) 'Politics and Economics of Defence Industries in a Changing World', in E. Inbar and B. Zilberfarb (eds.) *The Politics and Economics of Defence Industries* (Oxon/New York: Routledge): 1–28.

Art, R.J. (1991) 'A Defensible Defense: America's Grand Strategy after the Cold War', *International Security*, 15(4): 5–53.

ASD Europe (2016) 'Facts and Figures 2015'. See: www.asd-europe.org/sites/default/files/atoms/files/ASD_F_F2015_web_spreads_Nov.pdf.

ASD Europe (2015) 'Open Letter to the Presidents of the European Institutions and the Heads of State and Government of the European Union'. See: www.asd-europe.org/fileadmin/user_upload/Client_documents/ASD_Contents/2_COMMUNICATION/2.2_Press_Releases/ASD_Open_Letter.pdf.

ASD Europe (2013) 'Facts and Figures 2012'. See: www.asd-europe.org/fileadmin/user_upload/Client_documents/ASD_Contents/2_COMMUNICATION/2.5_Publications/2.5.2_Facts_and_Figures/ASD_Facts_and_Figures_2012.pdf.

ASD Europe (2007) 'ASD Broadly Welcomes the European Commission's Defence Directives'. See: www.defense-aerospace.com/articles-view/release/3/88856/industry,-eda-broadly-support-eu's-defense-proposals.html.

Ashley, R.K. (1984) 'The Poverty of Neorealism', *International Organization*, 38(2): 225–286.

Aspaturian, V.V. (1972) 'The Soviet Military–Industrial "Complex": Does it Exist?', *Journal of International Affairs*, 26(1): 1–28.

Augustine, N.R. (1982) *Augustine's Laws and Major System Development Programs* (Reston, VA: American Institute of Aeronautics and Astronautics).

Bach, L., Conde-Molist, N., Ledoux, M.-J., Matt, M. and Schaeffer, V. (1995) 'Evaluation of the Economic Effects of BRITE-EURAM Programmes on the European Industry', *Scientometrics*, 34(3): 325–349.

BAE Systems (2015) 'Strategic Report: 2014 at a Glance'. See: http://investors.baesystems.com/~/media/Files/B/Bae-Systems-Investor-Relations-V3/Annual%20Reports/bae-annual-report-2014.pdf.

BAE Systems (2014) 'Balance of Competences: Single Market: Free Movement of Services Review Defence Procurement'. See: www.gov.uk/government/uploads/system/uploads/attachment_data/file/332668/bis-14-987-free-movement-of-services-balance-of-competencies-report.pdf.

Bailer, S. (2010) 'What Factors Determine Bargaining Power and Success in EU Negotiations?', *Journal of European Public Policy*, 17(5): 743–757.

Baldwin, D.A. (1985) *Economic Statecraft* (Princeton, NJ: Princeton University Press).

Balis, C. and Heidenkamp, H. (2014) 'Prospects for the European Defence Industrial Base', *Occasional Paper* (London: Royal United Services Institute). See: https://rusi.org/sites/default/files/201409_prospects_for_the_edib.pdf.

Ball, N. (1986) 'Converting the Workforce: Defence Industry Conversion in the Industrialised Countries', *International Labour Review*, 125(4): 401–422.

Bangert, D., Davies, N. and Watson, R. (2017) 'Managing Defence Acquisition Cost Growth', *The RUSI Journal*, 162(1): 60–67.

Barrinha, A. (2010) 'Moving Towards a European Defence Industry? The Political Discourse on a Changing Reality and its Implications for the Future of the European Union', *Global Society*, 24(4): 467–485.

Bates, P. (1990) 'Defence Technology in Western Europe', in J.D. Drown, C. Drown and K. Campbell (eds.) *A Single European Arms Industry? European Defence Industries in the 1990s* (Oxford/New York: Brassey's): 97–120.

Bátora, J. (2009) 'European Defence Agency: A Flashpoint of Institutional Logics', *West European Politics*, 32(6): 1075–1098.

Baumgartner, F.R. and Jones, B.D. (2009) *Agendas and Instability in American Politics* (Chicago, IL: The University of Chicago Press).

BDSV (2013) 'Defence Exports'. See: www.bdsv.eu.

Beffa, J.-L. (2005) *Pour une nouvelle politique industrielle* (Paris: La documentation française).

Behr, T. and Siwiecki, A. (2004) 'EU Enlargement and Armaments: Defence Industries and Markets of the Visegrad Countries', *Occasional Paper*, No. 54 (Paris: EU Institute for Security Studies). See: www.iss.europa.eu/fr/publications/detail-page/article/eu-enlargement-and-armaments-defence-industries-and-markets-of-the-visegrad-countries/.

Belgian Government (2014) *The Value of the Belgian Defence* (Brussels: Federal Ministry of Defence). See: www.mil.be/sites/mil.be/files/files_library/waarde_belgische_defensie_-_uk.pdf.

Belgian Government (2008) *Policy on Industrial Participation in Defence Contracts* (Brussels: Federal Public Service for the Economy, SMEs, Self-Employed and Energy). See: http://economie.fgov.be/en/modules/publications/general/politique_industrielle_de_la_participation_dans_le_cadre_des_commandes_de_defense.jsp.

Belgian Government (2003) *Plan Directeur de la Défense* (Brussels: Federal Ministry of Defence). See: www.operationspaix.net/DATA/DOCUMENT/7885~v~Plan_directeur_de_la_Defense.pdf.

Bellais, R. (2013) 'Technology and the Defense Industry: Real Threats, Bad Habits, or New (Market) Opportunities?', *Journal of Innovation Economics & Management*, 12: 59–78.

Bellais, R. (2011) 'Restructuration et coopération, l'avenir des industries de défense française?', *Géoéconomie*, 57(2): 109–119.

Bellais, R. (2000) *Production d'Armes et Puissance des Nations* (Paris: L'Harmattan).

Bellais, R. and Droff, J. (2013) 'La nécessaire réorganisation de l'industrie de défense en Europe', *Revue Défense Nationale*, Comité d'études de défense nationale (Paris): 47–52. See: https://hal-ensta-bretagne.archives-ouvertes.fr/hal-01016989.

Bellais, R. and Guichard, R. (2006) 'Defense Innovation, Technology Transfers and Public Policy', *Defence and Peace Economics*, 17(3): 273–286.

Bellais, R., Foucault, M. and Oudot, J.-M. (2014) *Économie de la défense* (Paris: La Découverte).

Benes, V. and Karlas, J. (2010) 'The Czech Presidency', *Journal of Common Market Studies*, 48(S1): 69–80.

Benoit, E. (1978) 'Growth and Defense in Developing Countries', *Economic Development and Cultural Change*, 26(2): 271–280.

Béraud-Sudreau, L. (2015a) *The Extra-EU Defence Exports' Effects on European Armaments Cooperation* (Brussels: European Parliament). See: www.europarl.europa.eu/RegData/etudes/STUD/2015/549043/EXPO_STU(2015)549043_EN.pdf.

Béraud-Sudreau, L. (2015b) 'La France et la cooperation européenne sur le contrôle des exportations d'armement: l'adaptation aux mutations de l'économie de defense comme résultat de rapports de force domestiques', in F. d'Aude-Emmanuelle (ed.) *Quelles stratégies face aux mutations de l'économie de defense mondiale?* (Paris: Institut de recherche stratégique de l'École militaire): 42–55. See: www.defense.gouv.fr/content/download/367793/5349853/file/etude_irsem_n38.pdf.

Béraud-Sudreau, L. (2014) 'French Adaptation Strategies for Arms Export Controls since the 1990s', *Paris Papers*, No. 10 (Paris: Institut de recherche stratégique de l'École militaire). See: www.defense.gouv.fr/content/download/305828/4086800/file/Paris_paper_n%C2%B010_En.pdf.

Bertelli, A.M. and John, P. (2013) 'Public Policy Investment: Risk and Return in British Politics', *British Journal of Political Science*, 43(4): 741–773.

Betts, R.K. (1997) 'Should Strategic Studies Survive?', *World Politics*, 50(1): 7–33.

Bickerton, C., Hodson, D. and Puetter, U. (2015a) 'The New Intergovernmentalism: European Integration in the Post-Maastricht Era', *Journal of Common Market Studies*, 53(4): 703–722.

Bickerton, C., Hodson, D. and Puetter, U. (2015b) 'Something New: A Rejoinder to Frank Schimmelfennig on the New Intergovernmentalism', *Journal of Common Market Studies*, 53(4): 731–736.

Bickerton, C., Hodson, D. and Puetter, U. (2015c) *The New Intergovernmentalism: States and Supranational Actors in the Post-Maastricht Era* (Oxford: Oxford University Press).

Bickerton, C., Irondelle, B. and Menon, A. (2011) 'Security Co-operation Beyond the Nation-State: The EU's Common Security and Defence Policy', *Journal of Common Market Studies*, 49(1): 1–21.

Bieler, A. and Morton, A.D. (2001) 'The Gordian Knot of Agency-Structure in International Relations: A Neo-Gramscian Perspective', *European Journal of International Relations*, 7(1): 5–35.

Bigo, D. and Jeandesboz, J. (2008) *Review of Security Measures in the 6th Research Framework Programme and the Preparatory Action for Security Research* (Brussels: European Parliament). See: www.europarl.europa.eu/RegData/etudes/etudes/join/2008/393289/IPOL-LIBE_ET(2008)393289_EN.pdf.

Bijker, W., Hughes, T.P. and Pinch, T. (2012) (eds.) *The Social Construction of Technological Systems: New Directions in the Sociology and History of Technology* (Cambridge, MA: MIT Press).

Bischak, G. (1999) 'Contending Security Doctrines and the Military Industrial Base', in A.R. Markusen and S. Costigan (eds.) *Arming the Future: A Defence Industry for the 21st Century* (New York: Council on Foreign Relations Press): 37–73.

Biscop, S. (2018) 'European Defence: Give PESCO a Chance', *Survival: Global Politics and Strategy*, 60(3): 161–180.

Biscop, S. (2016) 'All or Nothing? The EU Global Strategy and Defence Policy after the Brexit', *Contemporary Security Policy*, 37(3): 431–445.

Biscop, S. (2015) *Peace without Money, War without Americans: Can European Strategy Cope?* (Farnham/Burlington, VT: Ashgate).

Biscop, S. (2011) 'Permanent Structured Cooperation and the Future of the ESDP: Transformation and Integration', *European Foreign Affairs Review*, 13(4): 431–448.

Biscop, S. (2005) *The European Security Strategy: A Global Agenda for Positive Power* (Farnham: Ashgate Publishing).

Biscop, S. and Andersson, J.J. (2008) 'Introduction', in S. Biscop and J.J. Andersson (eds.) *The EU and the European Security Strategy: Forging a Global Europe* (London/New York: Routledge): 1–4.

Biscop, S. and Coelmont, J. (2013) 'Military CSDP: The Quest for Capability', in S. Biscop and R.G. Whitman (eds.) *The Routledge Handbook on European Security* (London/New York: Routledge): 78–90.

Bishop, P. (2003a) 'Competition and Collaboration in the Provision of Public Services: The Case of the UK Defence Sector', *Journal of Finance and Management in Public Services*, 3(1): 13–24.

Bishop, P. (2003b) 'Collaboration and Firm Size: Some Evidence from the UK Defence Industry', *Applied Economics*, 35(18): 1965–1969.

Bishop, P. (1995) 'Diversification: Some Lessons from the UK Defence Industry', *Management Decision*, 33(1): 58–62.

Bitzinger, R.A. (2017) *Arming Asia: Technonationalism and its Impact on Local Defense Industries* (London/New York: Routledge).

Bitzinger, R.A. (2009) 'The European Defense Industry in the 21st Century', in R.A. Bitzinger (ed.) *The Modern Defense Industry: Political, Economic and Technological Issues* (Santa Barbara, CA: Praeger Security International): 175–195.

Bitzinger, R.A. (1999) 'Globalization in the Post-Cold War Defence Industry: Challenges and Opportunities', in A.R. Markusen and S. Costigan (eds.) *Arming the Future: A Defence Industry for the 21st Century* (New York: Council on Foreign Relations Press): 305–333.

Bitzinger, R.A. (1994) 'The Globalization of the Arms Industry: The Next Proliferation Challenge', *International Security*, 19(2): 170–198.

Black, J. (2013) *War and Technology* (Bloomington/Indianapolis, IN: Indiana University Press).

Blauberger, M. (2009) 'Of "Good" and "Bad" Subsidies: European State Aid Control through Soft and Hard Law', *West European Politics*, 32(4): 719–737.

Blauberger, M. and Weiss, M. (2013) '"If you can't beat me, join me!" How the Commission Pushed and Pulled Member States into Legislating Defence Procurement', *Journal of European Public Policy*, 20(8): 1120–1138.

Bleich, E. and Pekkanen, R. (2013) 'How to Report Interview Data', in L. Mosley (ed.) *Interview Research in Political Science* (Ithaca, NY/London: Cornell University Press): 84–108.

Blunden, M., Bissell, C. and Monk, J. (1989) 'Policy Making in Civil and Military Electronics: the Limits of Pragmatism', in M. Blunden and O. Greene (eds.) *Science and Mythology in the Making of Defence Policy* (London: Brassey's): 167–204.

Bowles, S. and Polanía-Reyes, S. (2012) 'Economic Incentives and Social Preferences: Substitutes of Complements?', *Journal of Economic Literature*, 50(2): 368–425.

Brandl, R. (2011) 'Die wichtigste Voraussetzung für die Umsetzung der Richtlinie 2009/43/EG ist für mich daher, dass die Mitgliedstaaten die Kontrolle über ihre eigenen Rüstungsexportkriterien behalten'. See: www.cducsu.de/themen/sicherheitspolitik/

die-wichtigste-voraussetzung-fuer-die-umsetzung-der-richtlinie-200943-eg-ist-fuer-mich-daher-dass-die-mitgliedstaaten-die.

Brauer, J. and Dunne, J-P. (2004) 'Introduction', in J. Brauer and J.-P. Dunne (eds.) *Arms Trade and Economic Development: Theory, Policy and Cases in Arms Trade Offsets* (London/New York: Routledge): 1–19.

Breant, C. and Karock, U. (2011) 'Defence and Security Research: Coexistence, Coherence and Convergence', in K. Thoma (ed.) *European Perspectives on Security Research* (Berlin: Springer): 55–66.

Breeze, R. (2011) 'Critical Discourse Analysis and its Critics', *Pragmatics*, 21(4): 493–525.

Breuer, F. (2006) 'Between Ambitions and Financial Constraints: The Reform of the German Armed Forces', *German Politics*, 15(2): 206–220.

Briani, V. (2013a) *The Costs of Non-Europe in the Defence Field* (Rome: Instituto Affari Internazionali). See: www.iai.it/sites/default/files/CSF-IAI_noneuropedefence_april 2013.pdf.

Briani, V. (2013b) 'Armaments Duplication in Europe: A Quantitative Assessment', *CEPS Policy Brief*, No. 297 (Brussels: Centre for European Policy Studies). See: www.ceps.eu/publications/armaments-duplication-europe-quantitative-assessment.

Briani, V. (2009) 'L'industria della difesa italiana', *Osservatorio di Politica Internazionale*, No. 3 (Rome: Instituto Affari Internazionali). See: www.iai.it/sites/default/files/pi_n_0003.pdf.

Briani, V., Marrone, A., Mölling, C. and Valasek, T. (2013) *The Development of a European Defence Technological and Industrial Base* (Brussels: European Parliament). See: www.europarl.europa.eu/RegData/etudes/etudes/join/2013/433838/EXPO-SEDE_ET(2013)433838_EN.pdf.

Britz, M. (2010) 'The Role of Marketization in the Europeanization of Defence Industry Policy', *Bulletin of Science, Technology and Society*, 30(3): 176–184.

Britz, M. and Eriksson, A. (2008) 'Analyzing the EU's Shared Strategy', in K. Englebrekt and J. Hallenberg (eds.) *The European Union and Strategy: An Emerging Actor* (Oxon/New York: Routledge): 56–70.

Bromley, M. (2011) 'The EU Common Position on Arms Exports and National Export Control Policies', in A.J.K. Bailes and S. Depauw (eds.) *The EU Defence Market: Balancing Effectiveness with Responsibility* (Brussels: Flemish Peace Institute): 39–46.

Bromley, M. and Brzoska, M. (2008) 'Towards a Common, Restrictive EU Arms Export Policy? The Impact of the EU Code of Conduct on Major Conventional Arms Exports', *European Foreign Affairs Review*, 13(3): 333–356.

Broomfield, N. (2000) *The Defence Industrial Base: European Rationalisation and Transatlantic Cooperation* (Chipping Norton: Ditchley Foundation). See: www.ditchley.co.uk/conferences/past-programme/2000-2009/2000/defence-industrial-base.

Bruff, I. (2010) 'European Varieties of Capitalism and the International', *European Journal of International Relations*, 16(4): 615–638.

Brune, S.-C., Dickow, M., Linnenkamp, H. and Mölling, C. (2010) 'The German Armed Forces and the Financial Crisis: Towards National Restructuring and European Economies of Scale', *SWP Comments*, No. 13 (Berlin: Stiftung Wissenschaft und Politik). See: www.files.ethz.ch/isn/117331/2010_German_Forces_Finances_E.pdf.

Brzoska, M., Wilke, P. and Wulf, H. (1999) 'The Changing Civil-Military Production Mix in Western Europe's Defense Industry', in A.R. Markusen and S. Costigan (eds.) *Arming the Future: A Defense Industry for the 21st Century* (New York: Council on Foreign Relations Press): 371–408.

Bulmer, S. (2008) 'Theorizing Europeanization', in P. Graziano and M.P. Vink (eds.) *Europeanization: New Research Agendas* (Basingstoke/New York: Palgrave Macmillan): 46–58.

Bundesverband der Deutschen Industrie (2013) 'Grundsatzpapier: Sicherheit für das Industrieland Deutschland'. See: http://bdi.eu/media/presse/publikationen/sicherheit-und-verteidigung/32782_BDI_Sicherheit_5.pdf.

Butler, C. (2005) 'Changes in Industry Structure and Competition: The Use of Strategic Alliances by UK Defence Manufacturing Firms', *Strategic Change*, 14: 15–24.

Butler, C., Kenny, B. and Anchor, J. (2000) 'Strategic Alliances in the European Defence Industry', *European Business Review*, 12(6): 308–322.

Calleja-Crespo, D. and Delsaux, P. (2012) 'Defending European Defence: The Commission's Role', *BEPA Monthly Brief*, No. 54 (Brussels: Bureau of European Policy Advisors). See: http://ec.europa.eu/internal_market/publicprocurement/docs/defence/task_force/article_defending_european_defence_en.pdf.

Caporaso, J. (1996) 'The European Union and Forms of State: Westphalian, Regulatory, or Post-Modern?', *Journal of Common Market Studies*, 34(1): 29–52.

Caruso, R. and Locatelli, A. (2011) 'Some Recent Development in Italian Defence Industry (with a Special Focus on Finmeccanica Group)', *European Integration Online Papers*. See: http://citeseerx.ist.psu.edu/viewdoc/summary?doi=10.1.1.168.4061.

Castellacci, F. and Fevolden, A.M. (2014) 'Capable Companies or Changing Markets? Explaining the Export Performance of Firms in the Defence Industry', *Defence and Peace Economics*, 25(6): 549–575.

Castellacci, F., Fevolden, A.M. and Lundmark, M. (2014) 'How are Defence Companies Responding to EU Defence and Security Market Liberalization? A Comparative Study of Norway and Sweden', *Journal of European Public Policy*, 21(8): 1218–1235.

Caverley, J.D. (2007) 'United States Hegemony and the New Economics of Defense', *Security Studies*, 16(4): 598–614.

Cevasco, F. (2009) 'Export Controls and their Relationship to National Defence Industries', in R.A. Bitzinger (ed.) *The Modern Defense Industry: Political, Economic and Technological Issues* (Santa Barbara, CA: Praeger Security International): 243–256.

Chang, T., Lee, C.-C. and Chu, H.-P. (2015) 'Revisiting the Defense-Growth Nexus in European Countries', *Defence and Peace Economics*, 26(3): 341–356.

Chang, F-C. (2011) 'European Defence Agency: Motor of Strengthening the EU's Military Capabilities?', *European Foreign Affairs Review*, 16(1): 59–87.

Child, J. (1972) 'Organization Structure, Environment and Performance: The Role of Strategic Choice', *Sociology*, 6(1): 1–22.

Cini, M. (2001) 'The Soft Law Approach: Commission Rule-Making in the EU's State Aid Regime', *Journal of European Public Policy*, 8(2): 192–207.

Coase, R. (1937) 'The Nature of the Firm', *Economica*, 4(16): 386–405.

Coen, D. and Dannreuther, C. (2003) 'Differentiated Europeanization: Large and Small Firms in the EU Policy Process', in K. Featherstone and C. Radaelli (eds.) *The Politics of Europeanization* (Oxford: Oxford University Press): 255–277.

Cogan, C. (2001) *The Third Option: The Emancipation of European Defence, 1989–2000* (London/Westport, CT: Praeger).

Comelli, M., Di Camillo, F. and Gasparini, G. (2004) 'Prospettive della politica europea di sicurezza e difesa: le missioni e l'Agenzia europea di difesa', *Quaderni europei e internazionali*, No. 4 (Rome: Instituto Affari Internazionali): 43–54. See: www.iai.it/sites/default/files/pi_a_c_008.pdf.

Comité Richelieu (2007) *Livre Blanc: Revelons l'Excellence*. See: www.comite-richelieu.org/wp-content/uploads/2014/03/livre-blanc-2007.pdf.

Conze, H. (1995) 'France's Defence Procurement Strategy: Looking to the Future', *The RUSI Journal*, 140(2): 48–51.

Cornish, P. (2004) 'NATO: The Practice and Politics of Transformation', *International Affairs*, 80(1): 63–74.

Cornish, P. and Edwards, G. (2001) 'Beyond the EU/NATO Dichotomy: The Beginnings of a European Strategic Culture', *International Affairs*, 77(3): 587–603.

Cosidó, I. (2005) 'The Spanish Defence Industry in the Face of Sector Consolidation in Europe', *Elcano Paper*, No. 44 (Madrid: Real Instituto Elcano). See: www.realinstitutoelcano.org/analisis/725/Cosido725.pdf.

Cothier, P. and Moravcsik, A. (1991) 'Defense and the Single Market: The Outlook for Collaborative Ventures', *International Defense Review*, 24(9): 949–964.

Council of the European Union (2016a) 'Implementation Plan on Security and Defence', *14392/16*. See: www.consilium.europa.eu/en/press/press-releases/2016/11/pdf/implementation-plan-on-security-and-defence_pdf/.

Council of the European Union (2016b) 'Council Conclusions on Implementing the EU Global Strategy in the Area of Security and Defence', *14149/16*. See: www.consilium.europa.eu/en/press/press-releases/2016/11/pdf/council-conclusions-on-security-and-defence_pdf/.

Council of the European Union (2014) 'Common Military List of the European Union', *2014/C 107/01*. See: http://eur-lex.europa.eu/legal-content/EN/TXT/?uri=OJ%3AC%3A2014%3A107%3AFULL.

Council of the European Union (2013) 'Council Approves Programme in Support of SMEs', *17443/13*. See: www.consilium.europa.eu/uedocs/cms_data/docs/pressdata/en/intm/139935.pdf.

Council of the European Union (2011a) 'Council Decision 2011/411/CFSP of 12 July 2011 Defining the Statute, Seat and Operational Rules of the European Defence Agency and Repealing Joint Action 2004/551/CFSP'. See: www.eda.europa.eu/docs/documents/eda_council_decision.pdf.

Council of the European Union (2011b) 'Press Release – Environment', *15321/11*. See: www.consilium.europa.eu/uedocs/cms_data/docs/pressdata/en/envir/125030.pdf.

Council of the European Union (2009) 'Directive of the European Parliament and the Council simplifying terms and conditions of transfers of defence-related products within the Community', *10399/09*. See: http://eur-lex.europa.eu/legal-content/EN/TXT/?uri=CELEX%3A32009L0043.

Council of the European Union (2003a) 'European Security Strategy: A Secure Europe in a Better World'. See: www.consilium.europa.eu/uedocs/cmsUpload/78367.pdf.

Council of the European Union (2003b) 'Decision creating a team to prepare for the establishment of the agency in the field of defence capabilities, research, acquisition and armaments', *2003/834/EC*. See: http://eur-lex.europa.eu/legal-content/EN/TXT/?uri=CELEX%3A32003D0834.

Council of the European Union (1997) 'Definition of Specific Characteristics of the Defence-Related Sector', *Appendix to Annex I in COM(97) 583 final*. See: http://ec.europa.eu/internal_market/publicprocurement/docs/defence/com97-583-final_en.pdf.

Countertrade & Offset (2014a) 'Poland's Largest Arms Procurements Will Not Be Based on Fully Competitive Tenders: "We Will Rely on Article 346"', 32(15): 1–8. See: https://cto-offset.com/issue/1343/.

Countertrade & Offset (2014b) 'Policy Paper Defines Poland's Robust Approach to the EC', 32(1): 1–8. See: http://cto-offset.com/issue/1258/.

Cowan, R. and Foray, D. (1995) 'Quandaries in the Economics of Dual Technologies and Spillovers from Military to Civilian Research and Development', *Research Policy*, 24(6): 851–868.

Cowen, D. (2010) 'A Geography of Logistics: Market Authority and the Security of Supply Chains', *Annals of the Association of American Geographers*, 100(3): 600–620.

Crollen, E. (2003) 'Prospects for Increased Cooperation in European Defence Industry', *European Security*, 12(2): 89–98.

Cross, M.A.K.D. (2015) 'The European Defence Agency and the Member States: Public and Hidden Transcripts', *European Foreign Affairs Review*, 20(2): 83–102.

Crouch, C. (2005) 'Models of Capitalism', *New Political Economy*, 10(4): 439–456.

Crumm, E.M. (1995) 'The Value of Economic Incentives in International Politics', *Journal of Peace Research*, 32(3): 313–330.

Czech Government (2009) '2009 Annual Report on the Czech Republic's Control of Exports of Military Equipment, Small Arms for Civilian Use and Dual-Use Items and Technologies'. See: download.mpo.cz/get/35863/60932/636048/priloha006.pdf.

Damro, C. (2012) 'Market Power Europe', *Journal of European Public Policy*, 19(5): 682–699.

Darnis, J-P. (2011) 'The Role of Italy's Strategic Industries in its Foreign Policy', in G. Giacomello and B. Verbeek (eds.) *Italy's Foreign Policy in the Twenty-First Century: The New Assertiveness of an Aspiring Middle Power* (Lanham, MD/Plymouth: Lexington Books): 197–214.

Darnis, J.-P., Gasparini, G., Grams, C., Keohane, D., Liberti, F., Maulny, J.-P. and Stumbaum, M.-B. (2007) 'Lessons Learned from European Defence Equipment Programmes', *Occasional Paper*, no. 69. See: www.infoeuropa.ciejd.pt/files/database/000040001-000041000/000040967.pdf.

Dassault Aviation (2016) 'Shareholding'. See: www.dassault-aviation.com/en/dassault-aviation/finance/shareholding/.

Davis, I., Smith, J., Close, H. and Isbister, R. (2007) 'Memorandum from British American Security Information Council and Saferworld', *Written evidence to the Select Committee on Defence*, House of Commons (15 November). See: www.publications.parliament.uk/pa/cm200708/cmselect/cmquad/memo/254/ucqm0902.htm.

DCNS (2015a) 'Key Figures'. See: http://en.dcnsgroup.com/group/en-profil/en-chiffres-cles/.

DCNS (2015b) 'Governance'. See: http://en.dcnsgroup.com/group/en-profil/en-gouvernance/.

DCNS (2014) 'Financial Report 2014'. See: http://en.dcnsgroup.com/push/annual-report-2013/.

Deakin, S. (2010) 'MoD PLC: New Labour, Managerialism, Marketisation and the Privatisation of British Defence Policy', in D. Brown (ed.) *The Development of British Defence Policy: Blair, Brown and Beyond* (Farnham/Burlington, VT: Ashgate Publishers): 139–152.

Defense-Aerospace (2004) 'The New European Defence Agency – Getting Above the Clouds'. See: www.defense-aerospace.com/article-view/release/40547/euro-ceos-want-arms-agency-funding-(june-15).html.

Defense-Aerospace (2003) 'It's Time to Act'. See: www.defense-aerospace.com/articles-view/release/3/17409/euro-majors-warn-%22it's-time-to-act%22.html.

De France, O., Mampaey, L. and Zandee, D. (2016) 'Defence Industrial Policy in Belgium and the Netherlands', *ARES Group Policy Paper*, No. 7 (Paris: Institut de Relations Internationales et Stratégiques). See: www.iris-france.org/wp-content/uploads/2016/10/Policy-Paper-Defence-Policy-Belgium-NL-October-2016.pdf.

Deger, S. and Sen, S. (1990) 'Military Security and the Economy: Defence Expenditure in India and Pakistan', in K. Hartley and T. Sandler (eds.) *The Economics of Defence Spending* (London: Routledge): 189–227.

Dehoff, K., Dowdy, J. and Sung Kwon, O. (2014) *Defence Offsets: From 'Contractual Burden' to Competitive Weapon* (McKinsey & Company). See: www.mckinsey.com/industries/public-sector/our-insights/defense-offsets-from-contractual-burden-to-competitive-weapon.

De La Brosse, G. (2017) 'Deploying Financial Tools in Support of European Defence Cooperation', *ARES Group Comment*, No. 14 (Paris: French Institute for International and Strategic Affairs). See: www.iris-france.org/wp-content/uploads/2017/03/ARES-Group-Comment-G-DelaBrosse-fev-17.pdf.

Deschaux-Beaume, D. (2012) 'Investigating the Military Field: Qualitative Research Strategy and Interviewing in the Defence Networks', *Current Sociology*, 60(1): 101–117.

De Vore, M. (2015a) 'Defying Convergence: Globalisation and Varieties of Defence-Industrial Capitalism', *New Political Economy*, 20(4): 569–593.

De Vore, M. (2015b) 'Organisations at War: The EDA, NATO and the European Commission', in N. Karampekios and I. Oikonomou (eds.) *The European Defence Agency: Arming Europe* (Oxon/New York: Routledge): 171–188.

De Vore, M. (2011) 'The Arms Collaboration Dilemma: Between Principal-Agent Dynamics and Collective Action Problems', *Security Studies*, 20(4): 624–662.

De Vore, M. and Eisenecker, S. (2010) 'The Three Ages of Armaments Collaboration: Determinants of Organizational Success and Failure', *Paper prepared for the SGIR Conference 9–11 September*. See: www.eisa-net.org/be-bruga/eisa/files/events/stockholm/The%20Three%20Ages%20of%20%20Collaboration%20SGIR.pdf.

Dickow, M. and Buch, D. (2012) 'Europäische Rüstungsindustrie: Kein Heil im Export', *SWP Aktuell*, No. 13 (Berlin: Stiftung Wissenschaft und Politik). See: www.swp-berlin.org/fileadmin/contents/products/aktuell/2012A13_dkw_bch.pdf.

Diehl Aerosystems (2016) 'Facts and Figures'. See: www.diehl.com/en/diehl-aero systems/company/facts-figures.html.

Diehl Group (2014) 'Annual Report 2014'. See: www.diehl.com/fileadmin/diehl-gruppe/upload/Annual_Report_2015_01.pdf.

Diez, T. (2001) 'Europe as a Discursive Battleground: Discourse Analysis and European Integration Studies', *Cooperation and Conflict*, 36: 5–38.

Diez, T. (1999) 'Speaking "Europe": The Politics of Integration Discourse', *Journal of European Public Policy*, 6(4): 598–613.

Di Lenna, N. (2009) *La Direttiva Europea sul Procurement Della Difesa* (Rome: Istituto Affari Internazionali). See: http://pubblicazioni.iai.it/pdf/Quaderni/Quaderni_33.pdf.

Dimaggio, P. and Powell, W. (1991) 'The Iron Cage Revisited: Institutional Isomorphism and Collective Rationality in Organizational Fields', in W. Powell and P. DiMaggio (eds.) *The New Institutionalism in Organizational Analysis* (Chicago, IL: University of Chicago Press): 63–82.

Dombrowski, P and Gholz, E. (2006) *Buying Military Transformation: Technological Innovation and the Defense Industry* (New York: Columbia University Press).

Dover, R. (2005) 'The Prime Minister and the Core Executive: A Liberal Intergovernmentalist Reading of UK Defence Policy Formulation, 1997–2000', *The British Journal of Politics & International Relations*, 7(4): 508–525.

Duke, S. (2017) *Europe as a Stronger Global Actor: Challenges and Strategic Responses* (Basingstoke: Palgrave Macmillan).

Dumbrell, J. (2009) 'The US–UK Special Relationship: Taking the 21st-Century Temperature', *The British Journal of Politics and International Relations*, 11(1): 64–78.

Dunne, J.P. (1995) 'The Defence Industrial Base', in K. Hartley and T. Sandler (eds.) *Handbook of Defence Economics – Volume 1* (Amsterdam: Elsevier): 399–430.

Dunne, J.P. and Nikolaidou, E. (2012) 'Defence Spending and Economic Growth in the EU15', *Defence and Peace Economics*, 23(6): 537–548.

Dunne, J.P. and the SIPRI Arms Production Program Staff (2009) 'Developments in the Global Arms Industry from the End of the Cold War', in R.A. Bitzinger (ed.) *The Modern Defense Industry: Political, Economic and Technological Issues* (Santa Barbara, CA: Praeger Security International): 13–37.

Dunne, J.P., Smith, R.P. and Willenbockel, D. (2005) 'Models of Military Expenditure and Growth: A Critical Review', *Defence and Peace Economics*, 16(6): 449–461.

Dussauge, P. and Garrett, B. (1995) 'The Future of the Defence Firm: Collaboration, Cooperation and Strategic Alliance', in A. Latham and N. Hooper (eds.) *The Future of the Defence Firm: New Challenges, New Directions* (Berlin: Springer Science): 121–132.

Dyson, T. (2016) 'Neoclassical Realism: Clarifying the Nature and Role of Systemic- and Domestic-level Variables in CSDP', in L. Cladi and A. Locatelli (eds.) *International Relations Theory and European Security: We Thought We Knew* (London/New York: Routledge): 28–47.

Dyson, T. (2015) 'Germany's Limited Leadership in the EDA: International and Domestic Constraints on Defence Cooperation', in N. Karampekios and I. Oikonomou (eds.) *The European Defence Agency: Arming Europe* (Oxon/New York: Routledge): 155–170.

Dyson, T. (2010) *Neoclassical Realism and Defence Reform in Post-Cold War Europe* (Basingstoke/New York: Palgrave Macmillan).

Dyson, T. (2007) *The Politics of German Defence and Security: Political Leadership and Military Reform in the Post-Cold War Era* (New York/Oxford: Berghahn Books).

Dyson, T. and Konstadinides, T. (2013) *European Defence Cooperation in EU Law and IR Theory* (Basingstoke/New York: Palgrave Macmillan).

EADS (2004) 'Ascending: EADS Annual Review 2004'. See: www.airbusgroup.com/int/en/investors-shareholders/Publications.html.

Ecorys (2012) *Study on Civil Military Synergies in the Field of Security* (Brussels: European Commission). See: http://ec.europa.eu/DocsRoom/documents/11427/attachments/1/translations/en/renditions/pdf.

Ecorys (2010) *Study on the Impact of Emerging Defence Markets and Competitors on the Competitiveness of the European Defence Sector* (Brussels: European Commission). See: http://citeseerx.ist.psu.edu/viewdoc/download?doi=10.1.1.231.7713&rep=rep1&type=pdf.

Edgar, A.D. (2001) 'Hurry Up and Wait? Intergovernmentalism and an Integrated European Defence Market', in G.A. Maclean (ed.) *Between Actor and Presence: The European Union and the Future of the Transatlantic Relationship* (Ottawa: University of Ottawa Press): 123–148.

Edwards, J. (2011) 'The EU Defence and Security Procurement Directive: A Step Towards Affordability?', *International Security Programme Paper*, No. 5 (London:

Chatham House). See: www.chathamhouse.org/sites/files/chathamhouse/0811pp_edwards.pdf.

Eilstrup Sangiovanni, M. (2003) 'Why a Common Security and Defence Policy is Bad for Europe', *Survival: Global Politics and Strategy*, 45(4): 193–206.

Ekelund, H. (2015) 'Institutionalist Approaches to Agency Establishment', in N. Karampekios and I. Oikonomou (eds.) *The European Defence Agency: Arming Europe* (Oxon/New York: Routledge): 11–26.

Eliassen, K.A. (2002) *European Defence Procurement and Industrial Policy: The Case of France* (Sandvika: Norwegian School of Management). See: www.bi.no/CenterFiles/CEAS%20files/02-12-France.pdf.

Englesson, M. (2006) 'Klartecken för ökad vapenexport', *Realtid* (30 June). See: www.realtid.se/klartecken-okad-vapenexport.

Eriksson, E.A., Axelson, M., Hartley, K., Mason, M., Stenérus, A.-S. and Trybus, M. (2007) *Study on the Effects of Offsets on the Development of a European Defence Industry and Market* (Brussels: European Defence Agency). See: https://zoek.officielebekendmakingen.nl/kst-22054-133-b2.pdf.

Estrup Ippolito, A. (2014) 'Government to Government Contracts in EU Defence Procurement', *Public Procurement Law Review*, 23(6): 249–265.

Eurocon (2010) *Study on State Control of Strategic Defence Assets* (Brussels: European Commission). See: www.iai.it/it/ricerche/eurocon-study-state-control-strategic-defence-assets#sthash.Lqu1wj11.dpuf.

Europe Economics (2009) *Study on the Competitiveness of European Small and Medium-sized Enterprises (SMEs) in the Defence Sector* (Brussels: European Commission). See: http://ec.europa.eu/DocsRoom/documents/10486/attachments/2/translations/en/renditions/native.

European Commission (2017) 'Launching the European Defence Fund', *COM(2017) 295 final*. See: https://eeas.europa.eu/sites/eeas/files/launching_the_european_defence_fund.pdf.

European Commission (2016) 'European Defence Action Plan', *COM(2016) 950 final*. See: http://ec.europa.eu/DocsRoom/documents/20372.

European Commission (2015a) 'In Defence of Europe: Defence Integration as a Response to Europe's Strategic Moment', EPSC Strategic Notes, 4 (Brussels: European Political Strategy Centre). See: https://ec.europa.eu/epsc/sites/epsc/files/strategic_note_issue_4_en.pdf.

European Commission (2015b) 'Roadmap: European Defence Action Plan'. See: http://ec.europa.eu/smart-regulation/roadmaps/docs/2016_grow_006_cwp_european_defence_action_plan_en.pdf.

European Commission (2013a) 'Towards a More Competitive and Efficient Defence and Security Sector: A New Deal for European Defence', *COM(2013) 542 final*. See: http://eur-lex.europa.eu/legal-content/EN/TXT/?uri=COM:2014:387:FIN.

European Commission (2013b) 'EU Competition Law: Merger Legislation', *Situation as at 1st July 2013*. See: http://ec.europa.eu/competition/mergers/legislation/merger_law_2013_web.pdf.

European Commission (2012a) 'EU State Aid Modernisation', *COM(2012) 209 final*. See: http://eur-lex.europa.eu/LexUriServ/LexUriServ.do?uri=COM:2012:0209:FIN:EN:PDF.

European Commission (2012b) 'Action Plan for an Innovative and Competitive Security Industry', *COM(2012) 417 final*. See: http://eur-lex.europa.eu/LexUriServ/LexUriServ.do?uri=COM:2012:0417:FIN:EN:PDF.

European Commission (2010a) 'An Integrated Industrial Policy for the Globalisation Era: Putting Competitiveness and Sustainability Centre Stage', *COM(2010) 614 final*. See: http://eur-lex.europa.eu/legal-content/EN/TXT/?qid=1475737489008&uri=CELEX:52010DC0614.

European Commission (2010b) 'EU Manufacturing Industry: What are the Challenges and Opportunities for the Coming Years?'. See: www.manufacturing-policy.eng.cam.ac.uk/futures-documents-folder/eu-eu-manufacturing-industry-what-are-the-challenges-and-opportunities-for-the-coming-years/view.

European Commission (2009a) 'Guidance Note on Field of Application'. See: http://ec.europa.eu/internal_market/publicprocurement/docs/defence/guide-scope_en.pdf.

European Commission (2009b) 'Guidance Note on Defence- and Security-Specific Exclusions'. See: http://ec.europa.eu/internal_market/publicprocurement/docs/defence/guide-exclusions_en.pdf.

European Commission (2009c) 'Guidance Note on Security of Information'. See: http://ec.europa.eu/internal_market/publicprocurement/docs/defence/guide-soi_en.pdf.

European Commission (2009d) 'Guidance Note on Offsets'. See: http://ec.europa.eu/internal_market/publicprocurement/docs/defence/guide-offsets_en.pdf.

European Commission (2009e) 'Guidance Note on Subcontracting'. See: http://ec.europa.eu/internal_market/publicprocurement/docs/defence/guide-subcontracting_en.pdf.

European Commission (2009f) 'Guidance Note on Research and Development'. See: http://ec.europa.eu/internal_market/publicprocurement/docs/defence/guide-research_en.pdf.

European Commission (2009g) 'Guidance Note on Security of Supply'. See: http://ec.europa.eu/internal_market/publicprocurement/docs/defence/guide-sos_en.pdf.

European Commission (2007a) 'A Strategy for a Stronger and More Competitive European Defence Industry', *COM(2007) 764 final*. See: http://eur-lex.europa.eu/legal-content/en/TXT/?uri=CELEX%3A52007DC0764.

European Commission (2007b) 'Commission Staff Working Document – Accompanying Document to the Proposal for a Directive of the European Parliament and of the Council on the Simplifying Terms and Conditions of Transfers of Defence-Related Products within the Community – Impact Assessment Summary', *SEC(2007) 1594*. See: http://eur-lex.europa.eu/legal-content/EN/ALL/?uri=CELEX:52007SC1594.

European Commission (2007c) 'Commission Staff Working Document: 2009/81/EC'. See: http://eur-lex.europa.eu/legal-content/EN/TXT/?uri=SWD:2013:0279:FIN.

European Commission (2007d) 'Proposal for a Directive on the Coordination of Procedures for the Award of Certain Public Works Contracts, Public Supply Contracts and Public Service Contracts in the Fields of Defence and Security', *COM(2007) 766 final*. See: www.europarl.europa.eu/registre/docs_autres_institutions/commission_europeenne/com/2007/0766/COM_COM(2007)0766_EN.pdf.

European Commission (2006a) 'Interpretative Communication on the Application of Article 296 of the Treaty in the Field of Defence Procurement'. See: http://ec.europa.eu/smart-regulation/impact/ia_carried_out/docs/ia_2006/sec_2006_1554_en.pdf.

European Commission (2006b) 'Consultation Paper on the Intra-Community Circulation of Products for the Defence of Member States'. See: http://ec.europa.eu/growth/tools-databases/newsroom/cf/itemdetail.cfm?item_id=32&lang=en&tpa_id=1051&title=Call-for-comments%3A-consultation-paper-on-the-intra-%0D%0Acommunity-circulation-of-defence-related-products.

European Commission (2005) 'Results of the Consultation Launched by the Green Paper on Defence Procurement and on the Future Commission Initiatives', *COM(2005) 626 final*. See: http://eur-lex.europa.eu/legal-content/en/ALL/?uri=CELEX%3A52005DC0626.

European Commission (2004) 'Green Paper on Defence Procurement', *COM(2004)608 final*. See: http://eur-lex.europa.eu/legal-content/EN/TXT/?uri=URISERV%3A122013.

European Commission (2003) 'European Defence – Industrial and Market Issues: Towards an EU Defence Equipment Policy', *COM(2003) 113 final*. See: http://eur-lex.europa.eu/legal-content/EN/TXT/?uri=URISERV%3An26028.

European Commission (1999) 'Resolution on the Communication from the Commission on Implementing European Union Strategy on Defence-Related Industries', *A4–0482/98*. See: http://eur-lex.europa.eu/legal-content/EN/TXT/?uri=celex%3A51998IP0482.

European Commission (1997) 'Implementing European Union Strategy on Defence-Related Industries', *COM(97) 583 final*. See: http://ec.europa.eu/internal_market/publicprocurement/docs/defence/com97-583-final_en.pdf.

European Commission (1996) 'The Challenges Facing the European Defence-Related Industry', *COM(96) 10 final*. See: http://ec.europa.eu/internal_market/publicprocurement/docs/defence/com96-10_en.pdf.

European Council (2013a) 'Defence in Europe: Pragmatically Forward', *EUCO 79/13*. See: www.consilium.europa.eu/uedocs/cms_data/docs/pressdata/en/ec/136394.pdf.

European Council (2013b) 'Council Conclusions on Common Security and Defence Policy'. See: www.consilium.europa.eu/uedocs/cms_data/docs/pressdata/en/foraff/139719.pdf.

European Defence Agency (2015) 'Annual Report 2014'. See: www.eda.europa.eu/docs/default-source/eda-annual-reports/eda-annual-report-2014.

European Defence Agency (2014a) 'Your Guide to European Structural Funds for Dual-Use Technology Projects'. See: www.eda.europa.eu/docs/default-source/brochures/esf-brochure.

European Defence Agency (2014b) 'Defence Data of France in 2014'. See: www.eda.europa.eu/info-hub/defence-data-portal/France/year/2014#2.

European Defence Agency (2009) 'Level Playing Field for European Defence Industries: The Role of Ownership and Public Aid Practices'. See: www.eda.europa.eu/docs/documents/level_playing_field_study.pdf.

European Defence Agency (2008) 'A Guide to the EDA's New European Defence Equipment Market'. See: www.eda.europa.eu/info-hub/publications/publication-details/pub/a-guide-to-the-eda-s-new-european-defence-equipment-market.

European Defence Agency (2007) 'A Strategy for the European Defence Technological and Industrial Base'. See: http://neweda/docs/documents/EDA_-_Strategy_for_the_European_Defence_Technological_and_Industrial_Base.pdf?sfvrsn=0.

European Defence Agency (2006a) 'Characteristics of a Strong Future European Defence Technological and Industrial Base'. See: www.eda.europa.eu/docs/documents/eda-characteristics-edtib.pdf.

European Defence Agency (2006b) 'The Code of Best Practice in the Supply Chain'. See: www.eda.europa.eu/docs/documents/CoBPSC_final.

European Defence Agency (2006c) 'European Defence Agency: 2005 Financial Report'. See: www.eda.europa.eu/docs/documents/financial_report_-_2005.

European External Action Service (2016) 'Shared Vision, Common Action: A Stronger Europe – A Global Strategy for the European Union's Foreign and Security Policy'. See: https://europa.eu/globalstrategy/sites/globalstrategy/files/regions/files/eugs_review_web.pdf.

European Parliament (2016) 'Report on the European Defence Union', *P8_TA(2016)0435*. See: www.europarl.europa.eu/sides/getDoc.do?type=TA&reference=P8-TA-2016-0435&language=EN&ring=A8-2016-0316.

European Parliament (2013) 'Report on the European Defence Technological and Industrial Base', *P7_TA(2013)0514*. See: www.europarl.europa.eu/sides/getDoc.do?pubRef=-//EP//TEXT+TA+P7-TA-2013-0514+0+DOC+XML+V0//EN.

European Parliament (2008a) 'Report on the proposal for a directive of the European Parliament and of the Council on simplifying terms and conditions of transfers of defence-related products within the Community', *A6–0410/2008*. See: www.europarl.europa.eu/sides/getDoc.do?type=REPORT&reference=A6-2008-0410&language=HR.

European Parliament (2008b) 'Opinion of the Committee on Foreign Affairs', *PE406.006*. See: www.europarl.europa.eu/meetdocs/2004_2009/documents/pa/722/722740/722740en.pdf.

European Parliament (2008c) 'Report on the proposal for a directive of the European Parliament and of the Council on the coordination of procedures for the award of certain public works contracts, public supply contracts and public service contracts in the fields of defence and security', *A6–0415/2008*. See: www.europarl.europa.eu/sides/getDoc.do?pubRef=-//EP//TEXT+REPORT+A6-2008-0415+0+DOC+XML+V0//EN.

European Parliament (2008d) 'Opinion of the Committee on Foreign Affairs', *PE406.137*. See: www.europarl.europa.eu/meetdocs/2004_2009/documents/pa/723/723874/723874en.pdf.

European Parliament (2005) 'European Parliament Resolution on the European Security Strategy', *P6_TA(2005)0133*. See: www.europarl.europa.eu/sides/getDoc.do?pubRef=-//EP//TEXT+TA+P6-TA-2005-0133+0+DOC+XML+V0//EN.

European Union (2012) 'Consolidated Version of the Treaty on the Functioning of the European Union'. See: http://eur-lex.europa.eu/legal-content/EN/TXT/?uri=celex%3A12012E%2FTXT.

European Union Global Strategy (2016) 'Shared Vision, Common Action: A Stronger Europe – A Global Strategy for the EU's Foreign and Security Policy'. See: https://eeas.europa.eu/top_stories/pdf/eugs_review_web.pdf.

European Union Institute for Security Studies (2016) *Report of the Group of Personalities on the Preparatory Action for CSDP-related Research* (Paris: EU Institute for Security Studies). See: www.iss.europa.eu/publications/detail/article/report-of-the-group-of-personalities-on-the-preparatory-action-for-csdp-related-research/.

Exadaktylos, T. and Radaelli, C. (2009) 'Research Design in European Studies: The Case of Europeanization', *Journal of Common Market Studies*, 47(3): 507–530.

Fairclough, N. (2013) *Critical Discourse Analysis: The Critical Study of Language* (Oxon/New York: Routledge).

Fairclough, N. (2005) 'Critical Discourse Analysis', *Marges Linguistiques*, 9: 76–94.

Fairclough, N. (1989) *Language and Power* (London: Longman).

Fallows, J. (2002) 'The Military-Industrial Complex', *Foreign Policy*, 133: 46–48.

Fearon, J. (1998) 'Domestic Politics, Foreign Policy and Theories of IR', *Annual Review of Political Science*, 1: 289–313.

Fincantieri (2015) 'Shareholders'. See: www.fincantieri.it/cms/data/pages_wide/000009.aspx.

Finland Prime Minister's Office (2004) 'Finnish Security and Defence Policy 2004', *Government Report 6/2004*, VNS 6/2004 vp. See: www.defmin.fi/files/311/2574_2160_English_White_paper_2004_1_.pdf.

Finmeccanica (2010) 'Finmeccanica Sustainability Report 2010'. See: www.leonardocompany.com/documents/63265270/66319503/ComFin_Sostenibilita_05_07_11_ING.pdf?download_file.

Fiott, D. (2017a) 'The CARD on the EU Defence Table', *Policy Alert*, No. 10 (Paris: European Union Institute for Security Studies). See: www.iss.europa.eu/content/card-eu-defence-table.

Fiott, D. (2017b) 'Promoting European Defence Cooperation and the Promise of Financial Incentives', *ARES Group Comment*, No. 16 (Paris: French Institute for International and Strategic Affairs). See: www.iris-france.org/wp-content/uploads/2017/05/ARES-16-Comment-DFiott-may-2017.pdf.

Fiott, D. (2016a) 'A Revolution Too Far? US Defence Innovation, Europe and NATO's Military-Technological Gap', *Journal of Strategic Studies*, 40(3): 417–437.

Fiott, D. (2016b) 'Europe and the Pentagon's Third Offset Strategy', *The RUSI Journal*, 161(1): 22–27.

Fiott, D. (2016c) 'Patriotism, Preferences and Serendipity: Understanding the Adoption of the Defence Transfers Directive', *Journal of Common Market Studies*, 55(5): 1045–1061.

Fiott, D. (2016d) 'Modernising NATO's Defence Infrastructure with EU Funds', *Survival: Global Politics and Strategy*, 58(2): 77–94.

Fiott, D. (2015a) 'European Defence-Industrial Cooperation: From Keynes to Clausewitz', *Global Affairs*, 1(2): 159–167.

Fiott, D. (2015b) 'The European Commission and the European Defence Agency: A Case of Rivalry?', *Journal of Common Market Studies*, 53(3): 542–557.

Fiott, D. (2014a) 'The Three Effects of Dual-Use: Firms, Capabilities and Governance', *Policy Brief*, No. 21 (Paris: European Union Institute for Security Studies). See: www.iss.europa.eu/uploads/media/Brief_21_Dual_use.pdf.

Fiott, D. (2014b) 'Autonomy Without Autarky: An EU "Roadmap" for Security of Supply', *Policy Alert*, No. 43 (Paris: European Union Institute for Security Studies). See: www.iss.europa.eu/uploads/media/Alert_43_security_of_supply.pdf.

Fiott, D. (2014c) 'Financing European Defence: Time to Call the European Investment Bank?', IES Policy Brief, No. 5 (Brussels: Institute for European Studies, VUB). See: www.ies.be/node/2522.

Fiott, D. (2013a) 'Improving CSDP Planning and Capability Development: Could There be a "Frontex Formula"?', *European Foreign Affairs Review*, 18(1): 47–62.

Fiott, D. (2013b) 'More Competitive, More Efficient? The 2013 European Commission Defence Communication', *Security Policy Brief*, No. 49 (Brussels: Egmont – Royal Institute for International Relations). See: www.egmontinstitute.be/wp-content/uploads/2013/09/SPB49-Fiott.pdf.

Fiott, D. (2013c) 'The "TTIP-ing Point": How the Transatlantic Trade and Investment Partnership Could Impact European Defence', *The International Spectator: Italian Journal of International Affairs*, 48(3): 15–26.

Fiott, D. (2012) 'Safeguarding the EDTIB: The Case for Supervising non-EU FDI in the Defence Sector', *Security Policy Brief*, No. 41 (Brussels: Egmont – Royal Institute for International Relations). See: www.egmontinstitute.be/wp-content/uploads/2013/09/SPB41.pdf.

Fiott, D. and Bellais, R. (2016) 'A "Game Changer"? The EU's Preparatory Action on Defence Research', *ARES Group Policy Paper*. See: www.iris-france.org/wp-content/uploads/2016/04/ARES-Group-Policy-Paper-Fiott-and-Bellais-04-16-OK.pdf.

Fiott, D. and Missiroli, A. (2016) 'Making Europe and Europeans Safer', *Policy Alert*, No. 39 (Paris: European Union Institute for Security Studies). See: www.iss.europa.eu/uploads/media/Alert_39_Defence.pdf.

Fiott, D., Missiroli, A. and Tardy, T. (2017) 'Permanent Structured Cooperation: What's in a Name?', *Chaillot Paper*, No. 142 (Paris: EU Institute for Security Studies). See: www.iss.europa.eu/sites/default/files/EUISSFiles/CP_142_ONLINE.pdf.

FitzGerald, B. and Sayler, K. (2014) Creative Disruption: Technology, Strategy and the Future of the Global Defense Industry (Washington, DC: Center for a New American Security). See: www.ndia.org/Policy/AcquisitionReformInitiative/Documents/CNAS FutureoftheGlobalDefeseIndustry.pdf.

Fleurant, A.-E. (2015) 'Quelles strategies face aux mutations de l'économie de défense mondiale?', *Etudes*, No. 38 (Paris: Institut recherches stratégiques l'École militaire). See: www.defense.gouv.fr/actualites/economie-et-technologie/quelles-strategies-face-aux-mutations-de-l-economie-de-defense-mondiale.

Fohlin, C. (2007) *Finance Capitalism and Germany's Rise to Industrial Power* (Cambridge/New York: Cambridge University Press).

Forster, A. (1998) 'Britain and the Negotiation of the Maastricht Treaty: A Critique of Liberal Intergovernmentalism', *Journal of Common Market Studies*, 36(3): 347–368.

Foucault, M. (2012) 'The Defence Budget in France: Between Denial and Decline', *Focus stratégique*, 36 (Paris: Institut français relations internationales). See: www.ifri.org/sites/default/files/atoms/files/fs36bisfoucault.pdf.

French Government (2017) 'France–India Defence Cooperation'. See: https://in.ambafrance.org/-Defence-Cooperation-.

French Government (2015) *Rapport au Parlement 2015 sur les exportations d'armement de la France*. See: www.defense.gouv.fr/salle-de-presse/dossiers-de-presse/rapport-au-parlement-2015-sur-les-exportations-d-armement-de-la-france.

French Government (2013a) *Preparatory Document for the French White Paper on Defence and National Security 2013*. See: www.sgdsn.gouv.fr/IMG/pdf/Doc_preparatoire_LBDSN_UK-2012-V2_WEB_Protected.pdf.

French Government (2013b) *French White Paper on Defence and National Security 2013*. See: www.defense.gouv.fr/content/download/215253/2394121/file/White%20paper%20on%20defense%20%202013.pdf.

French Government (2010a) *Project de loi relative au contrôle des importations et des exportations de matériels de guerre et de matériels assimilés, à la simplification des transferts des produits liés à la défense dans l'Union européenne et aux marchés de défense et de sécurité*. See: www.senat.fr/dossier-legislatif/pjl10-070.html.

French Government (2010b) *LOI n°2011–702 du 22 juin 2011 relative au contrôle des importations et des exportations de matériels de guerre et de matériels assimilés, à la simplification des transferts des produits liés à la défense dans l'Union européenne et aux marchés de défense et de sécurité*. See: www.legifrance.gouv.fr/affichTexte.do?cidTexte=JORFTEXT000024228630&categorieLien=id.

French Government (2008) *Le Livre Blanc: Défense et Sécurité nationale*. See: www.ladocumentationfrancaise.fr/var/storage/rapports-publics/084000341.pdf.

French Government (1994) *Livre Blanc sur la Défense*. See: www.ladocumentationfrancaise.fr/rapports-publics/944048700/index.shtml.

French Parliament (2015) *Rapport de Mme Patricia Adam sur le projet de loi, après engagement de la procédure accélérée, actualisant la programmation militaire pour les années 2015 à 2019 et portant diverses dispositions concernant la défense, n°2779* (Paris: Assemblée nationale). See: www.assemblee-nationale.fr/14/dossiers/actualisation_programmation_militaire_2015-2019.asp.

French Parliament (2014) *Rapport d'information de Mme Nathalie Chabanne et M. Yves Foulon déposé en application de l'article 145 du règlement, par la commission de la défense nationale et des forces armées, en conclusion des travaux d'une mission d'information sur le dispositif de soutien aux exportations d'armement, n° 2469* (Paris: Assemblée nationale). See: www.assemblee-nationale.fr/14/rap-info/i2469.asp.

French Parliament (2012a) 'Commission de la défense nationale et des forces armées', *Compte rendu n°23*, 21 November (Paris: Assemblée nationale). See: www.assemblee-nationale.fr/14/cr-cdef/15-16/index.asp.

French Parliament (2012b) 'Les capacities industrielles militaries critiques', 4 July (Paris: Sénat). See: www.senat.fr/notice-rapport/2011/r11-634-notice.html.

French Parliament (2011a) 'Contrôle des importations et des exportations de matériels de guerre et marches de défense et de sécurité', *Commission des affairs étrangères, de la défense et des forces armées*, séance du 12 janvier 2011: 1ère reunion (Paris: Sénat). See: www.senat.fr/dossier-legislatif/pjl10-070.html.

French Parliament (2011b) 'N° 3775 Avis – sur le projet de loi de finances pour 2012', *n°3809* (Paris: Assemblée nationale). See: www.assemblee-nationale.fr/13/dossiers/loi_finances_2012.asp.

French Parliament (2011c) 'Senace du mardi 01 mars 2011 (compte rendu integral des débats du Sénat)', 1 March (Paris: Sénat). See: www.senat.fr/seances/comptes-rendus.html.

French Parliament (2010) 'Transposition de la directive européenne 2009–43-CE relative à la coordination des procedures de passation de certains marches de travaux dans les domains de la défense et de la sécurite – communication', 6 October (Paris: Sénat). See: www.legifrance.gouv.fr/affichTexte.do?cidTexte=JORFTEXT000020983793&categorieLien=id.

French Parliament (2009) 'Avis de M. François Cornut-Gentille sur le project de loi de finances pour 2010', *n°1946* (Paris: Assemblée nationale). See: www.assemblee-nationale.fr/13/budget/plf2010/a1972-tVII.asp.

French Parliament (2003a) 'Agence européenne de l'armement', *12th legislature*, 24 July (Paris: Sénat). See: www.senat.fr/questions/base/2003/qSEQ030507243.html.

French Parliament (2003b) 'Question 11041 sur élargissement et préférence communautaire', *12th legislature*, 27 January (Paris: Assemblée nationale). See: http://questions.assemblee-nationale.fr/q12/12-11041QE.htm.

Frenzel, M. (2004) 'Bauanleitung für die Agentur', *DeutscheWelle* (28 May). See: www.dw.com/de/bauanleitung-für-die-agentur/a-1219259.

Fromion, Y. (2006) *Les exportations de défense et de sécurité de la France* (Paris: la documentation française).

Fursdon, E. (1980) *The European Defence Community: A History* (London: Macmillan Press).

Gabriel, M. and Weiner, K. (2010) 'The European Defence Procurement Directive: Toward Liberalization and Harmonization of the European Defence Market', *Procurement Lawyer*, 45(2): 1–23.

Galbreath, D.J. (2015) 'RMA, European Militaries and the Limits of Modernization', in J. Collins and A. Futter (eds.) *Reassessing the Revolution in Military Affairs: Transformation, Evolution and Lessons Learnt* (Basingstoke/New York: Palgrave Macmillan): 156–176.

Gallhöfer, P. (2013) *Effizienz und Effecktivität durch Verteidigungs-Kooperation: Auswirkungen innerhalb der Europäischen Union* (Wiesbaden: Springer VS).

Gallie, W.B. (1956) 'Essentially Contested Concepts', *Proceedings of the Aristotelian Society*, London (12 March). See: http://dx.doi.org/10.1093/aristotelian/56.1.167.

Garrett, G. and Weingast, B. (1993) 'Ideas, Interests, and Institutions: Constructing the European Community's Internal Market', in J. Goldstein and R.O. Keohane (eds.) *Ideas and Foreign Policy* (Ithaca, NY: Cornell University Press): 173–206.

Gasparini, G. (2004) 'Una Proposta di Lavoro per l'Agenzia Difesa', in G. Gasparini and S. Silvestri (eds.) *L'Agenzia Europea e lo Sviluppo delle Capacità di Difesa* (Roma: Centro Militare di Studi Strategici): 21–28.

Gegout, C. (2005) 'Causes and Consequences of the EU's Military Intervention in the Democratic Republic of Congo: A Realist Explanation', *European Foreign Affairs Review*, 10(3): 427–443.

Gegout, C. (2002) 'The French and British Change in Position in the CESDP: A Security Community and Historical–Institutionalist Perspective', *Politique Européenne*, 8(4): 62–87.

Gehring, T. and Oberthür, S. (2009) 'The Causal Mechanisms of Interaction Between International Institutions', *European Journal of International Relations*, 15(1): 125–156.

Gelderman, K., Ghijsen, P. and Schoonen, J. (2010) 'Explaining Non-Compliance with European Union Procurement Directives: A Multidisciplinary Perspective', *Journal of Common Market Studies*, 48(2): 243–264.

Gentiloni, P. (2016) 'EU needs "Schengen for defense"', *Politico Europe* (15 September). See: www.politico.eu/article/italian-foreign-minister-eu-needs-schengen-for-defense-paolo-gentiloni-islamic-state-migrants-security/.

George, A.L. and Bennett, A. (2005) *Case Studies and Theory Development in the Social Sciences* (Cambridge, MA: MIT Press).

Georgopoulos, A. (2011) 'Revisiting Offset Practices in European Defence Procurement: The European Defence Agency's Code of Conduct on Offsets', *Public Procurement Law Review*, 20(3): 29–42.

Georgopoulos, A. (2007) 'The Commission's Interpretative Communication on the Application of Article 296 EC in the Field of Defence Procurement', *Public Procurement Law Review*, 16(3): 1–21.

Gerber, J. (1990) 'The Political, Economic and Military Framework', in J. Drown, C. Drown and K. Campbell (eds.) *A Single European Arms Industry? European Defence Industries in the 1990s* (London/Oxford: Brassey's): 1–26.

German Government (2014a) *Report by the Federal Government on its Policy on Exports of Conventional Military Equipment in 2014* (Berlin: German Federal Ministry of Economics and Technology (BMWi)). See: www.bmwi.de/EN/Topics/Foreign-trade/export-controls-for-military-equipment.html.

German Government (2014b) *Zertifizierungsverfahren nach §9 AWG, 2 AWV und Art. 9 der Verteidigungsgüterrichtlinie (2009/43/EG)* (Eschborn: German Federal Office for Economic Affairs and Export Control (BAFA)). See: www.bafa.de/ausfuhrkontrolle/de/arbeitshilfen/merkblaetter/merkblatt_zertifizierungsverfahren.pdf.

German Government (2013) *Report by the Government of the Federal Republic of Germany on its Policy on Exports of Conventional Military Equipment in 2012* (Berlin: German Federal Ministry of Economics and Technology (BMWi)). See: www.bmwi.de/English/Redaktion/Pdf/2012-military-equipment-export-report,property=pdf,bereich=bmwi2012,sprache=en,rwb=true.pdf.

German Government (2011) *Report by the Government of the Federal Republic of Germany on its Policy on Exports of Conventional Military Equipment in 2010: 2010 Military Equipment Export Report* (Berlin: German Federal Ministry of Economics and Technology (BMWi)). See: www.bmwi.de/English/Redaktion/Pdf/2010-military-equipment-export-report,property=pdf,bereich=bmwi,sprache=en,rwb=true.pdf.

German Government (2006) *White Paper 2006 on German Security Policy and the Future of the Bundeswehr* (Bonn: German Federal Ministry of Defence (BMVg)). See: www.defesa.gov.br/projetosweb/livrobranco/arquivos/pdf/Alemanha%202006%20resumo.pdf.

German Government (2003) *Defence Policy Guidelines* (Berlin:

German Federal Ministry of Defence (BMVg)). See: www.bmvg.de/portal/a/bmvg/!ut/p/c4/TY1JDoMwDEXPwgUSEqsEdddTtHQXwA0WGVAwcP0mi0rVk56HL9nyLQvRnuQsU4rWy5ccJrqPlxjD6cRO04J5QeJ9S56YVmGjwzExijmtR8DIKJ_1yoxiShG5msuail22nLLYUmZfkyPnkgia5QAKbtBrBABdXCcotStd-0_Xdx-jQRkwxihQuv1Rn3onB4xyC6G_Hk3zBUEenVw!/.

German Government/Swedish Government (2010) 'Pooling and Sharing: German-Swedish Initiative – Food for Thought'. See: www.europarl.europa.eu/meetdocs/2009_2014/documents/sede/dv/sede260511deseinitiative_/sede260511deseinitiative_en.pdf.

German Parliament (2011) 'Beschlussempfehlung und Bericht des Ausschusses für Wirtschaft und Technologie (9. Ausschuss)', *Drucksache 17/5794*. See: http://dip21.bundestag.de/dip21/btd/17/057/1705794.pdf.

German Parliament (2005) 'Finanzierung des Europäischen Verteidigungsagentur', *Drucksache 16/332*. See: http://dip21.bundestag.de/dip21/btd/16/003/1600332.pdf.

Geuss, R. (1981) *The Idea of a Critical Theory* (Cambridge: Cambridge University Press).

Gholz, E. (2009) 'The RMA and the Defense Industry', in H.M. Sapolsky, B.H. Friedman and B. Rittenhouse Green (eds.) *US Military Innovation Since the Cold War: Creation without Destruction* (Oxon/New York: Routledge): 172–181.

Giegerich, B. and Nicoll, A. (2012) 'The Struggle for Value in European Defence', *Survival: Global Politics and Strategy*, 54(1): 53–82.

Gillespie, R. (2011) 'The Union for the Mediterranean: An Intergovernmentalist Challenge for the European Union?', *Journal of Common Market Studies*, 49(6): 1205–1225.

Gilli, A., Ungaro, A.R. and Marrone, A. (2015) 'The Italian White Paper for International Security and Defence', *The RUSI Journal*, 160(6): 34–41.

Giovachini, L. (2004) 'L'Agence européenne de défense: un progrès décisif pour l'Union?, *Politique étrangère*, 69(1): 177–189.

Glas, A.H. (2012) 'The German Defence Procurement and its Relation to Defence Industrial Policy', in Canadian Government (ed.) *National Shipbuilding Procurement Strategy: New Paradigms for Defence Procurement and Industrial Policy?* (Ottawa).

Glynos, J., Howarth, D., Norval, A. and Speed, E. (2009) 'Discourse Analysis: Varieties and Methods', *ESRC National Centre for Research Methods*. See: http://eprints.ncrm.ac.uk/796/1/discourse_analysis_NCRM_014.pdf.

Gneezy, U., Meier, S. and Rey-Biel, P. (2011) 'When and Why Incentives (Don't) Work to Modify Behavior', *The Journal of Economic Perspectives*, 25(4): 191–209.

Gordon, P.H. and Meunier, S. (2001) 'Globalization and French Cultural Identity', *French Politics, Culture & Society*, 19(1): 22–41.

Gorges, M.J. (2001) 'New Institutionalist Explanations for Institutional Change: A Note of Caution', *Politics*, 21(2): 137–145.

Gorton, G. and Schmid, F.A. (2000) 'Universal Banking and the Performance of German Firms', *Journal of Financial Economics*, 58(1–2): 29–80.

Gotkowska, J. (2014) 'New Market Conditions and "Exit Strategies" for the German Arms Industry', *OSW Commentary*, No. 130 (Warsaw: Osrodek Studiow Wschodnich): 1–9. See: www.osw.waw.pl/en/publikacje/osw-commentary/2014-03-12/new-market-conditions-and-exit-strategies-german-arms-industry.

Gray, J.N. (1977) 'On the Contestability of Social and Political Concepts', *Political Theory*, 5(3): 331–348.

Grevi, G., Helly, D. and Keohane, D. (2009) 'Introduction', in G. Grevi, D. Helly, and D. Keohane (eds.) *European Security and Defence Policy: The First 10 Years (1999–2009)* (Paris: EU Institute for Security Studies): 13–16. See: www.iss.europa.eu/uploads/media/ESDP_10-web.pdf.

Guay, T. (1998) *At Arm's Length: The European Union and Europe's Defence Industry* (London: Palgrave Macmillan).

Guay, T. (1996) 'Integration and Europe's Defence Industry: a "Reactive Spillover" Approach', *Policy Studies Journal*, 24(3): 404–419.

Guay, T. and Callum, R. (2002) 'The Transformation and Future Prospects of Europe's Defence Industry', *International Affairs*, 78(4): 757–776.

Guillou, S., Lazaric, N., Longhi, C. and Rocchia, S. (2009) 'The French Defence Industry in the Knowledge Management Era: A Historical Overview and Evidence from Empirical Data', *Research Policy*, 38(1): 170–180.

Guiraudon, V. (2000) 'European Integration and Migration Policy: Vertical Policy-making as Venue Shopping', *Journal of Common Market Studies*, 38(2): 251–271.

Gummett, P. and Stein, J.A. (1997) Introduction', in P. Gummett and J.A. Stein (eds.) *European Defence Technology in Transition* (Amsterdam, N.V.: Harwood Academic Publishers): 1–24.

Haas, E.B. (2001) 'Does Constructivism Subsume Neo-Functionalism?', in T. Christiansen, K.E. Jorgensen and A. Wiener (eds.) *The Social Construction of Europe* (London: Sage): 22–31.

Haas, E.B. (1970) 'The Study of Regional Integration: Reflections on the Joy and Anguish of Pretheorizing', *International Organization*, 24(4): 607–646.

Hacker, B. (2005) 'The Machines of War: Western Military Technology, 1850–2000', *History and Technology*, 21(3): 255–300.

Hagedoorn, J. (2002) 'Inter-Firm R&D Partnerships: An Overview of Major Trends and Patterns since 1960', *Research Policy*, 31(4): 477–492.

Hall, P. and Markowski, S. (1994) 'On the Normality and Abnormality of Offsets Obligations', in K. Hartley and T. Sandler (eds.) *Handbook of Defence Economics – Volume III* (Amsterdam: Elsevier): 220–234.

Hall, P. and Taylor, R. (1996) 'Political Science and the Three New Institutionalisms', *Political Studies*, 44(5): 936–957.

Hammersley, M. (1997) 'On the Foundations of Critical Discourse Analysis', *Language and Communication*, 17: 237–248.

Hansen, S.T. (2016) 'Taking Ambiguity Seriously: Explaining the Indeterminacy of the European Union Conventional Arms Export Control Regime', *European Journal of International Relations*, 22(1): 192–216.

Harland, C.M., Lamming, R.C. and Cousins, P.D. (1999) 'Developing the Concept of Supply Strategy', *International Journal of Operations and Production Management*, 19(7): 650–673.

Harrison, T. (2016) *Defense Modernization Plans through the 2020s: Addressing the Bow Wave* (Lanham, MD/New York: Rowman & Littlefield).

Hartley, K. (2014) *The Political Economy of Aerospace Industries: A Key Driver of Growth and International Competitiveness?* (Cheltenham: Edward Elgar).

Hartley, K. (2012) 'Options for the United Kingdom's Nuclear Weapons Programme – Defence-Industrial Issues: Employment, Skills, Technology and Regional Impacts', *Discussion Paper 2 of the BASIC Trident Commission* (London/Washington, DC). See:

www.basicint.org/sites/default/files/trident_commission_defence-industrial_issues_keith_hartley_0.pdf.

Hartley, K. (2011) *The Economics of Defence Policy: A New Perspective* (Oxon/New York: Routledge).

Hartley, K. (2008) 'Collaboration and European Defence Industrial Policy', *Defence and Peace Economics*, 19(4): 303–315.

Hartley, K. (2003) 'The Future of European Defence Policy: An Economic Perspective', *Defence and Peace Economics*, 14(2): 107–115.

Hartley, K. (1995) 'Industrial Policies in the Defense Sector', in K. Hartley and T. Sandler (eds.) *Handbook of Defence Economics – Volume 1* (Amsterdam: Elsevier): 459–489.

Hartley, K. (1991) *The Economics of Defence Policy* (London: Brassey's).

Hasik, J. (2008) *Arms and Innovation: Entrepreneurship and Alliances in the Twenty-First-Century Defense Industry* (Chicago, IL/London: University of Chicago Press).

Hay, C. and Wincott, D. (1998) 'Structure, Agency and Historical Institutionalism', *Political Studies*, 46(5): 951–957.

Hayward, K. (2001) 'The Globalisation of Defence Industries', *Survival: Global Politics and Strategy*, 43(2): 115–132.

Hébert, J.-P. (2006) 'Le débat stratégiques sur l'armement 1992–2005', *Cahier d'Etudes Stratégiques*, No. 38–39 (Paris: L'École des hautes études en sciences sociales). See: www.alternatives-economiques.fr/le-debat-strategique-sur-l-armement-1992-2005-par-jean-paul-hebert-dir-_fr_art_207_24514.html.

Heeg, S. (2014) 'The Erosion of Corporatism? The Rescaling of Industrial Relations in Germany', *European Union and Regional Studies*, 21(2): 146–160.

Heidenkamp, H. (2012a) 'A Sea Change in Germany's Defence Export Policy?', *RUSI Newsbrief*. See: https://rusi.org/publication/newsbrief/sea-change-germany's-defence-export-policy.

Heidenkamp, H. (2012b.) 'Assessing the Reform of German Defence Acquisition', *RUSI Defence Systems*. See: https://rusi.org/publication/rusi-defence-systems/assessing-reform-german-defence-acquisition.

Heidenkamp, H., Louth, J. and Taylor, T. (2013) 'The Defence Industrial Triptych: Government as Customer, Sponsor and Regulator', *Whitehall Paper*, No. 81 (London: Royal United Services Institute). See: https://rusi.org/publication/whitehall-papers/defence-industrial-triptych-government-customer-sponsor-and-regulator.

Heidenkamp, H., Thompson, G., Bontems, P., Carlier, B. and Pilottin, A. (2014) 'Foundations of International Defence Industrial Co-operation between Western States and Emerging Powers', *Occasional Paper* (London: Royal United Services Institute). See: https://rusi.org/sites/default/files/201405_op_defence_industrial_cooperation.pdf.

Heisbourg, F. (2016) 'Brexit and European Security', *Survival: Global Politics and Strategy*, 58(3): 13–22.

Heisbourg, F. (2004) 'The "European Security Strategy" is not a Security Strategy', in S. Everts, L. Freedman, C. Grant, F. Heisbourg, D. Keohane and M. O'Hanlon (eds.) *A European Way of War* (London: Centre for European Reform): 27–40.

Heuninckx, B. (2016) *The Law of Collaborative Defence Procurement in the European Union* (Cambridge: Cambridge University Press).

Heuninckx, B. (2015) 'Defence Procurement and the European Defence Equipment Market: The Virtues of Kissing the Frog', *Procurement Law Journal*, 4: 319–337.

Heuninckx, B. (2009) 'The European Defence Agency Capability Development Plan and the European Armaments Cooperation Strategy: Two Steps in the Right Direction', *Public Procurement Law Review*, 18(4): 136–143.

Hix, S. and Goetz, K. (2000) 'Introduction: European Integration and National Political Systems', *West European Politics*, 23(4): 1–26.

Hoeffler, C. (2012) 'European Armament Co-operation and the Renewal of Industrial Policy Motives', *Journal of European Public Policy*, 19(3): 435–451.

Hofmann, S. (2011) 'Why Institutional Overlap Matters: CSDP in the European Security Architecture', *Journal of Common Market Studies*, 49(1): 101–120.

Hofmann, S. (2009) 'Overlapping Institutions in the Realm of International Security: The Case of NATO and ESDP', *Perspectives on Politics*, 7(1): 45–52.

Hoffmann, S. (1966) 'Obstinate or Obsolete? The Fate of the Nation State and the Case of Western Europe', *Daedalus*, 95: 862–915.

Hoffmann, S. (1964) 'The European Process at Atlantic Crosspurposes', *Journal of Common Market Studies*, 3: 85–101.

Hollinger, P. and Wiesmann, G. (2008) 'In a Tangle', *Financial Times* (16 July). See: www.ft.com/cms/s/0/afebe46a-52cf-11dd-9ba7-000077b07658.html?ft_site=falcon&desktop=true#axzz4LxiSl2ZE.

Holtom, P., Bromley, M. and Béraud-Sudreau, L. (2011) 'Internal Compliance Programmes', *SEESAC/UN Development Programme*. See: www.sipri.org/sites/default/files/2016-03/Internal-Compliance-Programmes.pdf.

Hooper, N. and Cox, N. (1996) 'The European Union Konver Programme', *Defence and Peace Economics*, 7(1): 75–94.

Howorth, J. (2014) *Security and Defence Policy in the European Union* (Basingstoke/New York: Palgrave Macmillan).

Howorth, J. (2013a) 'European Security Institutions 1945–2010: The Weaknesses and Strengths of "Brusselsization"', in S. Biscop and R.G. Whitman (eds.) *The Routledge Handbook of European Security* (Oxon/New York: Routledge): 5–19.

Howorth, J. (2013b) 'The EU and NATO after Libya and Afghanistan: The Future of Euro–U.S. Security Cooperation', *Yale Journal of International Affairs*, 8(1): 30–39.

Howorth, J. (2007) *Security and Defence Policy in the European Union* (Basingstoke: Palgrave Macmillan).

Howorth, J. (2004) 'Discourse, Ideas, and Epistemic Communities in European Security and Defence Policy', *West European Politics*, 27(2): 211–234.

Hudson, V.M. (2014) *Foreign Policy Analysis: Classic and Contemporary Theory* (Lanham, MD/Plymouth: Rowman & Littlefield).

Hyde-Price, A. (2007) *European Security in the Twenty-First Century: The Challenge of Multipolarity* (Oxon/New York: Routledge).

Hyde-Price, A. (2004) 'European Security, Strategic Culture and the Use of Force', *European Security*, 13(4): 323–343.

Idiart, A. and Delaboudiniere, V. (2007) 'France', in Y. Aubin and A. Idiard (eds.) *Export Control Law and Regulations Handbook: A Practical Guide to Military and Dual-Use Goods* (Amsterdam: Kluwer Law): 127–158.

Ikegami, M. (2013) 'The End of a "National" Defence Industry? Impacts of Globalization on the Swedish Defence Industry', *Scandinavian Journal of History*, 38(4): 436–457.

Immergut, E.M. (1998) 'The Theoretical Core of the New Institutionalism', *Politics & Society*, 26(1): 5–34.

Indra Systems (2016) 'Shareholders Structure'. See: www.indracompany.com/en/accionistas/shareholders-structure.

Institut de relations internationales et stratégiques, Istituto Affari Internazionali and the University of Manchester (2010) *Study on the Industrial Implications in Europe of the Blurring of Dividing Lines between Security and Defence* (Brussels: European Commission). See: www.iai.it/en/pubblicazioni/study-industrial-implications-europe-blurring-dividing-lines-between-security-and.

Intriligator, M.D. (1998) 'The Economics of Defence Conversion', in E. Inbar and B. Zilberfarb (eds.) *The Politics and Economics of Defence Industries* (Oxon/New York: Routledge): 29–50.

Irondelle, B. (2008) 'European Foreign Policy: The End of French Europe?', *Journal of European Integration*, 30(1): 153–168.

Italian Government (2009) *Relazione annual sulla partecipazione dell'Italia all'Unione europea* (Rome: Presidenza del Consigilio dei Ministri). See: www.politichecomunitarie.it/file_download/1102.

James, A. (2008) 'The Defence Industry and "Transformation": A European Perspective', *Security Challenges*, 4(4): 39–55.

James, A. (2002) 'Comparing European Responses to Defence Industry Globalization', *Defence and Security Analysis*, 18(2): 23–143.

Joana, J. and Smith, A. (2006) 'Changing French Military Procurement Policy: The State, Industry and "Europe" in the Case of the A400M', *West European Politics*, 29(1): 70–89.

Jones, S.G. (2007) *The Rise of European Security Cooperation* (Cambridge/New York: Cambridge University Press).

Kambrod, M.R. (2007) *Lobbying for Defence: An Insider's View* (Annapolis, MD: Naval Institute Press).

Kapstein, E.B. (1991) 'International Collaboration in Armaments Production: A Second-Best Solution', *Political Science Quarterly*, 106(4): 657–675.

Karampekios, N. (2015) 'Understanding Greece's Policy in the European Defence Agency: Between National Interest and Domestic Politics', *Southeast European and Black Sea Studies*, 15(1): 37–52.

Kausal, T., Humily, G., Taylor, T. and Roller, P. (1999) *A Comparison of the Defence Acquisition Systems of France, United Kingdom, Germany and the United States* (Fort Belvoir, VA: Defence Systems Management College Press).

Kennedy-Loest, C. and Pourbaix, N. (2010) 'The New EU Defence Procurement Directive', *ERA Forum*, 11(3): 399–410.

Kenny, B. (2006) 'European Armaments Collaboration and Integration', *Leadership & Organization Development Journal*, 27(6): 484–500.

Keohane, D. (2004) 'Europe's New Defence Agency', *Policy Brief* (London: Centre for European Reform). See: www.cer.org.uk/sites/default/files/publications/attachments/pdf/2012/policybrief_defence_agency-5618.pdf.

Keohane, R.O. (1984) *After Hegemony: Cooperation and Discord in the World Political Economy* (Princeton, NJ: Princeton University Press).

King, A. (2011) *The Transformation of Europe's Armed Forces: From the Rhine to Afghanistan* (Cambridge/New York: Cambridge University Press).

Kingdon, J.W. (1984) *Agendas, Alternatives and Public Policies* (Boston, MA: Little Brown).

Kington, T. (2016) 'EU Sharply Reminds Members of Open Markets Policy', *Defence News* (6 March). See: www.defensenews.com/story/defense/policy-budget/industry/2016/03/06/eu-sharply-reminds-members-open-markets-policy/81217200/.

Kinsella, D. (2002) 'Rivalry, Reaction, and Weapons Proliferation: A Time-Series Analysis of Global Arms Transfers', *International Studies Quarterly*, 46(2): 209–230.

Kirkpatrick, D.L.I. (2004) 'Trends in the Costs of Weapon Systems and the Consequences', *Defence and Peace Economics*, 15(3): 259–273.

Kirkpatrick, D.L.I. (1997) 'The Affordability of Defence Equipment', *The RUSI Journal*, 142(3): 58–80.

Kirkpatrick, D.L.I. (1995) 'The Rising Unit Cost of Defence Equipment: The Reasons and the Results', *Defence and Peace Economics*, 6(4): 263–288.

Kirkpatrick, D.L.I. and Pugh, P.G. (1985) 'Towards the Starship Enterprise – are the Current Trends in Defence Unit Costs Inexorable?', *The Journal of Cost Analysis*, 2(1): 59–80.

Kiss, Y. (2014) *Arms Industry Transformation and Integration: The Choices of East Central Europe* (Oxford: SIPRI/Oxford University Press).

Kitschelt, H. (1986) 'Four Theories of Public Policy Making and Fast Breeder Reactor Development', *International Organization*, 40(1): 65–104.

Kolín, V. (2015) 'Towards Balanced Defence Industry in Europe: Main Specificities of Central and Eastern European Defence Industries', *IRIS Notes* (Paris: Institut des relations internationales et stratégiques). See: www.iris-france.org/wp-content/uploads/2015/03/IRIS-Note-March-2015-V-Kolin1.pdf.

Koutrakos, P. (2013) *The EU Common Security and Defence Policy* (Oxford: Oxford University Press).

Koutrakos, P. (2001) *Trade, Foreign Policy and Defence in EU Constitutional Law* (Oxford/Portland, OR: Hart Publishing).

Krasner, S. (1989) 'Sovereignty: An Institutional Perspective', in J. Caparaso (ed.) *The Elusive State: International and Comparative Perspectives* (Newbury Park, CA: Sage): 19–41.

Kuechle, H. (2006) *The Cost of Non-Europe in the Area of Security and Defence*. (Brussels: European Parliament). See: www.europarl.europa.eu/RegData/etudes/etudes/join/2006/381368/EXPO-SEDE_ET(2006)381368_EN.pdf.

Labbé, M.-H. (1994) 'French Export Control Policy', in G.K. Bertsch, R.T. Cupitt and S. Elliott-Gower (eds.) *International Cooperation on Nonproliferation Export Controls: Prospects for the 1990s and Beyond* (Ann Arbor, MI: The University of Michigan Press): 201–220.

Laclau, E. and Mouffe, C. (1985) *Hegemony and Socialist Strategy: Towards a Radical Democratic Politics* (London: Verso).

Ladrech, R. (1994) 'Europeanization of Domestic Politics and Institutions: The Case of France', *Journal of Common Market Studies*, 32(1): 69–88.

Laffan, B. (1997) 'From Policy Entrepreneur to Policy Manager: The Challenge Facing the European Commission', *Journal of European Public Policy*, 4(3): 422–438.

Leech, B. (2002) 'Interview Methods in Political Science', *Political Science and Politics*, 35(4): 663–664.

Leech, B., Baumgartner, F.R., Berry, J.M., Hojnacki, M. and Kimball, D.C. (2013) 'How to Report Interview Data', in L. Mosley (ed.) *Interview Research in Political Science* (Ithaca, NY/London: Cornell University Press): 209–224.

Leonardo-Finmeccanica (2016) 'Share Capital and Shareholders Base'. See: www.leonardocompany.com/en/investitori-investors/titolo-borsa-stock-quote/capitale-azionariato-share-capital-1.

Lequesne, C. and Rozenberg, O. (2008) 'The French Presidency of 2008: The Unexpected Agenda', *SIEPS Paper*, No. 3 (Stockholm: Swedish Institute for European Policy Studies). See: www.sieps.se/sites/default/files/422-20083op.pdf.

Levi, M. (1997) 'A Model, a Method, and a Map: Rational Choice in Comparative and Historical Analysis', in M. Lichbach and A. Zuckerman (eds.) *Comparative Politics: Rationality, Culture and Structure* (Cambridge: Cambridge University Press): 19–41.

Levi-Faur, D. (2008) 'Regulatory Governance', in P. Graziano and M.P. Vink (eds.) *Europeanization: New Research Agendas* (Basingstoke/New York: Palgrave Macmillan): 102–114.

Levy, J.D. (2008) 'From the Dirigiste State to the Social Anaesthesia State: French Economic Policy in the Longue Durée', *Modern & Contemporary France*, 16(4): 417–435.

Liberti, F., Matelly, S. and Maulny, J.-P. (2010) *Pratiques communautaires internes de contrôle des exportations et des transferts intracommunautaires de produits de defense* (Paris: Institut de relations internationales et stratégiques). See: www.iris-france.org/docs/kfm_docs/docs/analyses-iris/Controle-des-exportations-et-transferts-intra-communautaires-la-Bulgarie.pdf.

Lindberg, L. (1963) *The Political Dynamics of European Economic Integration* (Stanford, CA: Stanford University Press).

Lock, P. and Voβ, W. (1996) 'Germany', in P. Gummet and J.A. Stein (eds.) *European Defence Technology in Transition* (Amsterdam: Harwood Academic Publishers): 85–116.

Lock, P. and Voβ, W. (1994) 'The German Arms Industry in a European Context: A Study in Successful Downsizing', *Defence and Peace Economics*, 5(4): 341–348.

Longhurst, K. (2000) 'The Reform of the German Armed Forces: Coming of Age?', *European Security*, 9(4): 31–44.

Louth, J. (2013a) 'Defence Reform in the United Kingdom: A Twenty-First Century Paradox', *Focus stratégique*, No. 43 (Paris: Institut français des relations internationales). See: www.ifri.org/en/publications/enotes/focus-strategique/defence-reform-united-kingdom-twenty-first-century-paradox.

Louth, J. (2013b) ' "It's the Economy, Stupid!" ', *RUSI Defence Systems*. See: https://rusi.org/publication/rusi-defence-systems/"it's-economy-stupid".

Lovering, J. (1999) 'Which Way to Turn? The European Defense Industry after the Cold War', in A.R. Markusen and S. Costigan (eds.) *Arming the Future: A Defense Industry for the 21st Century* (New York: Council on Foreign Relations Press): 334–370.

Lundmark, M. (2004) 'To Be or Not to Be: The Integration and the Non-Integration of the French Defence Industry', *FOI Report*, No. 1291 (Stockholm; Swedish Defence Research Agency). See: http://foi.se/ReportFiles/foir_1291.pdf.

Lynn, W.J. (2014) 'The End of the Military–Industrial Complex: How the Pentagon is Adapting to Globalization', *Foreign Affairs* (Nov/Dec). See: www.foreignaffairs.com/articles/united-states/end-military-industrial-complex.

Lynn-Jones, S.M. (1995) 'Offense-Defense Theory and its Critics', *Security Studies*, 4(4): 660–691.

Macdonald, G. (1999) 'Reform of UK Defence Procurement and State/Industry Relationships During the 1980s and 1990s', *Defence Analysis*, 15(1): 3–25.

Mair, P. (2004) 'The Europeanization Dimension', *Journal of European Public Policy*, 11(2): 337–348.

Majone, G. (1997) 'From the Positive to the Regulatory State', *Journal of Public Policy*, 17(2): 139–167.

Major, C. and Mölling, C. (2013) 'The Dependent State(s) of Europe: European Defence in Year Five of Austerity', in S. Biscop and D. Fiott (eds.) *The State of Defence in Europe: State of Emergency?* (Gent: Academia Press/Egmont Institute): 13–18.

Mampaey, L., Moreau, V., Quéau, Y. and Seniora, J. (2014) *Study on the Implementation of Directive 2009/43/EC on Transfers of Defence-Related Products* (Brussels: Group de Recherche et d'Information Sur la Paix et la Securite). See: www.grip.org/en/node/1421.

Markowski, S. and Hall, P. (2005) 'The Defence Industry in Poland: An Offsets-based Revival?', in J. Brauer and J.P. Dunne (eds.) *Arms Trade and Economic Development: Theory, Policy and Cases in Arms Trade Offsets* (London/New York: Routledge): 171–184.

Markowski, S. and Wylie, R. (2007) 'The Emergence of European Defence and Defence Industry Policies', *Security Challenges*, 3(2): 31–51.

Marks, G., Hooghe, L. and Blank, K. (1996) 'European Integration from the 1980s: State-Centric v. Multi-level Governance', *Journal of Common Market Studies*, 34(3): 341–378.

Markusen, A.R. (1986) 'Defence Spending: A Successful Industrial Policy?', *International Journal of Urban and Regional Research*, 10(1): 105–122.

Markusen, A.R. and Brzoska, M. (2000) 'The Regional Role in Post-Cold War Military Industrial Conversion', *International Regional Science Review*, 23(1): 3–24.

Markusen, A.R. and Costigan, S.S. (1999) 'The Military Industrial Challenge', in A.R. Markusen and S.S. Costigan (eds.) *Arming the Future: A Defense Industry for the 21st Century* (New York: Council on Foreign Relations Press): 3–36.

Marrone, A. and Ungaro, A.R. (2014) 'Relations between the United States of America and Italy in the Post-Cold War Period: A Defense-Industrial Perspective', *Cahiers de la Méditerranée*, 88: 157–181.

Marsh, D. and Stoker, G. (eds.) (2010) *Theory and Methods in Political Science* (Basingstoke/New York: Palgrave Macmillan).

Martí Sempere, C., Römer, S., Missoweit, M., Trybus, M., Rubini, L., Sköns, E., Perlo Freeman, S. and Dyevre, A. (2009) *Level Playing Field for European Defence Industries: The Role of Ownership and Public Aid Practices* (Brussels: European Defence Agency). See: www.eda.europa.eu/docs/documents/level_playing_field_study.pdf.

Martin, S. (1996) 'Countertrade and Offsets: An Overview of the Theory and Evidence', in S. Martin (ed.) *The Economics of Offsets: Defence Procurement and Countertrade* (London/New York: Routledge): 15–48.

Martinage, R. (2014) *Toward a New Offset Strategy: Exploiting U.S. Long-Term Advantages to Restore U.S. Global Power Projection Capability* (Washington, DC: Center for Strategic and Budgetary Assessments). See: http://csbaonline.org/research/publications/toward-a-new-offset-strategy-exploiting-u-s-long-term-advantages-to-restore.

Masson, H. (2013) (ed.) 'Defining the "European Defence Technological and Industrial Base"', *Debates and Dilemmas*, No. 23 (Paris: Fondation pour la Recherche Stratégique). See: www.frstrategie.org/publications/notes/defining-the-european-defence-technological-and-industrial-base-debates-dilemmas-i-2013-23.

Masson, H. (2008) 'Union européenne et armement: des dispositions du traité de Lisbonne aux propositions de directive de la Commission européenne', *Recherches & Documents*, No. 9 (Paris: Fondation pour la Recherche Stratégique). See: www.frstrategie.org/publications/recherches-documents/web/documents/2008/200809.pdf.

Masson, H. and Martin, K. (2015) 'The Directive 2009/81/EC on Defence and Security Procurement under Scrutiny', *Recherches & Documents*, No. 3 (Paris: Fondation pour la Recherche Stratégique). See: www.frstrategie.org/publications/recherches-documents/the-directive-2009-81-ec-on-defence-and-security-procurement-under-scrutiny-2015-03.

Masson, H., Marta, L., Léger, P. and Lundmark, M. (2010) 'The "Transfer Directive": Perceptions in European Countries and Recommendations', *Recherches & Documents*, No. 4 (Paris: Fondation pour la Recherche Stratégique). See: www.files.ethz.ch/isn/119430/RD_201004.pdf.

Masson, H., Martin, K., Quéau, Y. and Seniora, J. (2015) *The Impact of the 'Defence Package' Directives on European Defence* (Brussels: European Parliament). See: www.europarl.europa.eu/RegData/etudes/STUD/2015/549044/EXPO_STU(2015)549044_EN.pdf.

Mastanduno, M., Lake, D.A. and Ikenberry, J.G. (1989) 'Toward a Realist Theory of State Action', *International Studies Quarterly*, 33(4): 457–474.

Matlary, J.H. (2009) *European Union Security Dynamics: In the New National Interest* (Basingstoke/New York: Palgrave Macmillan).

Matthews, R. (2014) 'The UK Offset Model: From Participation to Engagement', *Whitehall Report*, No. 1–14 (London: Royal United Services Institute). See: https://rusi.org/publication/whitehall-reports/uk-offset-model-participation-engagement-0.

Matthews, R. and Maharani, C. (2009) 'The Defense Iron Triangle Revisited', in R.A. Bitzinger (ed.) *The Modern Defense Industry: Political, Economic and Technological Issues* (Santa Barbara, CA: Praeger Security International): 38–59.

Mawdsley, J. (2015) 'France, the UK and the EDA', in N. Karampekios and I. Oikonomou (eds.) *The European Defence Agency: Arming Europe* (Oxon/New York: Routledge): 139–154.

Mawdsley, J. (2013) 'The A400M Project: From Flagship Project to Warning for European Defence Cooperation', *Defence Studies*, 13(1): 14–32.

Mazak, J. (2007) 'Conclusions de l'avocate general M. Jan Mazak présentées le 10 juillet 2007', *Case C-337/05*. See: http://eur-lex.europa.eu/legal-content/EN/TXT/?qid=1475688276403&uri=CELEX:62005CC0337.

MBDA (2015) 'Financial Results 2015'. See: www.mbda-systems.com/about-us/.

McGowan, F. and Wallace, H. (1996) 'Towards a European Regulatory State', *Journal of European Public Policy*, 3(4): 560–576.

McGowan, L. and Cini, M. (1999) 'Discretion and Politicization in EU Competition Policy: The Case of Merger Control', *Governance*, 12(2): 175–200.

McKinsey & Company (2012) 'The Future of European Defence: Tackling the Productivity Challenge'. See: www.mckinsey.com/~/media/mckinsey/industries/public%20sector/our%20insights/enlisting%20productivity%20to%20reinforce%20european%20defense/the%20future%20of%20european%20defence.ashx.

McNeill, W.H. (1982) *The Pursuit of Power: Technology, Armed Force, and Society since A.D. 1000* (Chicago, IL: University of Chicago Press).

Meiers, F.-J. (2001) 'The Reform of the Bundeswehr: Adaptation or Fundamental Renewal?', *European Security*, 10(2): 1–22.

Meijer, H.L.E. (2010) 'Post-Cold War Trends in the European Defence Industry: Implications for Transatlantic Industrial Relations', *Journal of Contemporary European Studies*, 18(1): 63–77.

Mesko (2016) 'O firmie'. See: www.mesko.com.pl/informacje-o-firmie.html.

Meunier, S. and Nicolaïdis, K. (2006) 'The European Union as a Conflicted Trade Power', *Journal of European Public Policy*, 13(6): 906–925.

Mintál, N. (2008) 'Export Control of Dual-Use Items During the Cold War and in Hungary Today', *AARMS*, 7(3): 397–406.

Missiroli, A. (2001) 'Italian Defence Policy: European Engagement and Domestic Reform', *International Spectator: Italian Journal of International Affairs*, 36(2): 27–38.

Mitrany, D. (1965) 'The Prospect of Integration: Federal or Functional?', *Journal of Common Market Studies*, 4(2): 119–149.

Molas-Gallart, J. (2002) 'Coping with Dual-Use: A Challenge for European Research Policy', *Journal of Common Market Studies*, 40(1): 155–165.

Molas-Gallart, J. (1997) 'Which Way to Go? Defence Technology and the Diversity of "Dual-Use" Technology Transfer', *Research Policy*, 26: 367–385.

Möller, J. (2014) 'Hartz IV and the Consequences: Did the Labour Market Reforms Destroy the German Model?', in S. Collignon and P. Esposito (eds.) *Competitiveness in the European Economy* (Oxon/New York: Routledge): 129–142.

Mölling, C. (2008) 'Options for an EU Regime on Intra-Community Transfers of Defence Goods', in D. Keohane (ed.) *Towards a European Defence Market*, Chaillot Paper, No. 113 (Paris: European Union Institute for Security Studies): 51–88. See: www.iss.europa.eu/uploads/media/cp113.pdf.

Moravcsik, A. (2005) 'The European Constitutional Compromise and the Neofunctionalist Legacy', *Journal of European Public Policy*, 12(2): 349–386.

Moravcsik, A. (2002) 'In Defence of the "Democratic Deficit": Reassessing Legitimacy in the European Union', *Journal of Common Market Studies*, 40(4): 603–624.

Moravcsik, A. (1999) 'A New Statecraft? Supranational Entrepreneurs and International Cooperation', *International Organization*, 53(2): 267–306.

Moravcsik, A. (1998) *The Choice for Europe: Social Purpose and State Power from Messina to Maastricht* (Ithaca, NY: Cornell University Press).

Moravcsik, A. (1997) 'Taking Preferences Seriously: A Liberal Theory of International Politics', *International Organization*, 51(4): 513–553.

Moravcsik, A. (1995) 'Liberal Intergovernmentalism and Integration: A Rejoinder', *Journal of Common Market Studies*, 33(4): 611–628.

Moravcsik, A. (1993a) 'Armaments among Allies: Franco-German Weapons Cooperation, 1975–1985', in P. Evans, H. Jacobson and R. Putnam (eds.) *Double-edged Diplomacy: International Bargaining and Domestic Politics* (Berkeley/Los Angeles, CA: University of California Press): 128–167.

Moravcsik, A. (1993b) 'Preferences and Power in the European Community: A Liberal Intergovernmentalist Approach', *Journal of Common Market Studies*, 31(4): 473–524.

Moravcsik, A. (1993c) 'Introduction: Integrating International and Domestic Theories of International Bargaining', in P. Evans, H. Jacobson and R. Putnam (eds.) *Double-edged Diplomacy: International Bargaining and Domestic Politics* (Berkeley/Los Angeles, CA: University of California Press): 1–42.

Moravcsik, A. (1991a) 'Arms and Autarky in Modern European History', *Daedalus*, 120(4): 23–45.

Moravcsik, A. (1991b) 'Negotiating the Single European Act: National Interests and Conventional Statecraft in the European Community', *International Organization*, 45(1): 19–56.

Moravcsik, A. (1990) 'The European Armaments Industry at the Crossroads', *Survival: Global Politics and Strategy*, 32(1): 65–85.

Moravcsik, A. and Nicolaïdis, K. (1999) 'Explaining the Treaty of Amsterdam: Interests, Influence, Institutions', *Journal of Common Market Studies*, 37(1): 59–85.

Moravcsik, A. and Schimmelfennig, F. (2009) 'Liberal Intergovernmentalism', in A. Wiener and T. Diez (eds.) *European Integration Theory* (Oxford: Oxford University Press): 67–87.

Morgenthau, H.J. (2000) 'The Intellectual and Political Functions of Theory', in A. Linklater (ed.) *Volume 1 – Critical Concepts in Political Science I* (London/New York: Routledge): 43–54.

Mörth, U. (2005) *Organizing European Cooperation: The Case of Armaments* (Lanham, MD: Rowman & Littlefield Publishers).

Mörth, U. (2000) 'Competing Frames in the European Commission: The Case of the Defence Industry and Equipment Issue', *Journal of European Public Policy*, 7(2): 173–189.

Mörth, U. and Britz, M. (2004) 'European Integration as Organizing: The Case of Armaments', *Journal of Common Market Studies*, 42(5): 957–973.

Mottier, V., Belleval, C., Seitz, K. and Sourdois, J.-L. (2009) *Comment donner un sens au made in European Countries*? (Paris: l'Institut hautes études de defence nationale). See: www.ihedn.fr/userfiles/file/larecherche/rapports/45sn-armement/SN45_T2_6.pdf.

Moura, S. (2008) 'The US Defence Industry Since 1945: Globalization Refused', in B. Jullien and A. Smith (eds.) *Industries and Globalization: The Political Causality of Difference* (Palgrave Macmillan): 129–148.

MTU Aero Engines (2015) 'Shareholder Structure'. See: www.mtu.de/investor-relations/mtu-share/shareholder-structure/.

Murphy, A.B. and Johnson, C.M. (2004) 'German Geopolitics in Transition', *Eurasian Geography and Economics*, 45(1): 1–17.

Neal, D.J. and Taylor, T. (2001) 'Globalisation in the Defence Industry: An Exploration of the Paradigm for US and European Firms and the Implications for being Global Players', *Defence and Peace Economics*, 12(4): 337–338.

Netherlands Government (2007) *Guidelines to an Industrial Benefits and Offsets Program in the Netherlands* (The Hague: Ministry of Economic Affairs). See: http://stingray consulting.nl/PDF/guidelines%20to%20an%20industrial%20benefits%20and%20offsets %20program.pdf.

Neuman, S. (2009) 'Power, Influence, and Hierarchy: Defense Industries in a Unipolar World', in R.A. Bitzinger (ed.) *The Modern Defense Industry: Political, Economic and Technological Issues* (Santa Barbara, CA: Praeger Security International): 60–94.

Neuman, S. (2006) 'Defense Industries and Global Dependency', *Orbis: A Journal of World Affairs*, 50(3): 429–451.

Nexter Group (2016) 'Governance'. See: www.nexter-group.fr/en/corporate-responsibility/governance-governance.

Niemann, A. and Schmitter, P. (2009) 'Neofunctionalism', in A. Wiener and T. Diez (eds.) *European Integration Theory* (Oxford: Oxford University Press, 2nd edn): 45–66.

Nones, M. and Marta, L. (2007) *Il Processo di Integrazione del Mercato della difesa Europeo e le sue implicazioni per l'Italia*. Senato, XV legislatura, No. 82. See: www.senato.it/application/xmanager/projects/leg16/attachments/dossier/file_internets/000/006/938/82.pdf.

Nones, M., Di Paola, S. and Ruggeri, S. (2003) 'Il processo di integrazione del mercato e dell'industria della difesa in Europa', *Quaderni*, No. 17 (Rome: Instituto Affari Internazionali). See: www.iai.it/it/pubblicazioni/il-processo-di-integrazione-del-mercato-e-dellindustria-della-difesa-europa.

Norheim-Martinsen, P.M. (2013) *The European Union and Military Force: Governance and Strategy* (Cambridge/New York: Cambridge University Press).

Nugent, N. and Rhinard, M. (2016) 'Is the European Commission *Really* in Decline?', *Journal of Common Market Studies*, 54(5): 1199–1215.

Oden, M. (1999) 'Cashing In, Cashing Out, and Converting: Restructuring of the Defense Industrial Base in the 1990s', in A.R. Markusen and S. Costigan (eds.) *Arming the Future: A Defence Industry for the 21st Century* (New York: Council on Foreign Relations Press): 74–105.

O'Hanlon, M.E. (2009) *The Science of War: Defense Budgeting, Military Technology, Logistics and Combat Outcomes* (Princeton, NJ/Oxford: Princeton University Press).

Ohmae, K. (1989) 'The Global Logic of Strategic Alliances', *Harvard Business Review* (March–April). See: https://hbr.org/1989/03/the-global-logic-of-strategic-alliances.

Olsen, J. (2002) 'The Many Faces of Europeanization', *Journal of Common Market Studies*, 40(5): 921–952.

Oredsson, M. and Winnerstig, M. (2005) 'Europeisk autonoi eller atlantisk integration? Dagens strukturer och framtida utvecklingslinjer inom ESFP och NATO', *Totalförsvarets Forskningsinstitut Report*, No. 1564 (Stockholm: Swedish Defence Research Agency). See: www.foi.se/rapport?rNo=FOI-R-1564-SE.

Ostwald, D.A., Schubert, S. and Knippel, J. (2012) *Economic Effects of the Security and Defence Industry* (Berlin: Wirtschaftsforschung). See: www.defenceandsecurity.ca/UserFiles/File/IE/KPMG.pdf.

Overhage, T. (2013) 'Pool it, Share it, or Lose it: An Economical View on Pooling and Sharing of European Military Capabilities', *Defense & Security Analysis*, 29(4): 323–341.

Pages, E. (1999) 'Defense Mergers: Weapons Cost, Innovation, and International Arms Industry Cooperation', in A.R. Markusen and S. Costigan (eds.) *Arming the Future: A Defense Industry for the 21st Century* (New York: Council on Foreign Relations Press): 207–223.

Palloni, E. and Lizza, P. (2014) 'Defense Procurement Reform in the EU: From an Italian Perspective', *Proceedings from the 5th International Public Procurement Conference*, Dublin. See: www.ippa.org/IPPC5/Proceedings/Part13/PAPER13-1.pdf.

Patria Group (2015) 'Financial Review 2015'. See: http://188.165.139.234/sites/default/files/file_attachments/patria_financial_review_2015_0.pdf.

Paukert, L. and Richards, P. (1991) 'Employment Impact of Industrial Conversion: A Comparative Analysis', in L. Paukert and P. Richards (eds.) *Defence Expenditure, Industrial Conversion and Local Employment* (Geneva: International Labour Organization): 205–229.

Perry, W.J. (2004) 'Military Technology: An Historical Perspective', *Technology in Society*, 26(2–3): 235–243.

Peters, G.B. and Pierre, J. (1998) 'Institutions and Time: Problems of Conceptualization and Explanation', *Journal of Public Administration Research and Theory*, 8(4): 565–584.

Pierson, P. (2000) 'Increasing Returns, Path Dependence, and the Study of Politics', *American Political Science Review*, 94(2): 251–267.

Pierson, P. (1996) 'The Path to European Integration: A Historical Institutionalist Perspective', *Comparative Political Studies*, 29(2): 123–163.

Pit-Radwar (2016) 'Structure'. See: www.pitradwar.com/en/about-us/structure/.

Polish Government (2013) 'Exports of Arms and Military Equipment from Poland: 2012 Report'. See: www.mfa.gov.pl/resource/ec44e6dc-653b-4fe7-97a9-bb40c1697502:JCR.

Politi, A. (2004) 'La Nascita dell'Agenzia Europea Difesa', in G. Gasparini and S. Silvestri (eds.) *L'Agenzia Europea e lo Sviluppo delle Capacità di Difesa* (Roma: Centro Militare di Studi Strategici): 11–19.

Pollack, M. (2003) *The Engines of European Integration: Delegation, Agency, Agenda Setting in the EU* (Oxford/New York: Oxford University Press).

Pollack, M. (1996) 'The New Institutionalism and EC Governance: The Promise and Limits of Institutional Analysis', *Governance: An International Journal of Policy and Administration*, 9(4): 429–458.

Portugal Government (2011) *Portugal: Industries and Logistics for the Defence 2012–2013* (Lisbon: Ministry of Defence). See: www.portugalglobal.pt/PT/Comprar Portugal/Documents/Industries%20and%20Logistics%20for%20Defence_final_digital.pdf.

Posen, B. (2006) 'European Union Security and Defense Policy: Response to Unipolarity?', *Security Studies*, 15(2): 149–186.

Posen, B. (2004) 'ESDP and the Structure of World Power', *The International Spectator: Italian Journal of International Affairs*, 39(1): 5–17.

Pugh, P.G. (2007) 'Retrospect and Prospect: Trends in Cost and their Implications for UK Aerospace', *Defence and Peace Economics*, 18(1): 25–37.

Pugh, P.G. (2004) 'Concept Costing for Defence Projects: The Problem and its Solution', *Defence and Peace Economics*, 15(1): 39–57.

Putnam, R.D. (1988) 'Diplomacy and Domestic Politics: The Logic of Two-Level Games', *International Organization*, 42(3): 427–460.

Quaglia, L., Neuvonen, M., Miyakoshi, M. and Cini, M. (2007) 'Europeanization', in M. Cini (ed.) *European Union Politics* (Oxford: Oxford University Press): 405–420.

Radaelli, C. (2006) 'Europeanization: Solution or Problem?', in M. Cini, and A.K. Bourne (eds.) *Palgrave Advances in European Union Studies* (Basingstoke: Palgrave): 56–76.

Radaelli, C. (2003) 'The Europeanization of Public Policy', in K. Featherstone and C. Radaelli (eds.) *The Politics of Europeanization* (Oxford: Oxford University Press): 27–56.

Randazzo, V. (2014) 'Article 346 and the Qualified Application of EU Law to Defence', *Policy Brief*, No. 22 (Paris: European Union Institute for Security Studies). See: www.iss.europa.eu/publications/detail/article/article-346-and-the-qualified-application-of-eu-law-to-defence/.

Rathbun, B.C. (2010) 'Is Anybody Not an (International Relations) Liberal?', *Security Studies*, 19(1): 2–25.

Raube, K., Wouters, J., Bicchi, F., De Man, P., Fiott, D., Helly, D., Kaunert, C., Lavallee, C., Mawdsley, J. and Simao, L. (2015) *Supporting European Security and Defence with Existing EU Measures and Procedures* (Brussels: European Parliament). See: www.europarl.europa.eu/RegData/etudes/STUD/2015/534993/EXPO_STU(2015)534993_EN.pdf.

Reppy, J. (1999) 'Dual-Use Technology: Back to the Future?', in A.R. Markusen and S. Costigan (eds.) *Arming the Future: A Defence Industry for the 21st Century* (New York: Council on Foreign Relations Press): 269–284.

Reynolds, C. (2007) 'Military Capability Development in the ESDP: Towards Effective Governance?', *Contemporary Security Policy*, 28(2): 357–383.

Robertson, P.L. and Yu, T.F. (2001) 'Firm Strategy, Innovation and Consumer Demand: A Market Process Approach', *Managerial and Decision Economics*, 22: 183–199.

Robertson, W.P. (1994) 'Economic Incentives and the Defense Procurement Process', *Journal of Economic Perspectives*, 8(4): 65–90.

Rogerson, W.P. (1994) 'Economic Incentives and the Defense Procurement Process', *The Journal of Economic Perspectives*, 8(4): 65–90.

Rosamond, B. (2005) 'The Uniting of Europe and the Foundation of EU Studies: Revisiting the Neofunctionalism of Ernst B. Haas', *Journal of European Public Policy*, 12(2): 237–254.

Rosenberg, N. (1990) 'Why do Firms do Basic Research (with their own Money)?', *Research Policy*, 19(2): 165–174.

Rosenkötter, A. and Fritz, A. (2008) *Legal Remedies in the Defence Procurement Directive* (Brussels: European Parliament). See: www.europe-economics.com/publications/defence_briefing.pdf.

Ruane, K. (2000) *The Rise and Fall of the European Defence Community: Anglo-American Relations and the Crisis of European Defence, 1950–55* (Basingstoke/New York: Palgrave).

Ruello, A. (2006) 'Exportation d'armements: l'État appelé à plus de volontarisme', *Les Echos* (6 July). See: www.lesechos.fr/06/07/2006/LesEchos/19703-097-ECH_exportation-d-armements-l-etat-appele-a-plus-de-volontarisme.htm.

Rumelt, R.P. (2003) 'Towards a Strategic Theory of the Firm', in N.J. Foss (ed.) *Resources, Firms and Strategies: A Reader in the Resource-Based Perspective* (Oxford/New York: Oxford University Press).

Rynning, S. (2011) 'Realism and the Common Security and Defence Policy', *Journal of Common Market Studies*, 49(1): 23–42.

Rynning, S. (2008) 'Why Not NATO? Military Planning in the European Union', *Journal of Strategic Studies*, 26(1): 53–72.

Saab Group (2016) 'Largest Shareholders'. See: http://saabgroup.com/investor-relations/the-share/ownership/.

Safran (2013) 'Document de référence 2013'. See: www.safran-group.com/fr/media/20140331_document-de-reference-2013.

Saggio, A. (1999) 'Opinion of Advocate General Saggio delivered on 18 March 1999', *Case C-414/97*. See: http://curia.europa.eu/juris/showPdf.jsf?text=&docid=44506&doclang=EN.

Sandler, T. and Hartley, K. (1999) *The Political Economy of NATO: Past, Present and into the 21st Century* (Cambridge: Cambridge University Press).

Sarotte, M.-E. (2001) 'Appendix', *The Adelphi Papers*, 41(340): 71–79.

Saurugger, S. (2014) *Theoretical Approaches to European Integration* (Basingstoke/New York: Palgrave Macmillan).

Schäfer, D. (2016) 'A Banking Union of Ideas? The Impact of Ordoliberalism and the Vicious Circle on the EU Banking Union', *Journal of Common Market Studies*, 54(4): 961–980.

Schake, K. (2016) 'Republican Foreign Policy After Trump', *Survival: Global Politics and Strategy*, 58(5): 33–52.

Scherner, J., Streb, J. and Tilly, S. (2014) 'Supplier Networks in the German Aircraft Industry during World War II and their Long-Term Effects on West Germany's Automobile Industry during the "Wirtschaftswunder" ', *Business History*, 56(6): 996–1020.

Schimmelfennig, F. (2015a) 'Liberal Intergovernmentalism and the Euro Area Crisis', *Journal of European Public Policy*, 22(2): 177–195.

Schimmelfennig, F. (2015b) 'What's the News in "New Intergovernmentalism"? A Critique of Bickerton, Hodson and Puetter', *Journal of Common Market Studies*, 53(4): 723–730.

Schimmelfennig, F. and Rittberger, B. (2004) 'Theories of European Integration: Assumptions and Hypotheses', in J. Richardson (eds.) *European Union: Power and Policy Making* (Oxon/New York: Routledge): 73–96.

Schmidt, V.A. (2010) 'Taking Ideas and Discourse Seriously: Explaining Change Through Discursive Institutionalism as the Fourth "New Institutionalism" ', *European Political Science Review*, 2: 1–25.

Schmidt, V.A. (2008) 'Discursive Institutionalism: The Explanatory Power of Ideas and Discourse', *Annual Review of Political Science*, 11: 303–326.

Schmitt, B. (2005a) *Defence Procurement in the European Union: The Current Debate* (Paris: EU Institute for Security Studies). See: www.iss.europa.eu/publications/detail/article/defence-procurement-in-the-european-union/.

Schmitt, B. (2005b) *Towards a European Defence Equipment Market* (Paris: EU Institute for Security Studies). See: www.iss.europa.eu/publications/detail/article/towards-a-european-defence-equipment-market/.

Schmitt, B. (2004) 'A Proposed Armaments, Research and Capabilities Agency', *EUISS Analysis* (Paris: European Union Institute for Security Studies). See: www.iss.europa.eu/de/publikationen/detail/article/a-proposed-armaments-research-and-capabilities-agency/.

Schmitt, B. (2003) 'Armaments Cooperation in Europe: Core Documents', *Chaillot Paper*, No. 59 (Paris: European Union Institute for Security Studies). See: www.iss.europa.eu/publications/detail/article/european-armaments-cooperation-core-documents/.

Schmitt, B. (2001) 'A Common European Export Policy for Defence and Dual-Use Items?', *Occasional Paper*, No. 25 (Paris: Western European Union Institute for Security Studies). See: www.iss.europa.eu/publications/detail/article/a-common-european-export-policy-for-defence-and-dual-use-items-1/.

Schmitter, P. (1969) 'Three Neo-Functional Hypotheses about International Integration', *International Organization*, 23(1): 161–166.

Schofield, S. (1995) 'The Levene Reforms: An Evaluation', *Defence Analysis*, 11(2): 147–174.

Scott, R. (1987) 'The Adolescence of Institutional Theory', *Administrative Science Quarterly*, 32(4): 493–511.

Searing, D. (1991) 'Role, Rules, and Rationality in the New Institutionalism', *American Political Science Review*, 85(4): 1239–1260.

Seibertz, J., Stähle, P. and Hensler, T. (2010) *Challenges for the German Defence Industry – CEO Agenda for 2030: Development of the Market – Strategies for the Industry* (Frankfurt am Main: PriceWaterhouseCoopers). See: www.pwc.de/de/industrielle-produktion/assets/ceo_agenda_for_2030.pdf.

Serfati, C. (2001) 'The Adaptability of the French Armaments Industry in an Era of Globalization', *Industry and Innovation*, 8(2): 221–239.

Serfati, C. (1997) 'France', in P. Gummett and J.A. Stein (eds.) *European Defence Technology in Transition* (Amsterdam: Harwood Academic Publishers): 51–84.

Serfati, C. (1995) *Production d'armes, croissance et innovation* (Paris: Economica).

Shepherd, A.J.K. (2015) 'EU Military Capability Development and the EDA: Ideas, Interests and Institutions', in N. Karampekios and I. Oikonomou (eds.) *The European Defence Agency: Arming Europe* (London/New York: Routledge): 65–84.

Shepherd, A.J.K. (2000) 'Top-Down or Bottom-Up: Is Security and Defence Policy in the EU a Question of Political Will or Military Capability?', *European Security*, 9(2): 13–30.

Simón, L. (2017) 'Neorealism, Security Cooperation and Europe's Relative Gains Dilemma', *Security Studies*, 26(2): 185–212.

Simón, L. (2016) 'The EU-NATO Conundrum in Perspective', in L. Cladi and A. Locatelli (eds.) *International Relations Theory and European Security: We Thought We Knew* (London/New York: Routledge): 138–158.

Simón, L. (2015) 'Britain, the European Union and the Future of Europe: A Geostrategic Perspective', *The RUSI Journal*, 160(5): 16–23.

Simón, L. (2014) *Geopolitical Change, Grand Strategy and European Security: The EU-NATO Conundrum in Perspective* (Basingstoke/New York: Palgrave Macmillan).

Simón, L. (2012) 'CSDP, Strategy and Crisis Management: Out of Area or Out of Business?', *The International Spectator: Italian Journal of International Affairs*, 47(3): 100–115.

Skowronek, S. (1982) *Building a New American State: The Expansion of National Administrative Capacity* (Cambridge: Cambridge University Press).

Slapin, J.B. (2008) 'Bargaining Power at Europe's Intergovernmental Conferences: Testing Institutional and Intergovernmental Theories', *International Organization*, 62(1): 131–162.

Slater, J. and Nardin, T. (1973) 'The Concept of Military–Industrial Complex', in S. Rosen (ed.) *Testing the Theory of the Military–Industrial Complex* (Lexington, MA: Lexington Books): 27–60.

Slocombe, W.B. (1992) *Lessons in Restructuring Defence Industry: The French Experience* (Washington, DC: US Congress).

Smith, D. and Smith, R. (2006) 'Corporate Strategy, Corporate Culture and Conversion: Adjustment in the Defence Industry', *Business Strategy Review*, 3(2): 45–58.

Smith, R.P. (2009) *Military Economics: The Interaction of Power and Money* (Basingstoke/New York: Palgrave Macmillan).

Smith, R.P. (1990) 'Defence Procurement and Industrial Structure in the UK', *International Journal of Industrial Organization*, 8: 185–205.

Society of British Aerospace Companies (2007) *European Commission's Defence Package*. See: www.defense-aerospace.com/articles-view/release/3/88856/industry,-eda-broadly-support-eu's-defense-proposals.html.

Soloch, K. (2015) 'Pologne: directive MPDS et Offsets, un compromis difficile', *Défense & Industries*, No. 4 (Paris: Fondation pour les recherches stratégiques): 23–24. See: www.frstrategie.org/publications/defense-et-industries/pologne-directive-mpds-et-offsets-un-compromis-difficile-4-6.

Spanish Government (2007) 'Spanish Export Statistics Regarding Defence Material, Other Material and Dual-Use Items and Technologies, 2007'. See: www.sipri.org/sites/default/files/research/armaments/transfers/transparency/national_reports/spain/SPA07.pdf.

Spanish Government (2004) 'National Defence Directive 1/2004'. See: www.defesa.gov.br/projetosweb/livrobranco/arquivos/pdf/Espanha%202004.pdf.

Stockholm International Peace Research Institute (2015) 'Arms Transfers Database'. See: www.sipri.org/databases/armstransfers.

Stoltenberg, J. (2016) '"No Contradiction" between EU Defence Plan and NATO: Stoltenberg', *European Defence Procurement*, 27 September 2016. See: www.eudefenceprocurement.com/single-post/2016/10/13/No-contradiction-between-EU-defence-plan-and-NATO-Stoltenberg.

Strange, S. (1970) 'International Economics and International Relations: A Case of Mutual Neglect', *International Affairs*, 46(2): 304–315.

Strikwerda, J. (2016) 'Sovereignty at Stake? The European Commission's Proposal for a Defence and Security Procurement Directive', *European Security*, 26(1): 19–36.

Svensson, A. (2006) 'Från nationellt försvar till internationell säkerhet', entrance speech to the Royal Swedish Academy of War Sciences, Stockholm (10 May). See: www.kkrva.se/wp-content/uploads/Artiklar/063/kkrvaht_3_2006_4.pdf.

Swedish Inspectorate of Strategic Products (2014) 'Annual Report 2014'. See: www.isp.se/documents/_English/Publications/AR/ISP_AnnualReport2014_web.pdf.

Tallberg, J. (2008) 'Bargaining Power in the European Council', *Journal of Common Market Studies*, 46(3): 685–708.

Taylor, C. (2011) 'EC Defence Equipment Directives. House of Commons Library', *SN/IA/4640*. See: http://researchbriefings.files.parliament.uk/documents/SN04640/SN04640.pdf.

Taylor, P. (1980) 'Interdependence and Autonomy in the European Communities: The Case of the European Monetary System', *Journal of Common Market Studies*, 18(4): 370–387.

Taylor, T. (1991) 'Procurement in European Defence', *Utilities Policy*, 1(2): 144–149.

Taylor, T. (1990) 'Defence Industries in International Relations', *Review of International Studies*, 16: 59–73.

Taylor, T. and Hayward, K. (1989) *The UK Defence Industrial Base: Development and Future Policy Options* (London: Brassey's).

Taylor, T. and Louth, J. (2012) 'The Defence Industrial Base – A Critical Component of Military Capability', *RUSI pre-conference paper* (28–29 June), London. See: www.rusi.org/downloads/assets/RUSI_DIS_Conference_2012_Pre-Read.pdf.

Teichler, T., Rapp-Jung, B., James, A.D., Maulny, J.P., di Camillo, F., Gari, M., Liberti, F., Mezzardi, S., Nones, M., Oscia, O. and Trybus, M. (2010) 'Study on State Control of Strategic Defence Assets', *ENTR/09/019*. See: http://ec.europa.eu/DocsRoom/documents/8585/attachments/1/translations/en/renditions/native.

Terlikowski, M. (2013) 'The Polish Defence Sector and the Liberalised European Defence Equipment Market', *Polish Institute for International Relations Bulletin*, 18(471): 1–2. See: www.pism.pl/publications/bulletin/no-18-471.

Thales Group (2015) 'Shareholders and Board of Director'. See: www.thalesgroup.com/en/worldwide/group/shareholders-and-board-directors.

Thales Group (2014) *Summary of Thales UK's Position. Public response to the UK Government's Balance of Competences Review*. See: www.gov.uk/government/uploads/system/uploads/attachment_data/file/332665/free-movement-of-services-competence-review-evidence-public-responses.pdf.

Thelen, K. and Steinmo, S. (1992) 'Historical Institutionalism in Comparative Politics', in S. Steinmo and K. Thelen (eds.) *Structuring Politics: Historical Institutionalism in Comparative Analysis* (Cambridge: Cambridge University Press): 1–32.

Thiele, R.D. (2012) 'On the Reorientation of the Bundeswehr: Meeting the Challenges Ahead', *Strategy Series: Focus on Defense and International Security*, No. 184 (Institut für Strategie-Politik-Sicherheits und Wirtschaftsberatung). See: www.files.ethz.ch/isn/140840/184_Thiele.pdf.

Thiele, R.D. (2001) 'Reforming the Bundeswehr', *The International Spectator*, 36(1): 75–81.

Thiem, A. (2011) 'Conditions of Intergovernmental Armaments Cooperation in Western Europe, 1996–2006', *European Political Science Review*, 3(1): 1–33.

Thoma, K. (ed.) (2011) *European Perspectives on Security Research* (Berlin: Springer).

Thoma, K., Hiller, D., Leismann, T. and Drees, B. (2011) 'A German Perspective on Security Research', in K. Thoma (ed.) *European Perspectives on Security Research* (Berlin: Springer): 27–44.

ThyssenKrupp (2016) 'Shareholder Structure'. See: www.thyssenkrupp.com/en/investors/shares-and-adr/shareholder-structure/.

TNO (2009) *Development of a European Defence Technological and Industrial Base*. See: http://ec.europa.eu/DocsRoom/documents/10488/attachments/2/translations/en/renditions/native.

Toje, A. (2005) 'The 2003 European Union Security Strategy: A Critical Appraisal', *European Foreign Affairs Review*, 10(1): 117–133.

Topcu, M. and Aras, I. (2015) 'Defense Spending and Economic Growth: Extended Empirical Analysis for the European Union', *Defence and Peace Economics*, 26(2): 233–246.

Treacher, A. (2001) 'Europe as a Power Multiplier for French Security Policy: Strategic Consistency, Tactical Adaptation', *European Security*, 10(1): 22–44.

Trybus, M. (2014) *Buying Defence and Security in Europe: The EU Defence and Security Procurement Directive in Context* (Cambridge: Cambridge University Press).

Trybus, M. (2013) 'The Tailor-Made EU Defence and Security Procurement Directive: Limitation, Flexibility, Descriptiveness and Substitution', *European Law Review*, 39: 2–29.

Trybus, M. (2009) 'Annotations to Case C-337/05, *Commission* v. *Italy* ("Augusta and Augusta Bell Helicopters"), judgment of 8 April 2008, nyr', *Common Market Law Review*, 46(3): 973–990.

Trybus, M. (2006) 'The New European Defence Agency: A Contribution to a Common European and Security and Defence Policy and a Challenge to the Community Acquis?', *Common Market Law Review*, 43(3): 667–703.

Trybus, M. (2005) *European Union Law and Defence Integration* (Oxford: Hart Publishers).

Trybus, M. (2002) 'The EC Treaty as an Instrument of European Defence Integration: Judicial Scrutiny of Defence and Security Exceptions', *Common Market Law Review*, 39: 1347–1372.

Udis, B. (2009) 'Offsets and International Industrial Participation', in R.A. Bitzinger (ed.) *The Modern Defense Industry: Political, Economic and Technological Issues* (Santa Barbara, CA: Praeger Security International): 257–271.

UK Government (2016) *UK Defence & Security Export Statistics for 2015* (London: UK Trade & Investment). See: www.gov.uk/government/uploads/system/uploads/attachment_data/file/541330/20160727_-_Official_Statistics_-_UKTI_DSO_Core_Slides_for_2015_-_Final_Version.pdf.

UK Government (2015) *UK Defence & Security Export Statistics for 2014* (London: UK Trade & Investment). See: www.gov.uk/government/uploads/system/uploads/attachment_data/file/444359/20150710_-_Defence_and_Security_Export_Statistics_for_2014_-_Core_Slides.pdf.

UK Government (2014) 'Free Movement of Services: Balance of Competences Review – Public Responses'. See: www.gov.uk/government/uploads/system/uploads/attachment_data/file/332668/bis-14-987-free-movement-of-services-balance-of-competencies-report.pdf.

UK Government (2013) *UKTI Defence & Security Organisation Market Brief: Portugal* (London: UK Trade & Investment). See: www.gov.uk/government/uploads/system/uploads/attachment_data/file/283294/UKTI_DSO_Market_Brief_Portugal.pdf.

UK Government (2012a) 'Implementation of the European Union Directive 2009/43/EC', *Notice to Exporters 2012/37*. See: http://webarchive.nationalarchives.gov.uk/20121017180846/http:/www.bis.gov.uk/assets/biscore/eco/docs/notices-to-exporters/2012/notice-to-exporters-2012-37-ict-directive-implementation.doc.

UK Government (2012b) 'Delay in UK Implementation of Directive 2009/43/EC (Intra-Community Transfer Directive) Concerning EU Trade in Military Goods', *Notice to Exporters – 2012/28*. See: http://webarchive.nationalarchives.gov.uk/20121017180846/

http:/www.bis.gov.uk/assets/biscore/eco/docs/notices-to-exporters/2012/notice-to-exporters-2012-28-delay-ict-directive.doc.

UK Government (2010) *Ministry of Defence Consultation Document on the Approach to Implementation of Directive 2009/81/EC of the European Parliament and of the Council of July 2009* (London: Ministry of Defence). See: www.gov.uk/government/uploads/system/uploads/attachment_data/file/35919/20101213Directive200981EC2ndCondoc_1.pdf.

UK Government (2003) *First Review of the Implementation of Defence Industrial Policy* (London: Ministry of Defence). See: www.kent.ac.uk/economics/documents/GES%20Background%20Documents/Defence/Defence%20Industrial%20Policy.pdf.

UK Parliament (2012) 'Inquiry into European Defence Capabilities: Lessons from the Past, Signposts for the Future – Oral and Written Evidence'. See: www.parliament.uk/documents/lords-committees/eu-sub-com-c/EUMilitaryCapabilities/EUMilCapEv.pdf.

UK Parliament (2008a) 'Conclusions and Recommendations', *12th Report*, House of Commons Select Committee on Defence. See: www.publications.parliament.uk/pa/cm200708/cmselect/cmdfence/254/254.pdf.

UK Parliament (2008b) 'Defence and Security Procurement', House of Commons European Committee B, Session 2007–08. See: www.publications.parliament.uk/pa/cm200708/cmgeneral/euro/081124/81124s01.htm.

UK Parliament (2008c) 'Scrutiny of Arms Export Controls (2009)', *House of Commons First Joint Report of Session 2008–09*. See: www.publications.parliament.uk/pa/cm200809/cmselect/cmquad/178/17802.htm.

UK Parliament (2008d) 'The EU and the International Perspective', *8th Report*, House of Commons Select Committee on Foreign Affairs. See: www.publications.parliament.uk/pa/cm200708/cmselect/cmquad/254/25411.htm.

UK Parliament (2008e) 'Current Developments in European Defence Policy: Report with Evidence', *20th Report of Session 2007–08*, European Union Committee, House of Lords Paper, No. 145. See: www.publications.parliament.uk/pa/ld200708/ldselect/ldeucom/145/145.pdf.

UK Parliament (2008f) 'Defence and Security Procurement', *39th Report*, House of Commons Select Committee on European Scrutiny. See: www.publications.parliament.uk/pa/cm200708/cmselect/cmeuleg/16-xxxv/16-xxxv.pdf.

UK Parliament (2007) 'European Defence Equipment Market', *13th Report*, House of Commons Select Committee on European Scrutiny. See: www.publications.parliament.uk/pa/cm200708/cmselect/cmeuleg/16xi/1603.htm.

UK Parliament (2005a) 'European Defence Agency: Report with Evidence', *9th Report of Session 2004–05*, European Union Committee, House of Lords Paper, No. 76. See: www.publications.parliament.uk/pa/ld200405/ldselect/ldeucom/76/7602.htm.

UK Parliament (2005b) 'Minutes of Evidence: 10 June 2004', *9th Report of Session 2004–05*, European Union Committee, House of Lords Paper, No. 76. See: www.publications.parliament.uk/pa/ld200405/ldselect/ldeucom/76/7602.htm.

UK Parliament (2005c) 'European Union', *Hansard*, vol. 669, cc396–408 (3 February). See: http://hansard.millbanksystems.com/lords/2005/feb/03/european-union.

UK Parliament (2005d) 'Minutes of Evidence: 17 January 2005', *9th Report of Session 2004–05*, European Union Committee, House of Lords Paper, No. 76. See: www.publications.parliament.uk/pa/ld200405/ldselect/ldeucom/999/euc1701.pdf.

UK Parliament (2004) 'European Defence Agency', *Hansard*, 21 June 2004 vol. 422, c71WS. See: http://hansard.millbanksystems.com/written_statements/2004/jun/21/european-defence-agency.

UK Parliament (2003) 'Defence Policy', *Hansard*, vol. 412, cc30–81 (27 October). See: www.publications.parliament.uk/pa/cm200203/cmhansrd/vo031027/debtext/31027-08.htm#31027-08_head1.

UK Parliament (2001) *Multinational Defence Co-operation* (London: Ministry of Defence). See: www.defense-aerospace.com/article-view/release/4527/uk-mod-details-cooperation-policy-(feb.-22).html.

UK Parliament (1997) 'European Defence Industrial and Armaments Co-operation', *House of Commons Research Paper*, 97/15. See: http://researchbriefings.files.parliament.uk/documents/RP97-15/RP97-15.pdf.

UK Parliament (1995) 'European Armaments Agency', *Hansard*, vol. 258, c229W (20 April). See: http://hansard.millbanksystems.com/written_answers/1995/apr/20/european-armaments-agency.

Ulanowski, A. (2012) *Polish Defence Yearbook 2012* (Warsaw: Magnum Publishers). See: https://issuu.com/zapfi/docs/polish_defence_yearbook_2012.pl.

Unisys (2005) *Intra-Community Transfers of Defence Products* (Brussels: European Commission). See: http://ec.europa.eu/enterprise/regulation/inst_sp/defense_en.htm.

Unite (2013) *Defending our Industry: A United Strategy for the UK Defence Sector* (London: Unite the Union). See: www.unitetheunion.org/uploaded/documents/(JN5990)%20A4%20Unite%20Defence%20Document%20(FINAL)%20201311-13444.pdf.

Uttley, M.R.H. and Wilkinson, B. (2016) 'A Spin of the Wheel? Defence Procurement and Defence Industries in the Brexit Debates', *International Affairs*, 92(3): 569–586.

Vail, M. (2003) 'Rethinking Corporatism and Consensus: The Dilemmas of German Social-Protection Reform', *West European Politics*, 26(3): 41–66.

Van Dijk, T. (1993) 'Principles of Critical Discourse Analysis', *Discourse & Society*, 4(2): 249–283.

Vink, M.P. and Graziano, P. (2008) 'Challenges of a New Research Agenda', in P. Graziano and M.P. Vink (eds.) *Europeanization: New Research Agendas* (Basingstoke: Palgrave Macmillan): 3–20.

Wagstyl, S. (2016) 'Wolfgang Schäuble calls for joint EU defence budget', *Financial Times* (18 October). See: www.ft.com/content/a20e8ade-9554-11e6-a1dc-bdf38d484582.

Walker, W. and Gummett, P. (1993) 'Nationalism, Internationalism and the European Defence Market', *Chaillot Papers*, No. 9 (Paris: European Union Institute for Security Studies). See: www.iss.europa.eu/publications/detail/article/nationalism-internationalism-and-the-european-defence-market/.

Walker, W. and Gummet, P. (1989) 'Britain and the European Armaments Market', *International Affairs*, 65(3): 419–442.

Walsh, K.A. (2009) 'The Role, Promise, and Challenges of Dual-Use Technologies', in R.A. Bitzinger (ed.) *The Modern Defense Industry: Political, Economic and Technological Issues* (Santa Barbara, CA: Praeger Security International): 123–152.

Waltz, K.N. (1979) *Theory of International Politics* (New York: McGraw Hill).

Watkins, T.A. (1990) 'Beyond Guns and Butter: Managing Dual-Use Technologies', *Technovation*, 10(6): 389–406.

Watts, B.D. (2008) *The US Defense Industrial Base: Past, Present and Future* (Washington, DC: Center for Strategic and Budgetary Assessments). See: http://csbaonline.org/research/publications/the-us-defense-industrial-base-past-present-and-future/publication.

Watts, B.D. and Harrison, T. (2011) *Sustaining Critical Sectors of the U.S. Defence Industrial Base* (Washington, DC: Center for Strategic and Budgetary Assessments).

See: http://csbaonline.org/research/publications/sustaining-critical-sectors-of-the-u-s-defense-industrial-base/publication.

Weiner, K. (2012) 'Towards European Preferences? Implications of Directive 2009/81/EC on Domestic Preferences in Defense Procurement', *Procurement Law*, 47(16): 16–18.

Weiss, M. (2014) 'Integrating the Acquisition of Leviathan's Swords? The Emerging Regulation of Defence Procurement within the EU', in P. Genschel and M. Jachtenfuchs (eds.) *Beyond the Regulatory Polity? The European Integration of Core State Powers* (Oxford: Oxford University Press): 27–45.

Weiss, M. and Blauberger, M. (2016) 'Judicialized Law-making and Opportunistic Enforcement: Explaining the EU's Challenge of National Defence Offsets', *Journal of Common Market Studies*, 54(2): 444–462.

Wendt, A. (1987) 'The Agent-Structure Problem in International Relations Theory', *International Organization*, 41(3): 335–370.

Western European Union (1998) 'Rome Declaration' (17 November). See: www.weu.int/documents/981116en.pdf.

Western European Union (1984) 'Rome Declaration' (24 October). See: www.cvce.eu/content/publication/2003/7/11/c44c134c-aca3-45d1-9e0b-04d4d9974ddf/publishable_en.pdf.

Whitman, R.G. (2004) 'NATO, the EU and ESDP: An Emerging Division of Labour?', *Contemporary Security Policy*, 25(3): 430–451.

Wight, C. (2004) 'State Agency: Social Action without Human Activity?', *Review of International Studies*, 30(2): 269–280.

Wincott, D. (1995) 'Institutional Interaction and European Integration: Towards an Everyday Critique of Liberal Intergovernmentalism', *Journal of Common Market Studies*, 33(4): 597–609.

Wolf, C. (1969) *Military-Industrial Complexities: Rand Report No. P-4177* (Santa Monica, CA: Rand Corporation).

Yost, D.S. (2000) 'The NATO Capabilities Gap and the European Union', *Survival: Global Politics and Strategy*, 42(4): 97–128.

Young, O.R. (1999) 'Comment on Andrew Moravcsik, "A New Statecraft? Supranational Entrepreneurs and International Cooperation"', *International Organization*, 53(4): 805–809.

Yukins, C.R. (2009) 'The European Defence Procurement Directive: An American Perspective', *The Government Contractor*, 51(41): 1–7.

Yustos Cordobés, R.L. (2010) 'The European Defence Agency: Involvement of Spain's Industry', in Spanish Ministry of Defence (ed.) *European Defence Agency: Past, Present and Future* (Madrid: Ministry of Defence): 205–240. See: www.portalcultura.mde.es/Galerias/publicaciones/fichero/European_Defence.pdf.

Zamelek, P. (2013) 'The Future of the European Defence Industry after the December Summit: Ten Polish Priorities', *PISM Policy Paper*, 35(83) (Warsaw: Polish Institute of International Affairs). See: www.pism.pl/files/?id_plik=15951.

Zandee, D. (2015) 'European Defence: About Neighbours and Distant Friends', in D. Fiott (ed.) *The Common Security and Defence Policy: National Perspectives* (Gent: Academia Press/Egmont – Royal Institute for International Relations): 105–108.

Zito, A.R. (2001) 'Epistemic Communities, Collective Entrepreneurship and European Integration', *Journal of European Public Policy*, 8(4): 585–603.

Index